CW00829819

THE LAW
AND
ELDERLY PEOPLE

Australia

The Law Book Company
Brisbane • Sydney • Melbourne • Perth

Canada

Carswell
Ottawa • Toronto • Calgary • Montreal • Vancouver

Agents

Steimatzky's Agency Ltd, Tel Aviv;
N.M. Tripathi (Private) Ltd, Bombay;
Eastern Law House (Private) Ltd, Calcutta;
M.P.P. House, Bangalore;
Universal Book Traders, Delhi;
Aditya Books, Delhi;
Macmillan Shuppan K.K., Tokyo;
Pakistan Law House, Karachi, Lahore

THE LAW
AND
ELDERLY PEOPLE

Ann McDonald, LL.B., M.A., C.Q.S.W.

and

Margaret Taylor, LL.B., Solicitor

LONDON
SWEET & MAXWELL
1995

Published in 1995 by Sweet and Maxwell Limited of South Quay Plaza,
183 Marsh Wall, London E14 9FT
Computerset by York House Typographic Ltd, London W13 8NT
Printed and bound in Great Britain by Butler and Tanner Ltd,
Frome and London

No natural forests were destroyed to make this product, only farmed
timber was used and replanted

A CIP catalogue record for this book is available from the
British Library

ISBN 0421 498501

PREFACE

We first met when practising in West Norfolk, Ann as a social worker with the elderly, and Margaret as a solicitor with a client base of predominantly older people. We found that we had many clients in common, but solutions to their practical and financial problems were not always easy to find. Subsequently Ann moved to become a lecturer in social work law, and later a lecturer in social work, at the University of East Anglia. We maintained our link through seminars for post-graduate social workers, most of whom were working with elderly people.

We began to write together and became increasingly aware of the lack of literature concerning the law and elderly people. When we were approached by Sweet & Maxwell to write this book, we were pleased to have the opportunity to pull together diverse areas of law all relevant to the needs of elderly people. This book is intended to be a practical guide covering welfare as well as financial issues which we hope will be of use both to the high street lawyer and to other people concerned with giving advice to elderly people and their families.

Ann would like to thank friends and colleagues in the School of Social Work at the University of East Anglia, and particularly Caroline Ball for her encouragement and support. Margaret would like to thank her partners and staff at Ward Gethin, particularly those of the private client department, for the willingness with which they have undertaken the extra work necessitated by her absences from the office whilst writing.

We would both like to thank our respective families and friends for their support, understanding and tolerance. Ann would like to thank Tina Marks and Barbara Loney in particular for their help. Margaret would like to thank Margaret Fox for the typing. We are also grateful to friends and colleagues in West Norfolk for their interest and willingness to share ideas and experiences.

Ann McDonald
Margaret E. Taylor
January 1995

CONTENTS

TABLE OF CASES

TABLE OF STATUTES

TABLE OF STATUTORY INSTRUMENTS

TABLE OF RULES OF THE SUPREME COURT

ABBREVIATIONS

A.C.	= Law Reports, Appeal cases
All E.R.	= All England Reports
B.M.L.R.	= Butterworths Medico-Legal Reports
C.A.	= Court of Appeal
C.C.R.	= County Court Rules
C.M.L.R.	= Common Market Law Review
C.O.D.	= Crown Office Digest
Ch.	= Chancery (Law Reports)
Cr. M. & R.	= Crompton and Meeson's Exchequer Reports
Cr.App.R.	= Criminal Appeal Reports
Cro. Eliz.	= Croke's K.B. Reports *temp.* Elizabeth I (1 Cro.)
FLR	= Family Law Reports
Fam. Law	= Family Law
H.C. Deb	= House of Commons' Debate
H.L.	= House of Lords
H.L.R.	= Housing Law Reports
J.P.	= Justice of the Peace Reports
J.P.N.	= Justice of the Peace Journal
K.B.	= Law Reports, King's Bench
L.G.R.	= Local Government Reports
L.J. Exch.	= Law Journal Exchequer
L.J.M.C.	= Law Journal Magistrates' Cases
L.R.C.P.	= Law Reports, Common Pleas
L.R.Eq.	= Law Reports, Enquiry Cases
L.R.Q.B.	= Law Reports, Queen's Bench
L.S. Gaz	= Law Society's Gazette
L.T.	= Law Times
Lew.	= Lewin's Crown Cases
M.L.R.	= Modern Law Review
Med. L.R.	= Medical Law Reports
New L.J.	= New Law Journal
Q.B.	= Law Reports, Queen's Bench
Q.B.D.	= Law Reports, Queen's Bench Division
R.S.C.	= Rules of the Supreme Court
S.J.	= Solicitors' Journal
TC	= Tax Cases

T.L.R.   = Times Law Reports

V.R.   = Victorian Reports

W.L.R.   = Weekly Law Reports

Chapter 1
Introduction

This book on the law and elderly people is designed to meet the needs of a growing elderly population for legal advice and assistance on a range of personal, social and financial issues. It brings together a number of topics which have importance in the lives of older people.

As with any section of society, it is impossible to say that all members of that group will have the same or similar needs. It can be argued that old age is predominantly a social construction, based upon society's views of what older people should do. Certainly retirement can be viewed in this way, less an individual choice than an artificial shortening of the working life. This book therefore seeks to take a developmental view of old age and tries to avoid a stereotypical view of the older person. "Old age" itself may cover a span of 30 years or more and includes a wide range of interests, abilities and needs.

In compiling a book of this sort the major obstacle is that there is no discrete body of law relating to elderly people as there is no distinct legal status of old age. This means that there are bound to be gaps in provision which leave some vulnerable people unprotected. At the same time there is an increasing emphasis on elderly people as users rather than passive recipients of services. The protective and enabling functions of the law are thus both relevant to the needs of elderly people. The solicitor, moreover, in his professional practice may have particular responsibilities to this client group.

DEMOGRAPHIC CHANGES

It is well known that we are an ageing society in the sense that there are more elderly people than ever before in the population and that individuals are living longer. In 1991 the age group 65 to 79 years comprised 12.0 per cent of the population, compared to 9.8 per cent in 1961. It is projected that this group will reduce to 11.4 per cent of the population in 2001, but will climb to 14.0 per cent in 2021 and 15.6 per cent in 2031. The greatest percentage change however will be in the number of those over 80 years. This sector accounted for 1.0 per cent of the population in 1961, and 3.7 per cent of the population in 1991. It is projected to increase to 4.2 per cent of the population in 2001, 5.2 per cent in 2021 and 6.9 per cent in 2031.[1] Elderly people thus comprise an increasingly significant proportion of the total population potentially in need of legal services.

GENDER DIFFERENCES

There is a predominance of women over men in the older age groups. Though numbers are equal for those aged 60 to 64 years, in the age group 65 to 74 years, 54.5 per cent are female rising to 62 per cent of those aged over 75 years.[2] Women are also twice as likely as men to be living alone in any of the older age groups. Taking both men and women together, 29 per cent of those aged 65 to 74 years live alone compared with 48 per cent of those aged 75 years or over. However, there are significant differences between ethnic groups: whereas 16 per cent of the white population is aged over 65 years, this is true for only 5 per cent of the Indian and black Caribbean population, but for 27 per cent of the Pakistani and Bangla-deshi population.

There is an imbalance between men and women in economic status which will affect the type of financial advice they seek. Though the proportion of men over 65 years in any socio-economic group is roughly the same as that for younger men, the number of women over 75 years in the "unskilled manual" or "semi-skilled manual" groups is especially marked, totalling 37 per cent. Women also lose out on pension scheme membership: 90 per cent of men at present over 55 years and in full-time employment belong to a pension scheme, but this is true for only 74 per cent of women.[3]

SOCIAL CHANGES

Social changes over the last two decades have had an important impact on older people. Early retirement has become the norm. In 1975 84 per cent of men aged 60 to 64 years were in employment, this dropped to 52 per cent in 1992: for men 65 years and over the figures are 16 per cent and 7 per cent respectively. Only 22 per cent of women aged 60 to 64 years and 3 per cent of those over 65 years were in employment in 1992.[4] Some of these people will have experienced redundancy or will have retire-ment lump sums to invest and therefore will be in need of financial advice. Advice on available benefits will also be important.

---

[1] *Social Trends* (H.M.S.O., 1994).
[2] *General Household Survey 1992* (H.M.S.O., 1994).
[3] *ibid.*
[4] *ibid.*

There is a high level of disability and chronic illness amongst older people. Fifty-nine per cent of those questioned by O.P.C.S. in 1992 aged 65 to 74 years admitted to a longstanding illness, which restricted their activities in 17 per cent of cases. 60 per cent of those aged over 75 years had a longstanding illness, restricting their activity in 21 per cent of cases. Of course this means that very many people are still fit and active but it does have implications in demands on medical and social services. It also means that many of the "young" elderly (60 to 75 years), who may have caring responsibilities to an older generation, do not themselves enjoy good health. Government policy on community care also means that many more older people will be remaining within the community rather than moving into residential or hospital care. This opens up a relatively unexplored area of work for the legal adviser in negotiating with predominantly social services departments for the provision of services to his client. The types of services available and access to those services is given considerable emphasis in Chapter 2—The Delivery of Social Services.

The Needs of Elderly People

There is a wide diversity in the social circumstances and economic status of people beyond retirement age; their need for legal services similarly will vary. In many cases the law will be enabling and legal advice will be sought on such matters as the writing of wills and the creation of powers of attorney. In other instances, the law will be used to enforce duties and to protect rights, particularly against public authorities. The law may also be protective in the face of abuse, or (more rarely) used as an instrument of compulsory intervention as where powers under the Mental Health Act 1983 are invoked.

The position of carers needs particular attention. Some may themselves be elderly and may have a need for services in their own right. They may not have undertaken the caring role voluntarily and may be under considerable stress. Difficulties may arise from a lack of clarity in the law if they have to make decisions on behalf of the person for whom they are caring. Conversely, elderly people may require support in making decisions for themselves with which their carers are less than happy. With married couples the question may arise of the extent to which one of them is authorised to give instructions on behalf of both.

Professional Responsibilities

The Law Society's *The Guide to the Professional Conduct of Solicitors*[5] raises both general and particular issues concerning practice with elderly

---

[5] *The Guide to the Professional Conduct of Solicitors* (6th ed., 1993). Hereafter referred to as *Professional Conduct*.

clients. The pertinent issues are "who is the client?" when an elderly person's wishes are conveyed, as they often are, by relatives; and "how do I protect my client from duress and undue influence?" Another important question (discussed below) is: "does my client have the legal capacity to enter into the type of transaction which is being proposed?"

A solicitor who has accepted instructions on behalf of a client is bound to carry out those instructions with diligence and must exercise reasonable care and skill.[6] Where instructions are received not from a client but from a third party purporting to represent that client, a solicitor should obtain written instructions from the client that he or she wishes the solicitor to act. If in doubt, the solicitor should see the client or take other appropriate steps to confirm instructions. In such circumstances a solicitor must advise the client without regard to the interests of the source from which he or she was introduced.[7] It may be necessary to see the client on his own to take or to confirm instructions.

A solicitor must not accept instructions which he suspects have been given under duress or undue influence: "particular care may need to be taken where clients are elderly or otherwise vulnerable to pressure from others."[8] Paragraph 12.12, which requires that a solicitor should keep his or her client's business and affairs confidential, prevents disclosure to relatives, except with the express consent of the client.

PROFESSIONAL SKILLS

The solicitor may need to proceed more slowly with the older client, taking into account any sensory impairment. Where mobility is limited a home visit may be desirable in order to see the client on his own, in surroundings where he feels more at ease. Asking "open" questions, which demand more than a "yes" or "no" answer, will encourage the client to talk more freely and more personally. Non-verbal communication is also important, and what is not said may be as important as what is said. Taking a "social history" may be useful to ascertain what relatives there are, and what status is accorded to them by the client. It is also important to ascertain whether the client is aware of the extent of his property and of its value when assessing testamentary capacity. Knowledge of the client's past and present lifestyle, values and priorities will assist in making decisions on behalf of incapacitated clients, for example under an enduring power of attorney.

Building up a relationship with the client over a period of time will provide essential background knowledge. Paragraph 12.05 of *Professional Conduct* is explicit that proper professional practice requires the solicitor,

---

[6] *ibid.* para. 12.11. See also *Groom v. Crocker* [1939] 1 K.B. 194 and Supply of Goods and Services Act 1982, s.13.
[7] *Professional Conduct*, para. 12.05.
[8] *ibid.* para. 12.04.

especially where the client is elderly, to obtain enough information about the client's circumstances to be able to act properly for the client. In addition, the client may feel more confident if they can deal with just one person in a practice across a range of issues rather than being referred from one department to another.

CAPACITY

One very pertinent issue when dealing with elderly clients is the question of mental capacity, to take action or indeed to give instructions. There is a presumption of capacity unless the contrary is proved on a balance of probabilities. Whether a client has capacity is a matter of law, and different levels of capacity are required for different types of transaction: for example, entering into a contract of marriage; making a will; and managing one's financial affairs without the compulsory intervention of the Court of Protection. It will be desirable in most cases to seek a doctor's opinion, in which case the doctor concerned should be given guidance on the relevant test of capacity to apply.[9] Where the client suffers mental incapacity the solicitor should take reasonable steps to ensure that the client's interests are still protected,[10] for example by an application to the Court of Protection.

The presence of mental disorder is not *per se* proof of incapacity, though a decline in cognitive ability may accompany some forms of mental disorder. A veneer of social skills or a retained ability to engage in social chit-chat may mask a cognitive decline. It is not uncommon for elderly people under the influence of alcohol or medication, or suffering from chest or urinary infections, to present in an acute confusional state, hence the importance of medical diagnosis. Persons recently bereaved or under severe stress may also find difficulty in concentrating or be emotionally labile. Depression is in fact the most common functional disorder encountered in old age, and, of course it is responsive to medical intervention. Dementia occurs in one in 20 of the population over 65, but one in five of those over 80.[11] Typical symptoms of dementia are loss of short-term memory, disorientation as to time and place, and misidentification (commonly not recognising relatives); auditory or visual hallucinations may also occur. People in the early stages of dementia may, however, retain legal capacity: therefore legal remedies must be sensitive to the different needs of people over the course of time in what is a progressive illness.

---

[9] *ibid.* para. 12.01.
[10] *ibid.* para. 12.17.
[11] Brayne and Ames, "The Epidemiology of Mental Disorders in Old Age" in *Mental Health Problems in Old Age* (Gearing B. *et al.*, 1988).

The Law Commission

The Law Commission[12] has endorsed the existing cognitive or "function" test of capacity, based upon the ability to arrive at a decision by
manipulating information and making a choice. Alternative formulations
rejected were a "rationality" test, based upon the outcome of decisions
made, and a "true choice" test, primarily aimed at those who had never
possessed capacity, or who were unduly swayed by the influence of
others.

The task of the Law Commission was to address deficiencies in both
public and private law concerning mentally incapacitated adults. No
effective machinery was seen to exist to resolve disputes, to offer
effective protection from abuse and neglect, and to legitimate substitute
decision-making. To this end, the Law Commission recommended "a
new jurisdiction", either a court or a tribunal, to resolve such issues. The
policy aims are clearly stated:

(1) People should be enabled and encouraged to take for themselves
     those decisions which they are able to take.
(2) Intervention should be as limited as possible, and should be based
     on what the person himself would have wanted.
(3) Proper safeguards should be provided against exploitation, neglect
     and abuse.

The Law Commission specifically rejected the introduction of a general
authority to take decisions for an incapacitated person simply on the
basis of a family relationship,[13] though it did endorse a power to do what
is reasonable in the circumstances.

Taking legal action

A person who is incapacitated must act in civil proceedings as a plaintiff
through his "next friend" or as a defendant through a guardian *ad litem*.[14]
In this context, an incapacitated person is one who, by reason of mental
disorder within the meaning of the Mental Health Act 1983, is incapable
of managing and administering his property and affairs, the same test
that is applied in relation to patients of the Court of Protection.

In the various chapters of this book reference will be made to the
differing tests of capacity relevant to each particular transaction under
discussion. The point at which relatives and other professionals may be
involved in decision-making is also highlighted.

---

[12] Consultation Paper No. 128, *Mentally Incapacitated Adults and Decision-Making: a New
Jurisdiction* (H.M.S.O., 1993).
[13] *ibid.* para. 2.9.
[14] see R.S.C., Ord. 80, r.1; C.C.R., Ord. 1, r.3; Family Proceedings Rules 1991 (S.I. 1991 No.
1247 (L.20)), r.9.

The proposals of the Law Commission have not yet been put into legislative form. Thus, the areas of uncertainty and deficiency, and the gaps in the law which were highlighted, remain.

STRUCTURE OF THE BOOK

This book is a result of the absence of any cohesive body of law relating solely or predominantly to elderly people. It is therefore eclectic in its approach, bringing together areas of the law relevant for practitioners dealing with an elderly client group. The law naturally divides into matters which concern the person (predominantly Chapters 2–9), and those which concern his property (Chapters 10–14). One of the consequences of this divergence is that there is no adequate mechanism or legal forum for bringing together decisions, for example about where a person should live and how he should pay for his care in that place. The other major division in the law is between voluntary and compulsory powers, a distinction based predominantly on whether or not an individual comes within the compulsory powers of the Mental Health Act 1983 (discussed in Chapter 8—Compulsory Intervention). Compulsory intervention is fortunately unusual. Greater emphasis is placed on enabling legislation, allowing people to plan their future with professional assistance and take advantage of a range of personal and financial services on offer.

Chapter 2
The Delivery of Social Services

THE STRUCTURE OF LOCAL AUTHORITIES

The legal responsibilities of local authorities towards those in need of assistance are defined in a number of welfare enactments, beginning with the National Assistance Act 1948, and culminating in the National Health Service and Community Care Act 1990. Not only is the provision of services described, but the means of assessment and mode of delivery are provided for in legislation.

The publication of the Seebohm Committee's report in 1968 heralded the introduction of social services departments, unitary in nature, and making provision across the whole range of client groups: children, elderly people, people with disabilities and the mentally ill.[1] The substantive duties that legislation placed on local authorities to provide welfare services were to be discharged through a social services committee which would appoint a Director of Social Services for its area. The scheme is contained within the Local Authority Social Services Act 1970. The relevant authorities were to be:

(i) the county councils,
(ii) the metropolitan boroughs, and
(iii) the London borough councils (Local Government Act 1972, s.195).

Internally, the organisation of social services departments follows a conventional pattern of area teams within divisional boundaries. In a local area teams may be either generic (or, more commonly) specialist — that is they may provide services for all client groups from within one team, or they may operate as separate teams for separate client groups. The advent of community care with the National Health Service and Community Care Act 1990 has seen a further division into purchasers and providers of services.

---

[1] Seebohm Committee, *Report of the Committee on Local Authority and Allied Personal Social Services*, Cmnd. 3703 (1968).

VOLUNTARY ORGANISATIONS

The voluntary sector has a long tradition of expertise, both in the direct provision of social services and as a catalyst for change. Thus an organisation like Age Concern may provide services such as day care, but also acts as a pressure group and information source on matters of relevance to older people. The type and level of voluntary provision varies greatly from one part of the country to another. The relationship between the voluntary sector and the statutory sector has recently been subject to change. Formerly, voluntary organisations would be funded on a grant-aided basis by the local authority: with the advent of community care, however, contracting for services has become the norm, and thus a more businesslike relationship, with greater emphasis on value for money, has emerged.

THE PRIVATE SECTOR

The promotion of a "mixed economy of care" has also brought the private sector into a closer relationship with the statutory sector. The provision of residential care has been the predominant contribution of the private sector, with a huge increase in the number of private residential establishments in the 1980s. The local authority continues to play a "watchdog" role as the registration authority for private residential care homes in its area, but it also now acts in partnership with the private sector in the placement of people seeking public funding in residential care. Private domiciliary care, though available in some areas, is not yet well-established.

PARTICULAR SERVICES

Though a continuum of care from domiciliary through day care, to respite and permanent residential care is available, it should be noted that it is only in respect of residential care and domiciliary care that the local authority has a duty to provide a service. Other services are phrased as powers and are discretionary. The existence of a power rather than a duty is the reason why services vary so much from one part of the country to another. Generally, a distinction is drawn between the provision of services to those ordinarily resident in the area of the local authority, and to those who are not ordinarily resident. Duties may be owed to the former but not to the latter.

The general power to promote the welfare of elderly people through the provision of support services is contained in the Health Services and Public Health Act 1968, s.45. This provides that a local authority may, with the approval of the Minister of Health and to such an extent as he may direct, shall make arrangements for promoting the welfare of old people. No directions have in fact been made under this section. Approval has been given for the provision of meals and recreational facilities, practical assistance in the home, the employment of wardens, transport needs and boarding out on the childcare model. Schemes may also be set up to identify elderly people in need and provide information about available services.[2]

Domiciliary Services

The term "domiciliary services" is here used to refer to services provided in the home such as home help, meals-on-wheels and recreational services. Social services authorities may use the power contained in section 45 of the Health Services and Public Health Act 1968 to provide such services. District councils, which are not social services authorities, also have a power under the Health and Social Services and Social Security Adjudication Act 1983, Sched. 9, Pt. II to provide meals and recreation for people in their homes or elsewhere.

Section 45(4)(a) of the 1968 Act precludes authorities from making payments of money to elderly people. This is an important provision because it prohibits local authorities from making cash payments to clients so that they are able to buy in their own care. Charges may however be levied for services provided (s.45(2)).

The duty to provide a home help service is contained in paragraph 3 of Schedule 8 to the National Health Service Act 1977 and covers a number of needy groups not just the elderly:

"It shall be the duty of every local authority to provide on such a scale as is adequate for the needs of their area, or to arrange for the provision on such a scale as is adequate of home help for households where such help is required owing to the presence of a person who is suffering from illness, lying-in, an expectant mother, aged, handicapped as a result of having suffered from illness or by congenital deformity or a child who has not attained the upper limit of compulsory school age [. . .] and every such authority shall have power to provide or arrange for the provision of laundry facilities for households for which home help is being or can be provided under this subsection."

Increasingly in recent years, the home help service has become a home care service, eligibility depending upon the need for personal care. Finding out about eligibility requirements and how to challenge assessments of individual need are discussed in Chapter 3—Community Care.

---

[2] D.H.S.S. Circular No. 19/71.

DAY CARE

Day care for elderly people may be provided by the public sector, the voluntary sector or, increasingly, the private sector. It may be provided in separate day care centres or as an additional service within residential care homes. Day care may also be provided as a preventative or as an after-care service under the provisions of section 21(1)(b) and paragraph 2(1) of Schedule 8 to the National Health Service Act 1977. Local authorities have been directed to provide such services only in respect of persons suffering from mental disorder.[3]

CHARGING FOR SERVICES

Particular rules relate to charging for residential care provided by or on behalf of local authorities (see Chapter 5—Residential Care). There is considerable discretion in charging for other services: section 17 of the Health and Social Services and Social Security Adjudication Act 1983 states that an authority may charge whatever it considers reasonable. A decreasing number of local authorities levy no charges at all for some services, others operate a sliding scale of payment. Where an authority is satisfied that an individual has insufficient means, it cannot require that person to pay more than is reasonably practicable (s.17(5)). However, DHSS Circular No. 94(1) advises that charges may be imposed on persons in receipt of income support. Where there is a duty upon the local authority to provide a service that service must be provided irrespective of the individual recipient's willingness to pay. Any charges will be recoverable as a civil debt. Local authorities may seek recovery in the magistrates' court under the provisions of Health and Social Services and Social Security Adjudication Act 1983, s.17(4).

SERVICES FOR PEOPLE WITH A DISABILITY

It has been estimated that 60 per cent of persons over the age of 65 are to some extent disabled[4]; the term "disability" in this context includes mental as well as physical handicap, and mental illness.[5] Those suffering from such chronic conditions as diabetes, arthritis or cardio-vascular disease are disabled, as are those suffering from more obvious physical dysfunctions. The terms "handicap" and "disability" are used almost interchangeably in the legislation, though as Michael Oliver argues, it is

---

[3] D.H.S.S. Circular No. 19/74.
[4] *Social Trends* (H.M.S.O., 1994).
[5] Circular LAC No. 13/74.

societal attitudes which can turn a physical handicap into a social disability.[6]

There are particular legal provisions relating to disability which are potentially applicable to a large number of elderly people. One advantage of emphasising the disability aspect of the situation is that services in this field are often mandatory as opposed to discretionary, and based upon assessments which are required by statute to be comprehensive and complete (Disabled Persons Act 1986, s.4). The thrust of the legislation is about need, and services adequately flexible to meet that need.

The relevant legislation in this area is section 29 of the National Assistance Act 1948; Chronically Sick and Disabled Persons Act 1970; the Disabled Persons (Services, Consultation and Representation) Act 1986; and section 47(5) of the National Health Service and Community Care Act 1990. However, the major difficulty in practice is that, although assessment procedures and eligibility criteria tend to be standardised, levels of provision are variable, and as paragraph 5 of Circular 12/70 makes clear "criteria of need are matters for the authority to determine in the light of resources."

Section 29 of the National Assistance Act 1948

Section 29(4) of the National Assistance Act 1948 sets out the general powers of the local authority towards people with a disability, but does not include any obligation to make any arrangements for the provision of particular services. It provides that:

> "A local authority social services authority may, with the approval of the Secretary of State, and to such an extent as he may direct in relation to persons ordinarily resident in the area of the local authority, shall make arrangements for promoting the welfare of persons [. . .] who are blind, deaf or dumb, and other persons who are substantially and permanently handicapped by illness, injury or congenital deformity or other such disability as may be prescribed by the Secretary of State."

Circular No. LAC 13/74 extends this definition to include the partially-sighted, and the hard-of-hearing and also confirms that, in this context, illness includes mental disorder. Section 29 thus provides a statutory definition of "disability" for the purposes of eligibility for local authority services. Circular No. LAC 93(10) calls upon district health authorities to give advice to local authorities on who is disabled within the meaning of the Act. There are separate and established registration procedures for blind and partially-sighted people, using form BD8.[7]

The provision of local authority services to people with disabilities is strengthened by Appendix 2 to Circular No. LAC 93(10), which refers back to section 29(1) of the Act and approves the making of arrangements under that section for all persons to whom that subsection applies (*i.e.* all

---

[6] Oliver, *The Politics of Disablement* (1990).
[7] L.A.S.S.L. (90)1.

disabled persons), but *directs* locals authorities to make arrangements for persons who are ordinarily resident in their area for all or any of the following purposes:

- (*a*) To provide a social work service and such advice and support as may be needed for people in their own homes or elsewhere.
- (*b*) To provide, whether at centres or elsewhere, facilities for social rehabilitation and adjustment in overcoming limitations of mobility or communication.
- (*c*) To provide, whether at centres or elsewhere, facilities for occupational, social, cultural or recreational activities.

Thus it appears that local authorities are required both to provide a social work service for people with disabilities and a range of day care opportunities.

Chronically Sick and Disabled Persons Act 1970

The passing of the Chronically Sick and Disabled Persons Act 1970 was a landmark insofar as it required the local authority to "inform themselves" (s.1) of the number of persons in their area to whom section 29 of the National Assistance Act 1948 applied, and to assess the extent of the need for the local authority to make arrangements for the provision of services under that section. In other words, the local authority is required to seek out people in need within their area and to make plans to meet that need: local authorities are directed to do this by keeping registers of disabled people within their area.[8] It is not however a legal requirement that people register as a prerequisite for their eligibility for services.[9] The 1970 Act contains a duty to publicise services and to inform users of any other local authority services which might be available to them (s.1(2)). The aim of the Act was to provide a comprehensive local authority service for the disabled: the Act thus not only addresses itself to social services departments (s.2), but also to housing departments and planning departments, concerning, for example, adaptations to property and the provision of special accommodation (see Chapter 10—Housing Matters), and access to public buildings.

Section 2(1), however, is central to the working of the Act. It imposes a duty (not a power) upon the local authority to meet the needs of an individual disabled person by the provision of any of a long list of services, namely:

- (*a*) The provision of practical assistance in the home.
- (*b*) The provision of, or assistance in, obtaining wireless, television, library or similar recreational activities (most often applied to

---

[8] Circular LAC No. 93(10), para. 2.
[9] *ibid.* para. 3.

people who are blind through the "talking books" or similar services).

(c) The provision of recreational activities outside the home, or assistance to that person in taking advantage of educational facilities available to him.

(d) The provision of or assistance with travel facilities to enable that person to participate in services provided by the authority, or equivalent services.

(e) The provision of any works of adaptation in the home or any additional facilities designed to secure his greater safety, comfort or convenience.

(f) Facilitating the taking of holidays, whether arranged by the local authority or otherwise.

(g) The provision of meals in the home or elsewhere.

(h) The provision for that person of, or assistance in obtaining, a telephone or any special equipment necessary to enable him to use a telephone.

Assessments for the provision of services under section 2 are usually carried out by occupational therapists employed by the local authority social services department. They will supply a variety of aids to daily living, ranging from bathing equipment to hoists to special cutlery. Wheelchairs are usually provided by the health authority.

Local authorities also operate the orange badge parking scheme under section 21 of the Chronically Sick and Disabled Persons Act and the Disabled Persons (Badges for Motor Vehicles) (Amendment) Regulations 1991.[10] The 1991 regulations have introduced a new "passport style" orange badge and have tightened eligibility for the scheme: those receiving the higher rate of the mobility component of disability living allowance (for which see Chapter 11 — Welfare Benefits and Finance) will automatically qualify for the scheme, but those people receiving the lower rate must also show that their disability is permanent and substantial and causes inability to walk or very considerable difficulty in walking. The Local Authorities' Traffic Orders (Exemptions for Disabled Persons) (England & Wales) (Amendment) Regulations 1991[11] detail the parking concessions available to orange badge users. A vehicle displaying an orange badge need not be driven by the disabled person themselves. There is a right of appeal to the Secretary of State against refusal or withdrawal of a badge.

Section 1(2)(a) of the Chronically Sick and Disabled Persons Act places the local authority under a duty to publicise the services that it provides, and section 1(2)(b) a duty to ensure that service users are informed of any other of those services "which in the opinion of the authority is relevant to his needs."

---

[10] S.I. 1991 No. 2708.
[11] S.I. 1991 No. 2709.

Disabled Persons (Services, Consultation and Representation) Act 1986

The Disabled Persons (Services, Consultation and Representation) Act 1986 imposes no new duties upon the local authority by way of service provision. What it does do is introduce a new procedure whereby the disabled person themselves or their representative may make representations to the local authority on the extent of their need for services and support (ss.1–3). The local authority must then provide a written and reasoned statement of the applicant's assessed need together with a statement of what services the authority is able to provide (s.3). Section 4 of the Act requires the local authority to assess the needs of a disabled person for any of the services listed in section 2 of the Chronically Sick and Disabled Persons Act 1970, if requested to do so by that person himself or by his carer. The needs of carers are specifically addressed by section 8 which requires the local authority to take into account, in their assessment, the ability of the carer to provide help on a regular basis. The section covers any person who is providing a substantial amount of care for a person living at home; it is not restricted to carers living in the same household as the disabled person.

Section 9 of the Act takes further the information-giving obligations upon the local authority under the Chronically Sick and Disabled Persons Act by requiring them to give information about services that not only they, but any other authority or organisation provide. It is worth noting moreover that relevant provisions of the Chronically Sick and Disabled Persons Act and the Disabled Persons (Services, Consultation Representation) Act apply equally to those who are resident in hospital or in residential care, as they do to those living in the community.

Though sections 4, 8 and 9 of the Act are in force, it was announced by the government in April 1991 that sections 1 to 3 of the 1986 Act would not be implemented in the light of developments in community care. Unfortunately, the National Health Service and Community Care Act 1990 in no way replicates the principles of advocacy and consumer involvement in the design of services which were the thrust behind the 1986 Act. Section 47(5) of that Act however makes it clear that any assessment of the need of a person appearing to be disabled should take place under section 4 of the Disabled Persons Act 1986. This is important because an assessment under that Act is a more thorough assessment than an assessment under section 47(2) of the National Health Service and Community Care Act need be. Assessments under the 1990 Act may be pitched at any one of six levels from a simple interview with the duty officer to a comprehensive assessment at level six.[12] Persons who are disabled, however, should always be offered the level six equivalent provided by section 4 of the Disabled Persons Act.

---

[12] *Managers' Guide to the Implementation of the Act* (H.M.S.O., 1991).

Discrimination against disabled people

The government has announced (November 16, 1994) that it now intends to bring in legislation to introduce new rights for disabled people. This follows a consultation exercise based on the document *A Consultation on Government Measures to Tackle Discrimination Against Disabled People* (1994). The key areas in which discrimination is likely to be addressed are: employment, building regulations, access to goods and services, financial services, and the appointment of a new advisory body to work closely with existing bodies representing the interests of disabled people.

RESIDENTIAL CARE

The local authority provision of residential care is governed by section 21(1) of the National Assistance Act 1948, and is available

> "for persons who by reasons of age, infirmity, or any other circumstances are in need of care and attention which is not otherwise available to them."

Section 21(1) has been amended by section 42 of the National Health Service and Community Care Act 1990. This substituted for the word "infirmity" the words "illness, disability".

As section 21 is the first section of Part III of the National Assistance Act, such accommodation has become commonly known as "Part III" accommodation. Directions made by the Secretary of State under section 21(1) impose a duty upon local authorities to provide such accommodation.[13]

Ordinary residence

The duty of any particular authority is limited, except in cases of "urgent need", to those who are "ordinarily resident" within the area of the local authority.[14] Being "ordinarily resident" usually involves a "settled intention" to reside in one particular area rather than elsewhere.[15] Where two or more authorities disagree specifically about the "ordinary residence" of a patient discharged from hospital, the matter must be referred for determination by the Secretary of State.[16]

Circular No. LAC 93(7) makes it clear that where an individual does not appear to have any settled residence, it is the responsibility of the authority where that person actually is to provide the residential care to meet their needs. Any disputes between authorities should be resolved at a later stage. Rules for determining the responsibilities of housing

---

[13] Circular No. LAC 13/74; Circular No. LAC (91)12.
[14] National Assistance Act 1948, s.24.
[15] *R. v. Waltham Forest, ex p. Vale, The Times,* February 25, 1985.
[16] National Assistance Act 1948, s.32(3).

authorities, *i.e.* the "local connection" provisions of Part III of the Housing Act 1985, specifically should not be used to identify ordinary residence for social services purposes.

Particular difficulties may arise where people have spent an extensive period of time in residential accommodation away from their home area. If the placement was made by the local authority, this will not normally change the ordinary residence of the person concerned. However, if it was a private arrangement that person would normally become ordinarily resident in their new area.[17]

Involving the private and voluntary sectors

The National Health Service and Community Care Act 1990 has enabled local authorities to seek placements in both the private and voluntary sectors, and, for the first time, to make placements in nursing homes. To this end section 42(2) of the 1990 Act inserts a new section 26(1A–D) into the National Assistance Act 1948. Section 26(1A) limits this power where board and personal care are provided to *registered* residential or nursing homes, and section 26(1C) forbids arrangements being made with any person who has been convicted of an offence under any provisions of the Registered Homes Act 1984 or regulations. Thus the contractual freedom of the local authority is statutorily limited, and residential home owners are given an additional incentive to comply with the provisions of the Registered Homes Act (discussed in Chapter 6—Inspecting Residential Care).

Changes in the funding arrangements for residential care, whereby monies are transferred from the Department of Social Security to local authorities, has meant that all applicants for residential care who are seeking public funding for placements must first pass through the local authority's own assessment procedures. This ensures that all alternatives to residential care are considered and that residential care is chosen only when a clear need is established. "Direct" placements, including placements arranged by relatives, are therefore no longer possible when "top-up" public funding is sought.

---

[17] Circular No. LAC 93(7), para. 7.

Chapter 3
Community Care

The National Health Service and Community Care Act 1990 is the legislative embodiment of the government's policy on community care. It is based upon the Griffiths Report *Community Care: Agenda for Action* (1988) and the White Paper *Caring for People* (1989). Frequent reference is still made to these documents in interpreting the scope of the legislation. The essence of the policy of community care is expressed in the Griffiths Report: enabling people to remain in the community for as long as possible, by making available a range of community care services, following a proper assessment of need including the needs of carers, and by extending choice through the use of the voluntary and private sectors. The Policy Guidance on the National Health Service and Community Care Act (1990) develops further what ought to be done by local authorities in order to meet what Griffiths established as the six key objectives of community care.[1] These are:

(1) To promote the development of domiciliary, day and respite services to enable people to live in their own homes wherever feasible and sensible.
(2) To ensure that service providers make practical support for carers a high priority.
(3) To make proper assessment of need and good care management the cornerstone of high quality care.
(4) To promote the development of a flourishing independent sector alongside good quality public services.
(5) To clarify the responsibilities of agencies and make it easier to hold them to account for their performance.
(6) To secure better value for taxpayer's money by introducing a new funding structure for community care.

---

[1] Griffiths, *Community Care: Agenda for Action* (1988).

The Influence of Central Government

Local authorities are cast as the "lead" authorities in developing policies and services: neither the White Paper nor the Act change the existing responsibilities of the National Health Service (see Chapter 4—The Provision of National Health Services), though co-ordination and co-operation between the two services are consistently emphasised. The process by which requests for services are assessed, implemented and reviewed is known as care management. The Department of Health and the Social Services Inspectorate jointly have published three guides which will serve to set standards for those involved in the provision of services:

(1) *Care Management and Assessment: Practitioners' Guide* (H.M.S.O., 1991).
(2) *Care Management and Assessment: Managers' Guide* (H.M.S.O., 1991).
(3) *Care Management and Assessment: Combined Guide* (H.M.S.O., 1991).

Although local authorities have considerable discretion in how to implement community care, central government influence is strong. Section 7 of the Local Authority Social Services Act 1970 provided generally that:

"Local authorities shall, in the exercise of their social services functions, including the exercise of any discretion [. . .] act under the general guidance of the Secretary of State."

Section 50 of the National Health Service and Community Care Act 1990, however, introduces a new section 7A into the 1970 Act which states that:

"(1) every local authority shall exercise their social services functions in accordance with such directions as may be given to them under this section by the Secretary of State.
(2) Directions under this section—
(a) shall be given in writing; and
(b) may be given to a particular authority or to authorities of a particular class, or to authorities generally."

The difference is that guidance ought to be followed, but that Directions must be followed. In addition, the default powers of the Secretary of State, are (by a new section 7D inserted by section 50 of the National Health Service and Community Care Act 1990) enforceable by mandamus, following the issue of Directions for the purpose of ensuring that the duty is complied with.

Community Care Plans

Section 46(1) of the National Health Service and Community Care Act 1990 requires each local authority to prepare and publish a plan for the provision of community care services in their area, and in so doing consult any district health authority, family health services authority, and local housing authority whose area is within the area of the local authority (s.46(2)). Furthermore, section 46(2)(*d*) requires it to extend consultation to:

> "such voluntary organisations as appear to the authority to represent the interests of persons who use or are likely to use any community care services within the area of the authority or the interests of private carers who within that area provide care to persons for whom, in the exercise of their social services functions, the local authority have a power or a duty to provide a service."

The duty to consult is enforceable by means of judicial review: see *R. v. Secretary of State for Social Services, ex p. Association of Metropolitan Authorities*[2]: "The essence of consultation in the communication of a genuine invitation to give advice and a genuine consideration of that advice."[3]

The first community care plans were produced in April 1992 in accordance with the Community Care Plans Direction 1991. Local authorities are required to publish modifications to the current plan, at intervals of not more than one year. Such plans are public documents and blueprints for the local authority's strategy for the coming year. In addition, they contain a wealth of information on eligibility for services, assessment criteria and local authority procedures.

CONTRACTING FOR CARE

The position of contractors

The requirement to put a range of local authority contracts out to tender under the Local Government Act 1988 does not apply to community care services. Nevertheless, there may be a fiduciary duty owed to ratepayers to enter into the best contract possible at the lowest cost. Where a number of service-providers exist in a given area, social services departments have the opportunity to choose between them in a number of ways:

(1) by open tendering,
(2) by select tendering, or
(3) by negotiating directly with one or more suppliers.

There is no obligation upon the local authority to act fairly in the selection of would-be contractors, and a statement of council policy in the

---

[2] [1986] 1 All E.R. 164.
[3] *per* Webster J. at 167.

selection of applicants would not amount to an "offer" in the contractual sense: *R. v. Knowsley Borough Council, ex p. Maguire and Others*.[4]

A variety of types of contract may co-exist:

(1) Individual or spot contracts, where the purchaser contracts for a service for an individual user for a specified time at an agreed price. These contracts are similar to those negotiated with private customers and provide flexible, tailored packages of care.
(2) Block contracts, where the purchaser buys access to a part of or the whole of a service or facility for a specified price. The provider is paid whether the facility is used or not; there is an incentive therefore for the purchaser to maximise the use of the service and to contract in the broadest of terms.
(3) Cost and volume contracts, where a volume of service and a total cost is agreed and any additional service is provided on an individual price basis.

Each of these contracts combines different risks for the provider, and varying degrees of flexibility for the user. What use is made of each of them will depend upon the amount of competition in the market and the policies of the local authority. Contracts should cover:

(1) a description of the type of service to be provided and a statement of the aims and objectives to be achieved;
(2) a statement of the quality of care expected;
(3) obligations of the care provider in respect of health and safety matters and anti-discriminatory practice;
(4) the complaints procedure that exists for the benefit of the consumer of the service;
(5) dispute resolution procedures; and
(6) the arrangements for contract monitoring and review.

(For an overview of contractual issues see *Diversification and the Independent Residential Care Sector* (H.M.S.O., 1993).)

The local authority may introduce any term that it wishes into the contract, provided that it is not unreasonable and is within the objects of the legislation (*R. v. Newcastle Upon Tyne City Council, ex p. Dixon*[5]). Where an agreement is terminable on notice, there is no right to be consulted before notice of termination is given (*R. v. Kent County Council, ex p. Ashford Borough Council*[6]).

---

[4] (1992) 90 L.G.R. 653.
[5] *The Times*, October 26, 1993.
[6] [1993] C.O.D. 47.

Users' rights

Various contractual arrangements may exist between the local authority and providers of services.[7] Ordinary contractual principles will apply to these arrangements. Though the emphasis is on quality assurance through contract specifications (and all local authorities now have their own contracts sections), the contractor, as in every commercial arrangement is obliged only to work to these specifications, and he is not liable if ultimately their design does not meet the user's requirements. The contract, moreover, is between the provider of services and the local authority. Thus, for example, if a person is placed in residential care by the local authority he himself cannot sue on the contract if the home owner is in breach, though he may have an action in negligence if there is a breach of a duty of care: *Midland Bank Trust Co. v. Hetts Stubbs and Kemp*.[8] The position would be otherwise if he could prove the existence of a collateral contract, either made explicit or inferred as a result of the dealings of the parties: *Shanklin Pier v. Detel Products*.[9] Legally, however, it does not appear that the individual user is well protected if the care arranged by the local authority is unacceptable to him.

In *Ephraim v. Newham London Borough Council*[10] an attempt was made to hold the local authority itself liable in negligence for damage suffered by the plaintiff in a fire at a lodging house, the address of which she had been given by the local authority's housing department. The local authority owed a duty to the plaintiff as a homeless person not in priority need to provide "such advice and assistance as they consider appropriate" (Housing Act 1985, s.65). The fact that the plaintiff sought and relied upon the advice of the borough council in securing accommodation showed that there was sufficient proximity between the plaintiff and the defendant for a duty of care to arise. However, the extent of the duty was held to be limited by section 365(1) of the Housing Act 1985 and regulations made thereunder. These required the local authority to ensure means of escape from multi-occupied houses only when they were three or more storeys high. The lodging house in question was only two storeys high and thus not within the scope of section 365(1). Would it have made a difference if the accommodation had been owned by the local authority? Glidewell L.J. (at p. 419) thought that it would have:

"in cases where the housing authority are under a duty to provide or secure accommodation to [*sic*] a homeless person who is in priority need, they may also be under a duty to ensure that the accommodation is reasonably safe. No doubt that it is correct where the housing authority themselves provide accommodation for such persons, in property which the authority own or in

---

[7] See Price Waterhouse, *Implementing Community Care: Purchaser, Commissioner and Provider Roles* (H.M.S.O., 1992).
[8] [1979] Ch. 384.
[9] [1951] 2 K.B. 854.
[10] (1993) 91 L.G.R. 412, C.A.

> which they have some other interest. But in cases where the authority secure accommodation for such persons in property controlled by some other person or body, for example, bed and breakfast accommodation, we express no opinion as to the extent of the housing authority's duty in this respect."

It will certainly be the case then that local authorities which provide community care services (including residential care) in premises that they own will be liable in negligence for harm suffered by the user of those services. This duty may also extend to premises which the local authority are under a duty to inspect (such as residential care homes under the Registered Homes Act 1984). However the position is unclear in respect of other premises or in respect of other services, for the provision of which the local authority has contracts with private providers.

COMMUNITY CARE ASSESSMENTS

Section 47 of the National Health Service and Community Care Act 1990 requires local authorities, for the first time, to carry out an assessment of need "where it appears to a local authority that any person for whom they may provide or arrange for the provision of community care services, may be in need of any such services." (s.47(1)(a)). Note, however, that the duty is not owed to all, but only to those who are prima facie in need of community care services (as defined in s.46(3)). The local authority "having regard to the results of that assessment, shall then decide whether his needs call for the provision by them of any such service" (s.47(1)(b)). As subsections (a) and (b) are distinct, the process is thus a two-stage one: first, the assessment of need, and secondly, a decision on the provision of service. It is clear therefore, that the duty to assess can stand alone, irrespective of the ability of the local authority to provide services. This may be of some use to those who wish to arrange their own services elsewhere, but who merely need advice and guidance on suitability. Those who wish to challenge the local authority (for example through the representations and complaints procedure) on the disparity between their assessed needs and the actual service provided should emphasise the distinction between the two stages.

Though the emphasis throughout is on "needs led assessment", this is not the same as "user led" assessment. In other words, what people say they want or would like may not be the same as that which a professional deems necessary. Disagreement may also exist between users and carers, in which case the *Practitioners' Guide* (1991), para. 3.34, states that it may be appropriate to offer carers the opportunity of a separate assessment of their needs.

Judicial review will potentially be available where a local authority acts unlawfully, irrationally or unfairly in refusing or failing to carry out an assessment properly, according to the principles laid down in *Associated*

Provincial Picture Houses v. Wednesbury Corporation.[11] An excellent analysis of the legal issues is provided by Richard Gordon in *Community Care Assessments: A Practical Legal Framework* (1993).

Once an apparent need is recognised, there seems to be no further onus upon the applicant to prove his case. The duty is then upon the local authority to carry out a proper assessment: *R. v. Reigate & Banstead Borough Council, ex p. Paris.*[12] So what are the elements of a proper assessment?

The *Managers' Guide* (1991) proposes six possible levels of assessment relating both to the complexity of the presenting problem and the degree of risk involved.[13] These range from what is termed a "simple assessment", where the need is simple and defined, such as a request for a bus pass or disabled car badge, to a comprehensive, multi-disciplinary assessment where care needs are inter-related and risk is high. The former assessment may be carried out by a member of the reception staff; the latter calls for a professionally qualified or specialist worker.

The following legal principles should apply to the making of an assessment:

(1) The authority must take all relevant matters but not any irrelevant matters into account. In particular, if medical evidence is provided, it must be taken into account by the receiving authority, or if they are inclined to disagree with it an alternative medical opinion must be sought: *R. v. Bath City Council, ex p. Sangermano.*[14]

(2) If the authority declines to make an assessment, it must give a reason for its decision: *R. v. Civil Service Appeal Board, ex p. Cunningham.*[15] A declaration may be sought that a refusal to consider a request for assessment is wrong in law, though there is no power in the court to award damages: *R. v. Ealing London Borough Council, ex p. Leaman.*[16]

(3) An unreasonable delay in making an assessment may be grounds for a judicial review, though the court may be reluctant to use mandamus in order to allow the applicant jump the queue: *R. v. Secretary of State for the Home Department, ex p. Phansopkar.*[17]

(4) Procedural impropriety in carrying out the assessment may be grounds for judicial review, particularly where an expectation is raised that a particular procedure will be followed: *R. v. Secretary of State for the Home Department, ex p. Asif Khan.*[18] Paragraph 3.18 of the

---

[11] [1948] 1 K.B. 223.
[12] (1984) 15 Fam.Law 28.
[13] *Managers' Guide to the Implementation of the Act* (H.M.S.O., 1991), p. 44.
[14] (1984) 17 H.L.R. 94.
[15] [1991] 4 All E.R. 310.
[16] *The Times*, February 10, 1984.
[17] [1976] Q.B. 606.
[18] [1984] 1 W.L.R. 1337.

Policy Guidance is of importance here. This advises local authorities to publish information not only about the services that they provide, but also about their assessment procedures and about how and where to apply for an assessment. Local authorities may be bound by a procedure which they have publicised in that way.

Although by virtue of section 47(4) of the National Health Service and Community Care Act the Secretary of State may give directions as to the manner in which an assessment is to be carried out and the form it is to take, no such directions have in fact been issued with the result that it "shall be carried out in such a manner and take such form as the local authority consider appropriate" (s.47(4)).

There may, of course, exist circumstances in which a detailed assessment is not possible, and section 47(5) provides for this by allowing a local authority to provide or arrange for the provision of community care services on a temporary basis without carrying out a prior assessment of need "if in the opinion of the authority, the condition of that person is such that he requires those services as a matter of urgency." In this situation, a proper assessment of his needs should be made as soon as is practicable thereafter (s.47(6)).

COMMUNITY CARE SERVICES

It is important to note, however, that the duty to assess under the National Health Service and Community Care Act 1990 relates to "community care services" alone. "Community care services" are defined in section 46(3) as:

> "services which a local authority may provide or arrange to be provided under any of the following provisions.
>
> (a) Part III of the National Assistance Act 1948;
> (b) Section 45 of the Health Services and Public Health Act 1968;
> (c) Section 21 of and Schedule 8 to the National Health Service Act 1977; and
> (d) Section 117 of the Mental Health Act 1983."

The substantive provisions of these Acts are discussed in Chapter 2 — The Delivery of Social Services but in brief, Part III of the National Assistance Act 1948 refers to the duty of the local authority to provide residential accommodation for people in need in their own area; section 45 of the Health Services and Public Health Act 1968 refers to the general power given to the local authority to promote the welfare of elderly people; section 21 of, and Schedule 8 to, the National Health Service Act 1977 places a duty upon the local authority to provide a home help service and also empowers the local authority to provide services for people suffering from either physical or mental illness; and section 117 of the Mental Health Act 1983 imposes aftercare duties in respect of people detained under section 3 of that Act. The National Health Service and Community Care Act therefore imposes no new substantive powers or duties upon local authorities to provide services that were not previously provided under existing legislation. Yet, it does provide new means of planning for, arranging and allocating these services. In other words, it imposes a new administrative and managerial structure, but does not fundamentally alter the range of services provided, which are still largely at the discretion of the local authority.

OTHER SERVICES

Services for people with a disability, provided by the local authority under section 2 of the Chronically Sick and Disabled Persons Act 1970, are outside the definition of community care services set out in section 46. This is because there is a duty upon the local authority to provide those services once the need for them is established. The Chronically Sick and Disabled Persons Act, moreover, has its own assessment regime under the Disabled Persons (Services, Consultation and Representation) Act 1986. The distinction is brought about by section 47(2) of the National Health Services and Community Care Act:

> "If at any time during the assessment of the needs of any person under subsection (1)(a) above it appears to a local authority that he is a disabled person, the authority —
>
> (a) shall proceed to make such a decision as to the services he requires as is mentioned in Section 4 of the Disabled Persons (Services, Consultation and Representation) Act 1986 without his requesting them to do so under that section; and
> (b) shall inform him that they will be doing so and of his rights under that Act."

An assessment of the needs of a disabled person is likely to involve a comprehensive multi-disciplinary assessment as detailed in the *Managers' Guide* (1991).[19]

Social care, health care and, in some circumstances, housing, are sometimes difficult to separate. There is no statutory definition of social care and health care needs to assist in the allocation of responsibility for meeting those needs, and boundaries between the two are often blurred. The emphasis instead is on multi-disciplinary assessments, but still with the local authority as the "lead" authority. Section 47(3) provides that:

> "If at any time during the assessment of the needs of any person under subsection 1(a) above, it appears to a local authority —

---

[19] *Managers' Guide to the Implementation of the Act* (H.M.S.O., 1991), p. 44.

(a) that there may be a need for the provision to that person by such District Health Authority as may be determined in accordance with regulations of any services under the National Health Service Act 1977, or

(b) that there may be a need for the provision to him of any services which fall within the functions of a local housing authority (within the meaning of the Housing Act 1985) which is not the local authority carrying out the assessment,

the local authority shall notify the District Health Authority or local housing authority and invite them to assist, to such extent as is reasonable in the circumstances, in the making of the assessment; and in making their decision as to the provision of the services needed for the person in question, the local authority shall take into account any services which are likely to be made available for him by that District Health Authority or local housing authority."

If either authority refuses to co-operate in the assessment, it would be open to the local authority to seek judicial review of that refusal on the grounds that it is based upon a misinterpretation of their statutory powers, or that the other authority is acting unreasonably in its refusal. In the converse situation where another authority provides information which is relevant to the assessment, such as medical information, the local authority will not be deemed to have discharged its own statutory responsibility properly unless it takes that information into account. Judicial review cannot however be used to impose co-operation between authorities if this would be tantamount to prejudicing that other authority's proper discharge of its functions, as where a social services authority sought to compel a housing authority to interpret its duty towards a homeless family in a particular way: *R. v. Northavon District Council, ex p. Smith.*[20]

THE PROVISION OF SERVICES

Having made an assessment of need for community care services under section 47(1)(a), subsection 1(b) then comes into operation, requiring the local authority to decide whether his needs call for them to provide any such services. This is where issues of targeting, rationing and prioritising come into play. Conceptually, the distinction between assessing need and deciding upon the allocation of available services follows the distinction drawn in the Children Act between local authorities' duties to assess children in need (s.17) and the provision of resources to meet that need (Sched. 2). Both the *Policy Guidance* (1990)[21] and the so-called Laming Letter[22] advocate priority being given to those whose needs are the greatest. An example of this would be the allocation of home care to

---

[20] [1994] 3 W.L.R. 403, H.L.
[21] *Community Care in the Next Decade and Beyond: Policy Guidance* (1990), para. 3.24.
[22] Circular C.I. (92)34, para. 14.

those with personal care rather than domestic needs. Although local authorities are encouraged to publish their criteria for determining when services should be provided,[23] the rigid application of a blanket policy, regardless of the assessed circumstances of each individual case, could amount to a fettering of discretion: *Stringer v. Minister of Housing and Local Government.*[24] Any discretion, moreover, must be within the policy and objects of the statute: *Padfield v. Minister of Agriculture, Fisheries and Food.*[25]

Where the statute is subjectively worded and leaves the decision to the local authority, as does section 47(1)(*b*), the courts have been reluctant to intervene: a good example is *Wyatt v. Hillingdon London Borough Council*[26] where the matter in dispute was the allocated number of home help hours to an elderly disabled woman. As long as the local authority have applied their minds to the question of providing resources to meet a need, a service may be refused on the grounds that it would be too expensive to provide: *R. v. Hertfordshire County Council, ex p. Three Rivers District Council.*[27] The *Policy Guidance* (1990), however, makes it clear that the service user's ability to make private provision is not a relevant factor (though of course he may be asked to contribute financially to the services provided).[28]

CARE MANAGEMENT

The implementation of the service delivery decision is by means of the process known as care management.[29] This process is not statutory but administrative; it covers the elements of assessment, care-planning, monitoring and reviewing.

Care planning

All users in receipt of a continuing service should have a care plan, even if only a brief one, which defines the user's needs and the objectives to be met by any service provider.[30] A care plan should contain the following:

   (*a*) the overall objectives,
   (*b*) the specific objectives of
      — users
      — carers
      — service providers,
   (*c*) the criteria for measuring the achievement of those objectives,

---

[23] *Community Care in the Next Decade and Beyond: Policy Guidance* (1990), para. 3.18 (hereafter *Policy Guidance* (1990)).
[24] [1970] 1 W.L.R. 1281.
[25] [1968] A.C. 997.
[26] (1978) 76 L.G.R. 727.
[27] (1992) 90 L.G.R. 526.
[28] *Policy Guidance* (1990), para. 3.1.
[29] *Care Management and Assessment: Practitioners' Guide* (1991).
[30] *ibid.* para. 4.3.

(*d*) the services to be provided by which personnel/agency,

(*e*) the cost to the user and the contributing agencies,

(*f*) the other options considered,

(*g*) any point of difference between the user, carer, care planning practitioner or other agency,

(*h*) any unmet needs with reasons—to be separately notified to the planning system,

(*i*) the names of person(s) responsible for implementing, monitoring and reviewing the care plan, and

(*j*) the date of the first planned review.[31]

Paragraph 4.37 says that care plans should be set out in concise written form, linked with the assessment of need. It is the care plan as the resource decision, however, and not the assessment of need, which legally constitutes the "decision" in any subsequent application for judicial review where certiorari is sought. However, there is a lack of clarity in the *Practitioners' Guide* as to the legal status of the care plan:

> "The care plan does not have a legal standing as a contract but, to reinforce the sense of commitment, contributors (including the user) may be asked to signify their agreement by signing. With or without signatures, the expectation is that contributors will honour their commitments and the care plan will be the means of holding them to account. As such a care plan may be used as evidence in the consideration of a complaint."[32]

If the care plan is not to be construed as a contract (giving rise to strict contractual liability), this does not mean, however, that it is incapable of giving rise to rights in private law. Although it was decided in *Cocks v. Thanet District Council*[33] that the duty to assess and determine need is a public law function, once a decision is reached, rights are created in private law which the public authority must then meet.

Implementing the care plan

It is in the implementation of the care plan that policy considerations figure most strongly. The philosophy of the Griffiths Report (1988) was that of the "enabling" state, where local authorities should be arrangers and purchasers of care services rather than monopolistic providers. A greater flexibility and choice for both purchasers and providers is thus built into the system.

(a) Residential accommodation

In particular, section 42 of the National Health Service and Community Care Act 1990 enables arrangements for the provision of residential accommodation to be made with the voluntary and the private sector by

---

[31] *ibid.* para. 4.37.

[32] *ibid.* para. 4.38.

[33] [1983] 2 A.C. 286.

introducing new sections 1A to 1D into section 26 of the National Assistance Act 1948. For the first time local authorities are enabled to arrange for accommodation to be provided in nursing homes, subject to obtaining the consent of the District Health Authority.[34] In practice, consent to such placement is normally given by the consultant or general practitioner responsible for the patient's care.

(b) Domiciliary care and day care
Private domiciliary care is less developed than private residential care, although a recent report from the Social Services Inspectorate encourages diversity of provision by the private residential care sector.[35] There is no requirement for such services to be registered except under the Employment Agencies Act 1973[35a] and the Nurses' Agency Act 1957. On the other hand, voluntary and private organisations providing day care services may have their premises subject to inspection by the local authority under section 48 of the National Health Service and Community Care Act.[36]

If assessment is to be truly needs led then services such as night sitting and housekeeping services, which were not conventionally provided by local authorities, may now be made available. Some local authorities are willing to expend resources that might have been used in paying for residential care to provide intensive domiciliary support instead.

Reviewing the care plan

Monitoring and reviewing the care plan are important aspects of care management. A review is defined[37] as "the mechanisms by which changing needs are identified and services adapted accordingly." It provides opportunities to reassess current needs[38] and redefine service requirements.[39] In procedural terms, therefore, it ought to be carried out as carefully as the original assessment. A difficulty may arise where the decision is taken to withdraw a service. If an entire service is to be discontinued, or an established practice withdrawn, there may well be a duty to allow representations to be made: *R. v. Secretary of State for the Home Department, ex p. Asif Khan.*[40] On an individual level, the Laming Letter counsels that in those cases where assessments have been undertaken, particularly under section 2(1) of the Chronically Sick and Disabled Person Act 1970, authorities must satisfy themselves before any

---

[34] See further the Residential Accommodation (Determination of District Health Authority) Regulations 1992 (S.I. 1992 No. 3182) and Circular No. LAC 92(22).
[35] *Diversification and the Independent Residential Care Sector* (H.M.S.O., 1993).
[35a] Employment agencies may however be subject to deregulation in future under the provisions of s.1. of the Deregulation Act 1994.
[36] See Chap. 6—Inspecting Residential Care.
[37] *Managers' Guide to the Implementation of the Act* (H.M.S.O., 1991), para. 7.1.
[38] *ibid.* para. 7.17.
[39] *ibid.* para. 7.20.
[40] [1984] 1 W.L.R. 1337.

reduction in service provision takes place that the user does not have a continuing need for it.[41] As long as there is a continuing need a service must be provided, although following review it is possible that an assessed need might be met in a different way.

PAYING FOR COMMUNITY CARE

The local authority should do its needs assessment under the National Health Service and Community Care Act 1990 first and establish what services it feels should be provided, and then decide whether to do a means assessment to work out what, if anything, the recipient of such services should pay.

Under the Health and Social Services and Social Security Adjudications Act 1983, s.17, a local authority providing services may recover such charge (if any) as it considers reasonable. Under the section, local authorities can, therefore, choose whether they wish to make charges for the services provided and, if so, how much. This inevitably means that charges vary from authority to authority and can amount from nothing, to a nominal amount for "home help" stamps (generally purchased from a local post office), to a more realistic price for the cost of the service provided.

Under the Health and Social Services and Social Security Adjudications Act 1983, s.17(3):

> "If a person:
>   (a)   avails himself of a service to which this section applies, and
>   (b)   satisfies the authority providing the service that his means are insufficient for it to be reasonably practicable for him to pay for the service the amount which he would otherwise be obliged to pay for it,
>   the authority shall not require him to pay more for it than it appears to them that it is reasonably practicable for him to pay."

If the care is provided by way of a place in a residential or nursing home, then, subject to the means test, the recipient pays for the care at the rate negotiated between the local authority and the care home. If the care plan is for services to be provided maintaining the individual in the community, the costs of comprehensive care in one's own home can be extremely expensive—more so than for a care home bed. Some local authorities are seeking to establish a rule whereby they will only provide care in the community up to the equivalent cost of a care home bed if it is the local authority itself which is responsible for a proportion of the ultimate cost as the recipient of care is not totally self-funding.

If the services are being provided under the Chronically Sick and Disabled Persons Act 1970, there is a duty on the local authority to provide the service, whether or not it is likely to be paid by the recipient

---

[41] Circular C.I. (92)34, para. 31.

for the supply of the service. The service cannot be withdrawn unless the need for the service no longer exists. Fees unpaid can, however, be recovered through the courts as a civil debt.

If care in the community is applicable, it is likely that the recipient of that care is eligible for the "needs" tested, as opposed to the "means" tested, benefits of either disability living allowance or attendance allowance.[42] The benefits are provided to help pay for care, but there is no requirement that the recipient must use the benefit for that purpose. It may also be that a carer is eligible for invalid care allowance or that a grant from the Independent Living Fund is applicable.[43]

In addition to services assessed and provided by the local authority (which may include provision from private agencies contracted to provide the service on behalf of the local authority), an individual can make his own private arrangements and employ his own care attendant, nurse or home help. These private arrangements may be additional to services provided under the assessment by the local authority or a purely private arrangement between individuals, without reference to the local authority or any form of needs assessment.

---

[42] See Chap. 11—Welfare, Benefits and Finance.
[43] ibid.

Chapter 4

The Provision of National Health Services

Though the National Health Service has undergone many reorganisations and internal changes since its inception in 1948, its legal mandate would still be familiar to its founders, insofar as it is the Secretary of State (for Health's) duty:

> "to continue the promotion in England and Wales of a comprehensive health service designed to secure improvement:
>
> (a)   in the physical and mental health of the people of those countries, and
> (b)   in the prevention, diagnosis and treatment of illness.
> and for the purpose to provide or secure the effective provision of services in accordance with this Act."[1]

Such a duty is owed to the public at large, and is not enforceable in individual cases: *R. v. Secretary of State for Social Services, ex p. Hincks*.[2]

Increasingly, the National Health Service is operating according to commercial principles, and parallels the changes in the delivery of social services by its reorganisation according to a purchaser/provider split. A good account of the National Health Service changes and of the availability of services for elderly people is provided by Christina Victor in *Health and Health Care in Later Life*.[3]

THE NATIONAL HEALTH SERVICE AND COMMUNITY CARE ACT 1990

The National Health Service and Community Care Act 1990 furthered the shift within the National Health Service from a hierarchical system to one based on relatively autonomous units. Regional health authorities exercise primarily a planning function; district health authorities remain both as purchasers and providers of services; and Family Practitioner

---

[1]   National Health Service Act 1977, s.1.
[2]   (1979) 123 S.J. 436 and see Chap. 7—Complaints Procedures at p. 92.
[3]   Victor, *Health and Health Care in Later Life* (1991).

Committees are renamed and reconstituted as Family Health Services Authorities (s.12), accountable to the regions. Section 5 of, and Schedules 2 and 3 to, the Act allow for the creation of "National Health Service Trusts" which are to be self-governing bodies within the larger framework of the National Health Service. Sections 14 to 17 establish "fund holding practices" and give other practices "indicative prescribing amounts" to be fixed by the Family Health Services Authorities. Crown immunities are removed from health authorities by section 60 of the Act.

The two basic principles of the old National Health Service remain; it is funded from general taxation, and it is (for the most part) free at the point of delivery. The great division is no longer between hospital and community services, but between purchasers or commissioners of services (such as district health authorities) and providers (such as the National Health Service Trusts); the result is the creation of what is known as the "internal market", and the arrangements thus made are known as "National Health Service contracts" (ss.3 and 4). This chapter covers some of the major changes enacted in 1990 as well as wider legal issues.

NATIONAL HEALTH SERVICE TRUSTS

National Health Service Trusts are bodies corporate within the National Health Service (National Health Service and Community Care Act 1990, s.5(a)), which are run by a board of directors (executive and non-executive) with a chairman appointed by the Secretary of State. The powers, responsibilities and assets of each self-governing unit thus created are vested in the trust, which has power to dispose of assets, set up its own management structures, and employ and pay its own staff. A trust may be a single unit, or a combination of neighbouring units. Trusts remain subject to the "medical audit" provisions of section 20 of and Schedule 4 to the National Health Service and Community Care Act 1990, and are also subject to National Health Service complaints procedures, and come within the jurisdiction of the Health Service Commissioner.

National Health Service Trusts provide services in the internal market on a contractual basis. This gives greater choice concerning where a patient will be treated, and introduces an element of competition into the supply of medical services. There are three types of contract in operation:

(1) *Block contracts.* These usually operate on a rolling three-year basis with district health authorities paying an annual fee, in instalments, for access to a defined range and level of service. Such contracts should also set performance targets, for example, about waiting times or length of stay.

(2) *Cost and volume contracts.* A fixed sum is paid for a baseline level of provision. Beyond that, payment is on a case-by-case basis.

(3) *Cost per case*. This type of contract is usually found where a district health authority or fund-holding general practitioner does not have a regular contract with that hospital.

NATIONAL HEALTH SERVICE CONTRACTS

National Health Service contracts are contracts *sui generis*. A National Health Service contract is defined in section 4 as:

> "an arrangement under which one health service body ('the acquirer') arranges for the provision to it by another health service body ('the provider') of goods and services which it reasonably requires for the purposes of its functions."

Such a contract operates wholly within the public sector. It is not subject to the ordinary principles of contract law, and in effect section 4(3) is an attempt to make such a contract unenforceable in the ordinary courts. Section 4(3) reads:

> "whether or not an arrangement which constitutes a National Health Service contract would, apart from this subsection, be a contract in law, it shall not be regarded for any purpose as giving rise to contractual rights and liabilities."

Instead, disputes within the internal market concerning contracts are to be referred to the Secretary of State, whose judgment will be within the sphere of public law and thus amenable to judicial review. For details of the arbitration system to be used, see the National Health Service Contracts (Dispute Resolution) Regulations 1991.[4]

This does not mean of course that there will be no liability except in contract. There will continue to be tortious liability in respect of health authorities, as well as individual practitioners, who display negligence in the provision of medical services. There may also be a duty of care placed upon the purchasing authority to contract only with providers who can maintain acceptable standards.

It is also arguable that the law of restitution may be invoked in respect of executed contracts for the performance of which renumeration has not been forthcoming, particularly after the recognition of the independent existence of the law of unjust enrichment by the House of Lords in *Lipkin Gorman v. Karpnale*.[5] It might therefore be possible to sue for a *quantum meruit*, despite the limitations on legal action apparently imposed by section 4(3) of the 1990 Act. For discussion see Kit Baker in *National Health Service Contracts, Restitution and the Internal Market*.[6]

---

[4] S.I. 1991 No. 725.
[5] [1991] A.C. 548.
[6] (1993) 56 M.L.R. 832.

GENERAL PRACTITIONERS

General practitioners remain independent contractors and have not become employees of the new Family Health Services Authorities. Their contract is to provide general medical services to those who register with them, not to work an agreed number of hours for a fixed salary. Fund-holding practices receive their funding directly from the regional health authority, and have budgets designed to cover surgical in-patient and day care treatment, and diagnostic investigations, as well as the cost of drugs, staff salaries and certain costs relating to the premises. Otherwise general practitioners' income is based on a mixture of capitation fees, a basic practice allowance, and audited performance-related payments. The introduction of new G.P.'s contracts has produced financial incentives, encouraging general practitioners to attain targets for such things as cervical cytology and immunisations: higher capitation fees are also payable for elderly patients. Disincentives, in the form of lower rates, were introduced for the use of deputising services.

Duties and obligations

General practitioners are obliged to provide a service 24 hours a day for 365 days of the year. They are responsible for the actions of those whom they employ (such as receptionists), and for those to whom they delegate treatment. Thus a receptionist who exercises discretion on the timing of appointments or the making of a home visit is in law deemed to be acting on the authority of the general practitioner.

If a home visit is requested, the general practitioner has a discretion whether or not to ask the patient to visit the surgery instead. He is not obliged to make "monitoring" visits to check on the progress of patients unless proper medical practice demands it, and may, for example, properly put the onus on a competent patient to contact him again if his circumstances change: *Durrant v. Burke.*[7]

General practitioners may register with the Family Health Services Authority as a dispensing doctor if there is no local access to a dispensing pharmacy. One general practitioner cannot refer a patient on to another general practitioner for National Health Service treatment unless they are within the same practice; even if that general practitioner is an expert in a particular area of practice. Also, within the National Health Service, "alternative" treatments such as homeopathy and hypnotherapy can only be provided by doctors registered with the General Medical Council. At common law there is an implied covenant of confidentiality in the doctor-patient relationship; doctors can pass on information about patients only when patients have given their permission, except to other professionals involved in their treatment. The confidentiality of medical

---

[7] [1993] 4 Med. L.R. 258.

records is thus preserved, subject to the rights of patients under the Access to Health Records Act 1990.[8]

Charges

There is no charge to patients for basic general practitioner or hospital treatment: National Health Service Act 1977, s.1(2). People over pensionable age are also entitled to free prescriptions under the National Health Service (Charges for Drugs and Appliances) Regulations 1980.[9]

Doctors' lists

The National Health Service (General Medical Services) Regulations 1992[10] clearly specify the responsibilities of general practitioners concerning both administrative and clinical matters; these regulations apply both to fund-holding and non-fundholding practices. Family Health Services Authorities are responsible under the regulations for compiling lists of doctors in their area who provide general medical services. There are also separate child health surveillance, obstetric and minor surgery lists. A full-time doctor is expected to provide general medical services for not less than 26 hours in any week (reg. 15(1)(a)). The Family Health Services Authority also maintains lists of patients accepted by doctors for inclusion on their lists (reg. 19). Any person living in the practice area who is refused acceptance by a doctor onto his list is still entitled to treatment by that doctor for up to 14 days (Sched. 2, para. 4(4)) and may apply to the Family Health Services Authority for assignment to a doctor thereafter (reg. 21). Regulations 22 and 23 govern the transfer from one doctor's list to another, subject only to acceptance by the receiving doctor; the principle of "open lists" is thus established. The position of temporary residents (up to three months) is dealt with in regulation 26; persons in this category who are refused acceptance onto a doctor's list will be entitled to assignment by the Family Health Services Authority under regulation 21(1)(b).

Terms of service for doctors

Doctors' terms of service are specified in Schedule 2 to the 1992 Regulations. Paragraph 3 defines the content of any duty of care owed under the regulations:

> "Where a decision whether any, and if so what, action is to be taken under these terms of service requires the exercise of professional judgment, a doctor shall not, in reaching that decision, be expected to exercise a higher degree of skill, knowledge than [. . .] that which general practitioners as a class may reasonably be expected to exercise."

---

[8] See p. 44.
[9] S.I. 1980 No. 1503.
[10] S.I. 1992 No. 635.

The services which a doctor is required to render include:

(a) giving advice, where appropriate, to a patient in connection with the patient's general health, and in particular about the significance of diet, exercise, the use of tobacco, the consumption of alcohol and the misuse of drugs or solvents;

(b) offering to patients consultations and, where appropriate, physical examinations for the purpose of identifying, or reducing the risk of, disease or injury;

(c) offering to the patients, where appropriate, vaccination or immunisation;

(d) arranging for the referral of patients, as appropriate, for the provision of any other services under the Act; and

(e) giving advice, as appropriate, to enable patients to avail themselves of services provided by a local social services authority.[11]

Considerable emphasis is thus placed on preventative services.

Practice leaflets

Doctors are required to produce a practice leaflet detailing, *inter alia*, the times at which they are available for consultation; the method of obtaining an urgent and a non-urgent appointment; the method of obtaining an urgent and non-urgent domiciliary visit; details of any clinics provided and staff employed; and of any arrangements for receiving patients' comments on the provision of general medical services.[12] A full list is given in Schedule 12 to the Regulations.

Consultations

Newly registered patients (para. 14) and patients aged 16 to 75 years not seen within three years (para. 15) should be invited to a consultation to discuss their medical history, social circumstances and lifestyle and should be offered a physical examination to include measurement of blood pressure and weight and the analysis of a urine sample.

Patients aged 75 years and over

Paragraph 16 of Schedule 2 requires all doctors, in addition to and without prejudice to any other obligations under their terms of service, once in each period of 12 months, beginning April 1 each year:

(a) to invite each patient on his list who has attained the age of 75 years to participate in a consultation; and

(b) to offer to make a domiciliary visit to each such patient,

---

[11] *ibid.* para. 12(2).
[12] *ibid.* para. 47.

for the purpose of assessing whether he needs to render personal medical services to that patient.

The doctor shall make note in the patient's records of any matter which appears to him to be affecting the patient's general health, including where appropriate the patient's

(a) sensory functions,
(b) mobility,
(c) mental condition,
(d) physical condition including continence,
(e) social environment, and
(f) use of medicines.[13]

The doctor shall furthermore offer to discuss with the patient the conclusions he has drawn, resulting from the consultation, as to the state of the patient's health, unless it is the opinion of the doctor that to do so would be likely to cause serious harm to the physical or mental health of the patient.[14]

Research by Tremellan and Jones in 1989 strongly favoured assessment in the patient's own home: 89 per cent of the general practitioners surveyed felt that the health visitor should be involved in the assessment. The conclusion was that social, environmental and daily living activities were a more appropriate basis for assessment than clinically based tests. Based on these criteria, significant levels of need, as yet unmet, could be discovered.[15]

Access to hospital treatment

A patient cannot demand that his general practitioner refer him to any particular hospital or consultant for specialist treatment. Unless one is a private patient, access to a consultant is available only through a general practitioner or a National Health Service Clinic such as a Family Planning or Child Health Clinic. Only casualty departments and special (genito-urinary) clinics at hospitals have open access to the public. It is the consultant himself who decides whether to see patients personally or to delegate the task to a member of his team. Patients who do not want to be examined in the presence of medical students should have their wishes respected.[16]

Treatment at an Accident and Emergency Unit will normally be funded by the district health authority which will contract with National Health Service Trusts for a minimum level of provision. Fund-holding general

---

[13] ibid. para. 16(5).
[14] ibid. para. 16(8).
[15] Tremellan, J., and Jones, D.A., "Attitudes and Practices of the Primary Health Care Team towards Assessing the Very Elderly" in Journal of the Royal College of General Practitioners, Vol. 39, pp. 142–144.
[16] Circular H.M. (73)8, para. 1.

practitioners may, however, be charged for the cost of a hospital admission following treatment at an Accident and Emergency Unit.

The distinction between fundholding and non-fundholding practices is most clearly seen at the point of referral to the hospital. Fundholding practices may use their budgets to shop around for the best available service at the best available price, and are able to buy into the private sector as well as the public sector. Non-fundholding practices usually only refer patients to hospitals with which their district health authority has a contract. There will be, however, upper limits on the cost to general practitioner fundholding budgets of hospital treatment in any given year; excessive costs will be met by the regional health authority. Once a patient is referred, decisions on the extent of treatment to be provided are for the hospital consultant not the general practitioner.

COMMUNITY NURSING SERVICES

Community nursing services (district nurses, health visitors and community psychiatric nurses) are employed and managed by the district health authority or community health trusts, but often work as part of a primary health care team. As well as providing direct nursing services, community nurses have an important assessment and monitoring role.[17]

Health visitors

Health visitors are primarily concerned with preventative work and promoting better health. Their role has a strong educational element and they may hold clinics in doctors' surgeries or health centres. Though the majority of health visitors work with children, their training also equips them to work with elderly people and some are specialists in this field.

Community psychiatric nurses

Community psychiatric nurses provide specialist nursing services to people with mental health problems living in the community. Often there will be a specific nurse, or team of nurses, allocated to the care of elderly people. The services they provide include the monitoring of medication, counselling, and arranging respite care in National Health Service resources. They may also be linked to day hospitals, providing specialist care for the elderly mentally infirm.

---

[17] *Nursing in Primary Health Care*, Circular C.N.O. (77)8.

Practice nurses

General practitioners may also employ practice nurses to undertake assessments as well as to deal with practical medical procedures such as giving vaccinations and taking blood. In *Stockdale v. Nicholls*,[18] a doctor who sent his practice nurse instead of himself in response to a request for a home visit was held on the facts not to be negligent when judged by the standards of the ordinary general practitioner. Practice nurses may in fact play an important role in the health care of many elderly people, and often themselves carry out assessments of person aged 75 years and over.

Nurse practitioners

The White Paper *Working for Patients* supported the idea of nurse practitioners to whom the public would have direct access and who would have the power to prescribe a limited range of medication.[19] Though many practice nurses may come close to performing the diagnostic part of this role, the title "nurse practitioner" is not yet formally recognised by the Royal College of Nursing as having distinct legal status. The Medicinal Products: Prescription by Nurses, etc., Act 1992 will allow certain classes of nurses to be specified by regulations as "appropriate practitioners" in relation to specified descriptions or classes of medicinal products under section 58 of the Medicines Act 1968; the Act however awaits further implementation.

COMMUNITY HEALTH COUNCILS

Community Health Councils are consumer organisations representing people who use, or may wish to use, National Health Service services. They have a statutory right to be consulted concerning any substantial development of health services or variation in provision which takes place within their district: Community Health Council Regulations 1985,[20] reg. 19(1). The Community Health Councils (Access to Information) Act 1988 also extends sections 100A to 100D of the Local Government Act 1972 (access by the public to meetings and documents) to Community Health Councils.

There is also a role for Community Health Councils in representing people in complaints procedures, and part of their task is to monitor satisfaction with the range and type of services available, the quality of

---

18 [1993] 4 Med. L.R. 191.
19 *Working for Patients*, Cm. 555 (1987).
20 S.I. 1985 No. 304.

care provided, and the accuracy and accessibility of information that people are given by the National Health Service.[21]

ACCESS TO HEALTH SERVICE RECORDS

The Access to Health Records Act 1990 enables patients to see and to take copies of information manually recorded on their health service records since November 1991. Section 1(1) of the Act defines a "health record" as one which:

(a) consists of information relating to the physical or mental health of an individual who can be identified from that information or from that and other information in the possession of the holder of the record; and

(b) has been made by or on behalf of a health professional in connection with the care of that individual.

"Health professionals" include medical practitioners, dentists, opticians, pharmacists, nurses, midwives, health visitors, occupational therapists, physiotherapists and clinical psychologists. Both the National Health Service and the private sector are covered. In the case of a person incapable of managing their own affairs section 3(1) enables "any person appointed by the court to manage the affairs of the patient", in effect a receiver appointed by the Court of Protection, to apply to see the records of that person. Relatives are given no automatic right of access to records unless they are authorised to do so (s.3(1)(b)) and presumably only by a person capable of giving consent. Access may be refused to information which would cause serious harm to the physical or mental health of the patient or some other person.

Records held on computer are covered by the Data Protection Act 1984. Access is subject to similar limitations relating to the risk of harm to oneself or others: see the Data Protection (Subject Access Modification) (Health) Order 1987.[22]

In *R. v. Mid-Glamorgan Family Health Services Authority, ex p. Martin*[23] the applicant was refused judicial review of the decisions of two health authorities not to disclose to him medical reports and records made before the Access to Health Records Act 1990 came into force. It was held that the statute itself militated against the existence of any common law right of access to records prior to 1991. The doctor's common law duty to act in the best interests of his patient militated against harmful disclosure, but did require records to be made available to his legal adviser for proceedings in which he was involved.

---

[21] See Chap. 7—Complaints Procedures, at pp. 87, 89.
[22] S.I. 1987 No. 1903.
[23] *The Times*, August 16, 1994.

ACCESS TO MEDICAL REPORTS

A further step towards openness in health care was made by the Access to Medical Reports Act 1988. This established a general right of access by individuals to reports relating to themselves which are provided by medical practitioners for employment and insurance purposes. Section 3 of the Act in fact requires the patient's consent to be given before the applicant (as he is called) is supplied with a report, and section 4 enables the patient to have sight of that report before it is passed on. Furthermore these rights are enforceable by application to the county court (s.8). The only exceptions to disclosure are where serious harm would be caused to the physical or mental health of the patient, where there is information concerning third parties, or where there is information that "would indicate the intentions of the practitioner in respect of the individual" (s.7(1)).

CONSENT TO TREATMENT

Common law

Older people are quite likely to come across medical treatment of various types as the years go by. The rules in respect of consent to treatment are the same as for any adult.

Under the Patients' Charter everyone has a right "to be given a clear explanation of any treatment proposed, including any risks and alternatives, before you decide whether you will agree to the treatment."

The doctor is under a duty of care to his patient to impart the facts about a particular course of treatment. It obviously depends on the complexity of the treatment, the ability of the patient to understand and what questions the patient asks as to how much the doctor needs to say. A minimal risk or side-effect need not be disclosed, a sizeable statistical risk (say 10 per cent) should be mentioned; if not the doctor could be liable in negligence.[24]

Consent to treatment can be determined in several ways. It can be inferred by turning up for appointments or continuing to take the tablets. For other treatments, the patient will generally sign a consent form. This should specify, as best it can, the nature of the treatment to be carried out and its extent.

Consent is personal to the patient. It cannot be given by an agent under a power of attorney or receivership, or by a relative, however close.[25] As part of its consideration of the law in relation to mentally incapacitated adults, the Law Commission is looking at medical powers of attorney but

---

[24] See *Sidaway v. Board of Governers of the Bethlem Royal Hospital and the Maudsley Hospital* [1985] A.C. 871.
[25] See *Re T. (Adult: Refusal of Medical Treatment)* [1992] 4 All E.R. 649.

no decision has been taken as to whether to introduce them or in what form. Meanwhile, the involvement of relatives in discussion should be encouraged as it will help the clinicians to reach their decision as to treatment in any particular case.

Except for patients who are unconscious or severely demented, if time is taken and the treatment explained in simple terms, it should be possible for the patient to be able to make a decision as to whether or not he will accept the treatment proposed. Each patient has the right to refuse treatment, even if the refusal might seem illogical, just as he can discharge himself from hospital if he so wishes. Recent cases have confirmed this right. In *Re T.*[26] the Court of Appeal held, on the facts, that the patient had not been fit to make a genuine treatment decision due to the undue influence of her mother, her weakened state and that she had not fully appreciated the seriousness of her illness or the effectiveness of alternative courses of treatment. Even so, all three judgements clearly upheld the rights of capable adults to make their own treatment decisions, even if this decision was contrary to medical advice and what might be regarded as "sensible". In *Re C.*[27] a patient at Broadmoor Hospital had his decision to refuse the amputation of a gangrenous leg upheld, the court considering that he was fully aware of the implications of his decision and that his mental illness had not affected his competence to make that particular treatment decision.

Technically, there is an assault if treatment is given without consent, but there are circumstances where this is inevitable and damages would be unlikely to be awarded if any case were brought. Such situations arise where the patient is unconscious, affected due to a stroke and unable to communicate, or severely demented. Faced with such a patient the doctor will do that which is necessary to save his life or alleviate symptoms, particularly where the inability to consent may be temporary, for example a stroke, when consent may be obtained at a later date for such treatment as can reasonably be postponed. If the patient is known to have a view about a particular form of treatment, such as Jehovah's Witnesses and blood transfusions, then this would be taken into account by the clinician at the time.

There are situations when the doctor has to balance the control of pain against the possibility of life being shortened by the medication prescribed. As the prosecution of Dr. Nigel Cox in 1992 showed, that can be a difficult line to tread. It is unlawful to kill or be a party to the attempted killing of a patient, but there may come a time when struggling too hard to keep a patient alive is not clinically necessary and other considerations, such as the patient's wishes or pain control come into play.

In *Airedale National Health Service Trust v. Bland*[28] Lord Goff stated:

[26] *ibid.*
[27] [1994] 1 W.L.R. 290.
[28] [1993] 1 All E.R. 821 at 867.

"that the law draws a crucial distinction between cases in which a doctor decides not to provide, or to continue to provide, for his patient treatment or care which could or might prolong his life and those in which he decides, for example by administering a lethal drug, actively to bring his patient's life to an end."

Part IV of the Mental Health Act 1983

This applies to a patient "liable to be detained" under the act, therefore not to informal patients or those subject to guardianship. In such cases, the act does not apply to treatment for physical illness where the common law as detailed above applies, but it does cover treatment given to the patient in respect of the mental disorder from which he is suffering. Treatment such as naso-gastric feeding (which might be considered as medical treatment for physical symptoms) can be given under the Act where it is treatment in respect of the patient's mental condition: *Re K.B. (Adult) (Mental Patient: Medical Treatment)*.[28a] The treatment must be given by or under the direction of the Responsible Medical Officer.

Under the Mental Health Act 1983, s.57, the patient's consent must be obtained along with a second opinion. This section applies to any surgical operation for destroying brain tissue or for destroying the functioning of brain tissue and such other forms of treatment as may be specified by regulation. A certificate in writing is produced to the effect that the patient is capable of understanding the nature, purpose and likely effects of the treatment and is signed by three independent people, a registered doctor (not being the responsible officer) and two others (not being registered medical practitioners), all of whom are either members of, or appointed by, the Mental Health Act Commission.

The Mental Health Act 1983, s.58, applies to treatments specified either by regulation or to the administration of medicine to a patient, by any means and at any time, during a period for which he is liable to be detained as a patient to whom Part IV of the Act applies. It must also be the case that three months or more have elapsed since the first occasion in that period when medicine was administered by any means for his mental disorder.

There must be a certificate in writing stating that the patient consents, but if the patient is incompetent to consent or does not consent then the treatment can still be given under written certificate if it is considered that the treatment will alleviate or prevent a deterioration in the patient's condition.

The patient can withdraw his consent to treatment, when given, under section 57 and section 58 above, at any time before the treatment is completed and the sections then apply as if the continuation of treatment were a new treatment.

Treatment can be given without consent under the Mental Health Act 1983, s.62, in urgent cases where it is immediately necessary:

[28a] (1994) 19 B.M.L.R. 144. See also *B. v. Croydon Health Authority*, *The Times*, December 1, 1994, C.A.

(a) to save the patient's life;
(b) (not being irreversible) to prevent a serious deterioration in condition;
(c) (not being irreversible or hazardous) to alleviate serious suffering by the patient; or
(d) (not being irreversible or hazardous) represents the minimum interference necessary to prevent the patient behaving violently or being a danger to himself or others.

Treatment cannot be carried on beyond the point when the emergency has come to an end.

DISCHARGE OF PATIENTS FROM HOSPITAL

It has been stated in the Department of Health Circular No. LAC (89)5 and the accompanying booklet *Discharge of Patients from Hospital* that when discharge arrangements are made they should be in good time and acceptable to the patient. Everything should be fully explained and, if the discharge is into nursing or residential care which has to be paid for privately, this must have been explained in writing and accord with the patient's wishes. Pressure is often brought to bear on elderly patients to be discharged because the hospital is unable to improve or cure their condition and there is a shortage of beds. That alone is not an acceptable reason for them to be moved out of an National Health Service bed and should be resisted until an acceptable alternative can be found.

The annual report of the Health Service Commissioner for both 1992 to 1993 and 1993 to 1994 has been critical of the way discharge procedures are often implemented. Partly because of this criticism, draft guidance (HSG(94)) was produced by the National Health Service Executive in August 1994 for consultation. This is seeking to change discharge policy with the effect that, if a patient's condition is unlikely to be improved by continuing care in hospital, then the patient can be discharged into the community (probably feepaying residential or nursing care), if need be against his wishes.

If the discharge is back home, Circular No. LAC (89)5 states that any necessary assessment of home circumstances should have been done. This should ensure that any support, help or equipment required to enable the patient and any carer to cope at home is available by the time the patient leaves hospital. It may include ensuring that a patient going home alone has food provided and the heat already switched on. This may mean liaison with the local authority, in which case a firm timetable of events should be made.

The discharge arrangements should involve the patient, any carer, other relatives, the consultant and nursing staff, possibly social services and any specialist service which may be needed in the community. The patient's general practitioner should be informed, in writing and possibly by telephone, of relevant details including medication and the degree of patient management which may be required of him.

LIVING WILL/ADVANCE DIRECTIVE

The status of the living will or advance directive is uncertain in English law, there being no statutory provision for such a document, and the validity of one not yet having been considered, as such, by the courts. It is a document whereby the signatory sets out, in advance, his wishes should he be in a position in the future when he cannot be consulted about treatment decisions because of lack of capacity and there is no reasonable prospect of recovery. Such documents exist in several states in the United States of America, and the Law Commission is considering them in relation to the law and mentally incapacitated adults. Several charitable organisations are promoting them and/or have produced suggested forms, the Terence Higgins Trust being one example. Whilst they have an uncertain legal validity, such documents can help the clinicians to reach a treatment decision when the patient is no longer able to give consent.

The current position is that where a decision is necessary as to whether treatment and care are to be discontinued and the patient is unable to consent, an application should be made to the courts for a declaration as to how the medical practitioners should proceed and treatment continues until the court proceedings have been determined. This has been confirmed by the judgment in *Airedale NHS Trust v. Bland*,[29] where there are suggestions that the views expressed in a living will might be taken into account:

> "it has been held that a patient of sound mind may, if properly informed, require that life support should be discontinued [. . .] Moreover, the same principle applies when the patient's refusal to give his consent has been expressed at an earlier date, before he becomes unconscious or otherwise incapable of communicating it; though in such circumstances especial care may be necessary to ensure that the prior refusal of consent is still properly to be regarded as applicable in the circumstances which have subsequently occurred."

The most sophisticated forms in the United States of America cover a range of possible treatment and the individual's wish in each case. Great care needs to be taken to ensure that the patient's wishes are seen to be his own and not merely the reflection of someone else's vested interest. There are also suggestions that a patient's views alter depending on his state of health at the time a question is posed or if advances are made in medical science. The Law Commission has suggested limiting the period

---

[29] *ibid.* Lord Goff at p. 866.

for which an advance directive might last, after which it would need to be renewed, and that it take a specific form.

The possibility of being able to appoint a medical attorney to be consulted with regard to treatment decisions is also under consideration. At present the likelihood of legislation to recognise either concept appears remote.

Chapter 5
Residential Care

LOCAL AUTHORITY CARE

Residential care is provided by the local authority directly, by the voluntary sector, and by the private sector. Part III of the National Assistance Act 1948 still governs local authority provision of care, and the D.H.S.S. Circular No. LAC 13/74 sets out current ministerial directions under section 21(1) of that Act so as to impose a duty upon the local authority to make provision for all those in need who are ordinarily resident within the area of the local authority.

Circular No. LAC 13/74 further regulates the conduct of local authority homes by requiring authorities, *inter alia*, to:

(a) make arrangements for supervising hygiene in the accommodation provided,
(b) obtain medical and nursing attention,
(c) provide necessary services and amenities, and
(d) review the arrangements thus made.

Inspection of standards was made possible by the National Assistance (Powers of Inspection) Regulations 1948.[1] Standards of care in local authority homes were, however, largely uncontrolled, except for the demands of professionalism and political accountability, until section 48 of the National Health Service and Community Care Act 1990 gave a power to inspect premises used for the provision of "community care services", which include local authorities' own accommodation. Though there is pressure now to achieve parity of standards with the private sector, local authority homes are not subject to the Registered Homes Act 1984.

---

[1] S.I. 1948 No. 1445.

THE VOLUNTARY SECTOR

Voluntary organisations and non-profitmaking organisations such as Age Concern, the Sue Ryder Foundation and Cheshire Homes have long been involved in the provision of care, either exclusively for elderly people or for people of all ages who have particular disabilities or needs. These organisations may be either registered charities, or limited companies.

The National Assistance Act 1948, s.21(10), enabled local authorities to discharge their duty to provide residential care by entering into arrangements with the voluntary sector. Section 42(1) of the National Health Service and Community Care Act has extended this power to include the private sector as well. Residential care homes and nursing homes managed by bodies established by Act of Parliament or incorporated by royal charter are exempt from the requirement to register under the Registered Homes Act 1984.[2] Section 37 of the Registered Homes Act also gives the Secretary of State power to exempt Christian Scientist nursing and mental nursing homes from registration under that Act.

THE PRIVATE SECTOR

The private sector of care expanded greatly in the 1980s supported, as the Audit Commission (1986) saw it, by the "perverse incentive" of public funding being available to enter residential or nursing home care, but not to support services in the community.

The private sector is regulated by the Registered Homes Act 1984 and regulations such as the Residential Care Homes Regulations 1984 and the Nursing Homes and Mental Nursing Homes Regulations 1984.[3] Considerable influence on patterns of availability and standards, however, will be introduced as a result of local authorities' new powers to make placements in the private sector by way of "contracting for care", and, effectively, to ration the availability of public funding for placements.

RESIDENTIAL CARE AND NURSING CARE DISTINGUISHED

No clear distinction between residential and nursing care exists, except for the differential requirements for registration discussed in Chapter 6 — Inspecting Residential Care. There is a further category of mental nursing home for which separate registration is required. Whilst local authorities

---

[2] See ss.1(5), 21(3) and 22(2).
[3] S.I. 1994 No. 1345 and S.I. 1994 No. 1578 respectively; see also Chap. 6—Inspecting Residential Care.

register and inspect residential care homes, it is health authorities that register and inspect all types of nursing home, though dual registration of premises is also possible. Though one would expect significant differences in dependency levels between residents in nursing homes and residential care homes, in practice this is not always the case. The choice of placement will be guided by the extent to which invasiveness in procedures is necessary or by the amount and quality of supervision required. Only a minority of people will move between one sector and another.

Guidance seeks to ensure that medical care from the National Health Service is available to people who are in residential care, as it would be if they were living in the community. Local authorities paying for placements in private nursing homes will also want to ensure that adequate nursing care is in fact being provided within the establishment.

HEALTH CARE NEEDS IN RESIDENTIAL CARE

Circular No. LAC (92)24 seeks to clarify the position.[4] Local authorities should ensure that the nursing home care that is funded by them includes the provision of all "general nursing care services", defined as including incontinence services and aids, but not specialist incontinence advice.[5] If specialist nursing services are required for any individual client, or class of clients, it is the responsibility of the placing agency to discuss and agree with National Health Service purchasers the arrangements for their provision.[6] Continence advice and stoma care, together with diabetic liaison, are given as primary examples of specialist nursing services which may be provided in this way. Other community health services (primarily physiotherapy, speech and language therapy and chiropody) should also be subject to negotiation between the placing authority and the National Health Service provider units. Local agreements may be drawn up between local authorities and health authorities as to which of them will provide occupational therapy services to residents.

The Annex to Circular No. LAC (92)24 makes it clear, in paragraph 2, that local authorities' contracts for independent sector residential care should not include the provision of any services which it is the responsibility of the National Health Service to provide. Such community health services must be delivered free of charge, though their availability will be subject to local priorities (para. 10).

---

[4] *Local Authority Contracts for Residential and Nursing Home Care: N.H.S. Related Aspects*, Circular No. LAC (92)24 and for health authorities, Circular No. HSG (92)50.
[5] *ibid.* para. 2(i).
[6] *ibid.* para. 2(ii).

Health authorities, in addition, are expected to play their part in maintaining standards of care. Those who do not make services available should be referred to paragraph 9:

> "Health authorities are reminded that good quality community health services involve multi-disciplinary working; and that geriatricians and psycho-geriatricians have specialist expertise which should be readily available to purchasers when looking at quality assurance. The community health services which health authorities are expected to provide would include advice to homes on issues such as the management of continence, maintenance of mobility and the management of behavioural disorders in elderly people."

"Dowry" Payments and Discharge from Long-Term Hospital Care

Section 28A of the National Health Service Act 1977 enables health authorities to make "dowry" payments to (predominantly) local authorities in respect of patients formerly in long-term hospital care. Such payments are intended to pay for the care of such people in the community. Capital payments made in this way may result in the joint financing of projects to provide new community resources. The discharge of patients from long-stay mental handicap hospitals has been facilitated in many cases by the use of such payments. Directions by the Secretary of State as to the conditions governing payments by health authorities to local authorities and other bodies under section 28A of the National Health Service Act 1977, limit the use of such discretion:

> "Before making a payment under s.28A, the health authority shall be satisfied that the payment is likely to secure a more effective use of public funds than the deployment of an equivalent amount on the provision of services under s.3(1) of the Act."[6a]

Circular No. LAC 92(17), *Health Authority Payments in respect of Social Services Functions*, deals with the situation where a dowry has not been paid, and care arrangements in the community break down. In those instances the local authority should look to the district health authority responsible for the person before discharge "to assist in resecuring those arrangements."[7]

[6a] Directions by the Secretary of State as to the conditions governing payments by health authorities to local authorities and other bodies under s. 28A of the National Health Service Act 1977, published as Annex C to Circular No. LAC (92)17, para. 3(2).

[7] *Health Authority Payments in Respect of Social Services Functions*, Circular No. LAC 92(17), para. 1(iii).

CHOICE IN RESIDENTIAL CARE

New provisions for residential care have prompted two questions in particular: What choice does any individual resident have about where he is placed? and, what is his position if he is required to leave the home where he has been resident for some time?

The choice of accommodation for those who are not privately funded ultimately rests with the local authority. The situation is thus akin to that of children in the care of or accommodated by the local authority, and it is likely that, if challenged, the decision of the House of Lords in *A. v. Liverpool City Council*[8] (refusing to place limits on the discretion of the local authority) would be followed. Through the system of contracting for care it is possible that choices will be limited to homes with which the local authority has a pre-existing relationship. This discretion, however, is limited by the National Assistance Act (Choice of Accommodation) Directions 1992,[9] which aim to provide the would-be resident with a more "genuine choice" whether the care is temporary (for example, for respite) or permanent. If the individual concerned expresses a preference for particular accommodation (known as "preferred accommodation") within the United Kingdom the authority must arrange for care in that accommodation, provided that:

(1) The accommodation is suitable in relation to the individual's assessed needs.
(2) To do so would not cost the authority more, unless the individual or a third party is willing to meet the difference in cost.
(3) The accommodation is available.
(4) The person in charge of the accommodation is willing to provide it subject to the authority's usual terms and conditions for such accommodation.

If the individual client is unable to express a preference, carers may do so on that person's behalf, unless that would be against his best interests. Wishing to move nearer to relatives would be a relevant factor in overriding limitations on cost.[10]

What if the preferred move is to accommodation in Scotland? The original [1992] regulations were technically flawed insofar as they referred to placements in the United Kingdom but overlooked the fact that the Registered Homes Act 1984 applied only to England and Wales. The conundrum for local authorities was that the Community Care (Residential Accommodation) Act 1992 allowed them to make placements only in registered homes, if board and care were to be provided. Placements in Scotland therefore appeared not to be legally possible. The

---

[8] [1981] 2 W.L.R. 948.
[9] Issued with Circular No. LAC (92)27.
[10] *ibid.* para. 7.6.

National Assistance Act 1948 (Choice of Accommodation) (Amendment) Directions 1993[11] therefore restricted "preferred accommodation" in the 1992 Directions to that within England and Wales. Those seeking accommodation in Scotland therefore will have to rely on "liaison" between the English and Scottish authorities.[12] There are no such reciprocal arrangements with Northern Ireland.

Complaints about the application of the directions and decisions taken in individual cases will fall within the scope of the authorities' statutory complaints procedures.[13]

CLOSURE OF HOMES

Local authority homes

If a local authority home itself is threatened with closure, then the authority is under a duty, enforceable through judicial review, to handle the whole process fairly.[14] Fairness involves:

(1) Giving the residents clear notice that closure is under consideration.
(2) Allowing enough time for residents to make representations about the closure.
(3) Giving proper consideration to any representations made.

It is not necessary, however, for each individual resident to be consulted face-to-face by either officers or elected members of the council.

Some local authorities have sold off their residential accommodation to the independent sector. This action has raised fears about security for existing residents, particularly those who require an increasing amount of care. Directions contained in Circular No. LAC (91)12, *Community Care: Review of Residential Homes Provision and Transfers*, make it clear in paragraph 7, that the transfer of a local authority home to the independent sector does not alter the status of the existing residents. This does not, however, guarantee security of tenure in that particular home for any given resident as their status remains that of a licensee whose licence to occupy is terminable on reasonable notice. What it does mean, however, is that the local authority remains under a duty to make arrangements to provide accommodation, perhaps in a different home.

---

[11] Circular No. LAC (93)18.
[12] *Ordinary Residence*, Circular No. LAC 93(7).
[13] See Chap. 7—Complaints Procedures.
[14] *R. v. Devon County Council, ex p. Baker; R. v. Durham County Council, ex p. Curtis*, (1993) 91 L.G.R. 479.

Private sector homes

Section 42 of the National Health Service and Community Care Act 1990 prohibits local authorities from "making arrangements" for the placement of persons already resident in the private sector before April 1, 1993. However, difficulties may arise when such private homes close or decide that they can no longer accommodate a particular resident, either because he can no longer meet the fees or because he is no longer suitable for the type of care they provide.

A limited solution is provided by the Residential Accommodation (Relevant Premises, Ordinary Residence and Exemptions) Regulations 1993.[15] These regulations entitle local authorities to make arrangements for the accommodation of people who after April 1, 1993 either:

(a) are evicted from a residential care home; or
(b) are not allowed to return there after a period of absence; or
(c) who have been served with a notice to quit.

The financial implications of the local authority assuming responsibility for such people are explained in Circular No. LAC 93(6) which accompanies the regulations.[16] Basically, any preserved rights which the resident may have to income support will accrue to the benefit of the local authority for the placement of that resident in alternative accommodation. The local authority is thus compensated financially for acting as a safety net for other sectors of residential care. However, it cannot make a placement in a home which is under the same management or ownership as that from which the resident has been evicted.[17] The resident therefore ultimately pays the penalty, in having to move to new accommodation in circumstances where he changes from being independently funded to becoming dependent upon the local authority for funds. There is no comparable power to make arrangements to accommodate people in nursing homes who are threatened with closure or eviction unless those persons were placed there by the local authority after April 1, 1993. All other residents must look to the National Health Service to fund new placements.

PAYING FOR RESIDENTIAL CARE

The systems for paying for residential care vary depending on the type of care, residential or nursing home, permanent or respite, and whether or

---

[15] S.I. 1993 No. 477.
[16] *Local Authorities' Powers to Make Arrangements for People who are in Independent Sector Residential Care and Nursing Homes on March 31, 1993,* Circular No. LAC (93)6.
[17] The Residential Accommodation (Relevant Premises, Ordinary Residence and Exemptions) Regulations 1993, reg. 9(2).

not the resident first entered permanent residential care before April 1, 1993. If the client is in receipt of the mobility component of disability living allowance, this will continue to be paid whatever the type of home, but if he is in receipt of the attendance allowance or the care component of disability living allowance, then this will be lost after four weeks in a local authority home, previously known as "Part III".

PERMANENT RESIDENTS ON MARCH 31, 1993

Private sector

If the elderly person was a permanent resident in a private or voluntary residential, or nursing home on March 31, 1993 then they have "pre-served rights" under the income support rules. The "preserved rights" arise under the National Health Service and Community Care Act 1990, s.43, which inserts section 26A into the National Assistance Act 1948 and prohibits local authorities from making residential accommodation arrangements for people who on March 31, 1993 are in "relevant premises", for example:

(a) premises in respect of which any person is registered under the Registered Homes Act 1984;
(b) premises in respect of which such registration is not required by virtue of their being managed or provided by an exempt body;
(c) premises which do not fall within the definition of a nursing home in section 21 of that Act by reason only of their being maintained or controlled by an exempt body; and
(d) such other premises as the Secretary of State may prescribe by regulations.

The definition has been extended to include residents of small residential care homes and premises run by the Abbeyfield Society (Residential Accommodation (Relevant Premises, Ordinary Residence and Exemptions) Regulations 1993[18]).

Preserved rights are relevant to people temporarily absent on that date whose absence did not exceed four weeks (if then a temporary resident), 13 weeks (if then a permanent resident) or 52 weeks (if absence is in hospital). If the resident is paying privately, arrangements will continue as before, with annual increases as agreed with the home. If the Benefits Agency was paying income support on March 31, 1993 it will continue to do so at prevailing income support rates (subject to preset maximums depending on the type of care) so long as eligibility for income support continues (capital of less than £3,000 for full income support, on a sliding scale for capital between £3,000 and £8,000). Where the resident was

---

[18] S.I. 1993 No. 477.

paying full fees privately, but his capital has started to run down, then it is to the Benefits Agency that he applies for income support once the capital gets below £8,000 because of his "preserved rights". If the Benefits Agency is paying income support and the resident is temporarily absent, a retaining fee is paid, generally of 80 per cent, for up to 52 weeks if the absence is due to hospitalisation or 13 weeks for other reasons.

The amount of income support due is calculated by reference to the resident's income (private pension as well as National Insurance). The resident's capital is assumed to earn a notional income of £1 for every £250 over £3,000. If the only or main residence is still owned, claimants are expected to place this on the market for sale and will then receive income support for 26 weeks with the Benefits Agency extending this period if it is reasonable in the circumstances, for example, the general state of the housing market (Income Support (General) Regulations 1987[19]). Once the property is sold, the capital is taken into account and will almost certainly take the resident over the £8,000 capital limit. The residence is only ignored if occupied by the claimant's partner, by someone aged 60 or over, or by an incapacitated relative, as their only or main home. Furthermore, if the local authority had been "topping up" fees, it can continue to do so.

Preserved rights will apply to most people in "relevant premises" on March 31, 1993 but for those not covered or who subsequently lose such rights, local authorities have powers to make residential arrangements for them under the Residential Accommodation (Relevant Premises, Ordinary Residence and Exemptions) Regulations 1993, reg. 5.[20]

People in residential or nursing homes owned or managed by close relatives on March 31, 1993 do not have "preserved rights" as they were not eligible for higher rates of income support, but should they move to another residential home or their current home be taken over by a non-relative, they will become entitled to preserved rights because of the change in circumstances.

The local authority has the power to help residents of residential care homes but not nursing homes even if they have preserved rights, the home is to close or they are threatened with eviction (Residential Accommodation (Relevant Premises, Ordinary Residence and Exemptions) Regulations 1993, regs. 8 and 9[21]).

Preserved rights are maintained if the elderly person moves to a new home (for example, from residential care to nursing care) but such rights may be lost if they move out of an independent sector home for more than 13 weeks, except for a hospital stay which can be for up to 52 weeks (see Diagram 1 — Preserved Rights Entitlement, at page 68).

---

[19] S.I. 1987 No. 1967, Sched. 10.
[20] S.I. 1993 No. 477.
[21] *ibid.*

Housing benefit

Housing benefit is only payable to those in residential care if they were either in receipt of housing benefit, or entitled to it on March 31, 1993, or living in a small home which has now had to be registered and were entitled to, or getting housing benefit, on March 31, 1993.

Small homes

If the resident is in a home for less than four people and meeting the full fees, limited preserved rights are available, in that the resident must have been entitled to the higher rates of income support on March 31, 1993, to qualify. If he was not, he needs to look to the local authority for financial help once his capital gets down to £8,000 (see Diagram 2—Preserved Rights for People in Small Homes, at page 69).

Local authority homes: "Part III"

A resident on March 31, 1993, does not have "preserved rights" but the capital rules changed on that date and are being phased in over three years for people already in Part III accommodation on that date. It may mean that people with over £8,000 capital will eventually pay the full fee, when previously they might not have done.

RESIDENTS AFTER APRIL 1, 1993

If, after carrying out its assessment of need under the National Health Service and Community Care Act 1990, s.47, the local authority has concluded that a place in residential or nursing home care is what is required, the local authority takes legal responsibility for paying the fees. There will usually be a number of homes in the private sector who have negotiated contracts with the local authority detailing the charges and the care to be provided but if the resident prefers another home he is allowed that choice provided it will not cost the local authority more (National Assistance (Choice of Accommodation) Directions 1992[22]). If the resident or a third party is prepared to meet any difference in cost, then the alternative accommodation can be entered into, but thought must be given to future increases and the continued likelihood of funds to "bridge" the gap.

The local authority carries out a means assessment to calculate how much the resident pays towards the care home's fees. The charging rules are to be found by reference to the National Assistance Act 1948, ss.21 and 26, as amended by the National Assistance (Assessment of

---

[22] D.O.H. Circular No. LAC (92)27.

Resources) Regulations 1992[23] and subsequently amended by the National Assistance (Assessment of Resources) Amendment Regulations 1993[24] and the National Assistance (Assessment of Resources) (Amendment No. 2) Regulations 1993.[25]

The local authority's specific right to charge is in the National Assistance Act 1948, s.22, which requires it to fix a standard rate for the accommodation, assess the resident's ability to pay, and decide what lesser amount to charge if the resident is unable to pay the full charge.

The "standard rate" for a local authority managed home is the full cost of providing the accommodation (National Assistance Act 1948, s.22(3)), whilst for a home in the private sector it is the gross cost to the local authority of providing or purchasing the accommodation under a contract with the home (National Assistance Act 1948, s.26(2)). In effect, this can make local authority homes more expensive for the resident compared with private sector ones, and the resident can be further out of pocket because of the ineligibility for attendance allowance. The resident is liable to pay the "standard rate" fee until his savings have reduced to £8,000 or less. Thereafter, both income and capital are taken into account to calculate the amount to be paid.

Capital

Capital covers the expected range of assets which an individual might own in his own right, from cash and stocks and shares to land. So far as accounts in joint beneficial ownership are concerned, the monies are treated as owned in equal shares and assessed accordingly. If the actual ownership is different, it will only be assessed as such once the investment is split and each owner has invested in their sole name their actual share (National Assistance (Assessment of Resources) Regulations 1992, reg. 27[26]).

A resident with capital of more than £8,000 is liable to pay the standard charge if in local authority accommodation, or the contracted fee if in the private sector. There is no need to make a wider assessment of the ability to pay (reg. 20). Capital of less than £3,000 is fully disregarded.

Where capital is between £8,000 and £3,000, "tariff income" is calculated and taken into account as weekly income on the basis of £1 for every £250 or part of £250 over £3,000 (reg. 28).

Schedule 4 of the Regulations lists a large number of capital assets to be disregarded:

(*a*) indefinitely:
    (i)   Surrender value of life policy.
    (ii)   Payment in kind from a charity.

---

[23] S.I. 1992 No. 2977.
[24] S.I. 1993 No. 964.
[25] S.I. 1993 No. 2230.
[26] S.I. 1992 No. 2977.

    (iii) Personal possessions such as paintings or antiques unless purchased with the intention of reducing capital for the purpose of reducing the local authority charge.

    (iv) Value of a right to receive outstanding instalments under an agreement to repay a capital sum.

    (v) Reversionary interests.

(b) for 26 weeks or longer:

    (i) Money acquired for repairs to or replacement of a resident's home or possessions, provided it is used for that purpose.

    (ii) Capital from sale of a former home to be used to buy a replacement.

(c) for 52 weeks:

    arrears of various state benefits.

Land

There are circumstances when, if there is a house or land amongst the capital assets, it will be ignored. First, if the stay in residential care is temporary, the only or main dwelling is ignored.[27] Secondly, should the dwellinghouse be occupied in whole or in part by the resident's spouse (but not a separated or divorced spouse), or a relative who is aged 60 or over, or aged under 16 and is a child whom the resident is liable to maintain, or incapacitated, then the value of the property is ignored (Sched. 4, para. 2). Relative in this context means:

parent	
parent in law	
child or child's spouse	the spouse or any unmarried partner of
step parent	any of these
stepchild	
brother or sister	
grandparent	
grandchild	
uncle or aunt	
nephew or niece	

In addition, where it is reasonable to do so, the value of such a property can be ignored by the local authority. For example, if it is occupied by a relative who had given up their own accommodation to care for the elderly person or someone who had acted as an elderly companion.

---

[27] National Assistance (Assessment of Resources) Regulations (S.I. 1992 No. 2977) Sched. 4, para. 1.

Incapacitated is not defined but is likely to include those in receipt of or eligible for social security benefits such as invalidity benefit, severe disablement allowance, disability living allowance or attendance allowance.

If land is liable to be taken into account and is not sold, the local authority have power to secure a charge against it (Health and Social Services and Social Security Adjudications Act 1983, s.22). This may arise where the resident has refused to place the property on the market, or the resident owns a share in a property jointly held with others. Even if the property passes on survivorship to co-owners, the co-owners receive the deceased's share subject to a charge for an amount not exceeding the amount of the charge to which the interest of the deceased joint tenant was subject.

Deprivation of capital

If a resident has deliberately deprived himself of a capital asset in order to reduce his liability to pay for accommodation charges, the local authority can treat the resident as still possessing the asset. It may depend on the nature of the asset disposed of and the purpose behind the disposal. If, on moving into care, a parent gives some of his chattels to a child, this would be ignored as personal possessions are generally not counted in any event (National Assistance (Assessment of Resources) Regulations 1992, Sched. 4, para. 8[28]). If the disposal was to discharge a debt not due for repayment at the time, was the purpose to reduce liability to accommodation charges to a significant degree?

If the resident was fit and healthy at the time of the disposal and could not foresee a move into residential care, the disposal will be allowed if it appears reasonable to do so.

Should the local authority decide deprivation of assets has occurred in order to avoid or reduce liability to charges it then has to decide whether to treat the resident as still having the capital (notional capital) and assess the charge payable accordingly. The question is then how to recover the assessed charge either from the resident or, if he is unable to pay, to use the limited relief of the Health and Social Services and Social Security Adjudications Act 1983, s.21, and transfer the liability to the person or persons to whom the asset has been transferred to the extent of the benefit accruing to the beneficiary as a result of the transfer. The section specifically states that, where:

(a) a person avails himself of Part III accommodation (meaning accommodation in any sector as arranged under the National Assistance Act 1948 as amended); and

---

[28] S.I. 1992 No. 2977.

(b) that person knowingly and with the intention of avoiding charges for the accommodation:
   (i) has transferred any asset to which this section applies to some other person or persons not more than six months before the date on which he begins to reside in such accommodation; or
   (ii) transfers any such asset to some other person or persons while residing in the accommodation; and
(c) either:
   (i) the consideration for the transfer is less than the value of the asset; or
   (ii) there is no consideration for the transfer

the person or persons to whom the asset is transferred by the person availing himself of the accommodation should be liable to pay to the local authority providing the accommodation or arranging for its provision, the difference between the amount assessed as due to be paid for the accommodation by the person availing himself of it, and the amount which the local authority receives from him for it.

If the gift was made more than six months prior to the move into residential care, section 21 will not help the local authority. Some local authorities are suggesting that they will continue to levy the full fee on the resident and, on remaining unpaid for any length of time, will sue the resident for the unpaid debt, eventually involving the bankruptcy legislation in an attempt to have the gift or any transfer at an undervalue set aside and the asset brought back into the resident's estate.

Income

Income can be taken fully into account or partly or fully disregarded in the assessment.

Most state benefits, occupational pensions, annuity income and trust income are taken fully into account. Income from capital is generally not treated as income, the notional income calculations being substituted, however income from disregarded capital is taken fully into account for as long as the capital is disregarded. Furthermore, there is a £10 disregard in respect of certain charitable or voluntary payments, payments made under German or Austrian law to victims of National Socialist persecution, war/disablement pensions and war widow's pension. Other income may be disregarded, depending on special circumstances, for example, monthly income from a home income plan, if being paid to a partner remaining in the matrimonial home when the other partner moves into permanent care. Fully disregarded income includes the £10 Christmas bonus paid with state benefits, war widows' special payments and payments from the Macfarlane Trusts or the Independent Living Funds.

As there are rules for treating as notional capital that which the resident has deprived himself of, in the same way a resident can be treated as possessing income of which he has deprived himself for the purpose of paying a reduced charge (National Assistance (Assessment of Resources) Regulations 1992, reg.17(1)[29]).

Once more, the local authority may be able to use the Health and Social Services and Social Security Adjudications Act 1983 to transfer the liability for that part of the charges assessed as a result of the notional income, to the person to whom the income has been passed.

Income support

Income support may be payable where capital is less than £8,000 if other pensions, annuities, etc., are inadequate to meet the total fee, to the extent of the income support personal allowance, any applicable pensioner premium (if between 60 and 74 years), enhanced pensioner premium (if between 75 and 79 years) or higher pensioner premium (if over 80 or between 60 and 79 years if fulfilling the disability conditions for disability premium) and the residential allowance (£57 if in London or £51 elsewhere for the year beginning April 1995).

Trust funds

Where a resident has a beneficial interest in the capital of a trust fund, he is assessed as owning the actual amount. Where the entitlement is to income, it is the amount of income paid, or which would be paid if the resident applied to the trustees for it, which is assessed.

If the resident is only a discretionary beneficiary of a trust fund, it is only actual payments made out to him which are assessed.

Personal expenses

In assessing a resident's ability to pay for his accommodation, the local authority is required to ensure than an amount is retained by the resident for their personal expenses: (National Assistance Act 1948, s.22(4)). This sum is the same, be the resident in a local authority home or private sector care, and is laid down each year in the National Assistance (Sums for Personal Requirements) Regulations (£13.10 for the year commencing April 1995[30]).

In special circumstances, local authorities have a power to allow a different amount from that prescribed, for example, if a person is in residential care temporarily and is receiving income support for a partner who remains at home; the needs of the person at home should be considered in setting the allowance.

---

[29] *ibid.*
[30] S.I. 1994 No. 826.

Method of payment

The normal method of payment is that the local authority pays the full fee to the care home directly and collects from the resident the sum he is assessed as liable to pay.

If the local authority, resident and proprietor all agree, the resident of a non-local authority home can pay the home direct (s.26(3A)). The local authority is responsible for meeting the balance of the fees over and above the resident's contribution, and if the resident fails to pay his contribution, the local authority remains liable for the full charge, and may pursue the resident accordingly.

Couples

A local authority has no power to assess a couple according to their joint resources under the National Assistance Act 1948. Each person entering residential care is assessed according to their individual means.

If income support is paid to, or in respect of, one person, whom another person is liable to maintain, then a complaint can be made to a Magistrates' Court by the Department of Social Security for an order that an amount of maintenance be paid (Social Security Administration Act 1992, s.106).

Liability of relatives

Under the National Assistance Act 1948, s.42, spouses are liable to maintain each other, but this does not apply to unmarried couples. The local authority can, therefore, approach the non-resident spouse (liable relative) to contribute towards the residential fees of the resident spouse. Where possible, the amount of any payment is agreed between the liable relative and the local authority, but if this proves impossible, then the local authority can apply to the court. The liable spouse need not agree any assessment prepared by the local authority and can use the complaints procedure for any such calculations to be reviewed.

Temporary residents

If the stay in residential care is likely to be temporary, for example for respite care or convalescence, the charges are assessed differently. No assessment of ability to pay is required for the first eight weeks of a temporary stay, it is for the local authority to decide in each case whether or not to make an assessment. If no assessment is made, the charge is the amount the local authority deems reasonable for the resident to pay (National Assistance Act 1948, s.22(5A)). Often this is equivalent to the basic national insurance pension less the personal expenses allowed.

After eight weeks, the charge is the "standard rate" for the accommodation and an assessment of ability to pay is carried out. Such an assessment should take into account that as the stay is temporary, it is unreasonable to apply those rules which would have affected a permanent resident. Therefore the resident's principal dwelling is disregarded, provided he intends to return to occupy it and it is available to him (National Assistance (Assessment of Resources) Regulations 1992, Sched. 4, para. 1[31]). If the resident's stay was thought to be permanent initially, but turns out to be temporary, his permanent home should be treated as if his residence had been temporary from the start.

Placements without assessment

An elderly person can make his own arrangements as to a placement in residential or nursing home care and then reach his own arrangements direct with the home as to the payment of fees and the like without requesting an assessment of needs from the local authority under the National Health Service and Community Care Act 1990. If, in the future, the resident's capital falls to below £8,000 and there is insufficient income to meet the fees, then an approach is made to the local authority for help at that time. An assessment will be made and the local authority may not wish to continue funding the care previously agreed privately if it does not consider it appropriate for the resident's needs, or regards it as too expensive. It is unlikely that a local authority will be prepared to commit itself to accepting responsibility for future fees in such cases without a full assessment of needs. Therefore, people placing themself in care in this way run the risk of being moved in the future if their finances are liable to run down.

Some residents whose only asset is their home, are currently placing themselves direct into residential care without first going through the assessment procedure. They are placing their property on the market and claiming income support, which if they are eligible for attendance allowance and the severe disability premium, produces enough to pay the fees of the lower charges of some homes. The advantage is that under income support the Department of Social Security does not recover money paid out whilst the property was on the market whereas the local authority will recover the fees which it pays out after placing someone under an assessment and will probably have taken a legal charge to protect its chances of repayment.

---

[31] S.I. 1992 No. 2977.

DIAGRAM 1: PRESERVED RIGHTS ENTITLEMENT[32]

Note: this chart gives general guidance only and should not be treated as a complete and authoritative statement of the law.

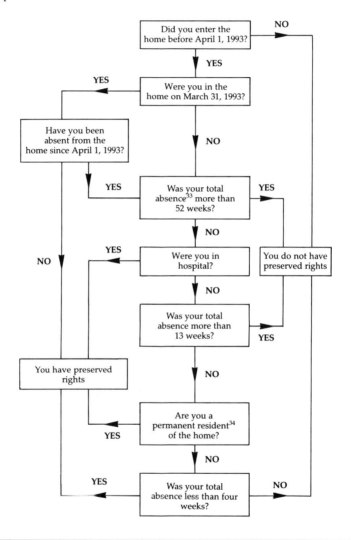

---

[32] This flowchart does not apply to people who live in small homes (with fewer than four residents). See following flowchart. These flowcharts are reproduced from D.O.H. Circular No. LAC (93)6, *Local Authorities' Powers to Make Arrangements for People who are in Independent Sector Residential Care and Nursing Homes on 31 March, 1993.*

[33] *Total absence* means the period between the day you left home up to and including the day before you returned.

[34] You are a *permanent resident* if the home is your usual address. If you have another address where you spend as much or more time then you are classed as a temporary resident.

DIAGRAM 2: PRESERVED RIGHTS FOR PEOPLE IN SMALL HOMES

Note: this chart gives general guidance only and should not be treated as a complete and authoritative statement of the law.

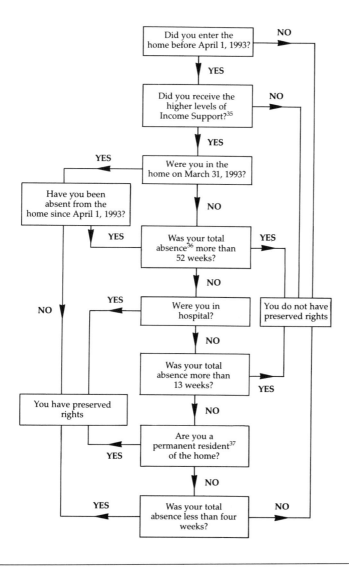

---

[35] The higher levels are *not* payable if the home is run by someone related to you or if it did not meet the care criteria laid down before April 4, 1993.

[36] *Total absence* means the period between the day you left home up to and including the day before you returned.

[37] You are a *permanent resident* if the home is your usual address. If you have another address where you spend as much or more time then you are classed as a temporary resident.

Chapter 6
Inspecting Residential Care

The registration of both residential and nursing homes in the voluntary and private sector is governed by the Registered Homes Act 1984. "Small" residential homes, with fewer than four residents, which were previously outside the system, are now governed by the Registered Homes (Amendment) Act 1991, though the provisions of this Act are somewhat less stringent than those of the 1984 legislation. A dual system is in operation whereby the registration of residential care homes is the responsibility of the social services authority under Part I of the 1984 Act, whilst nursing homes fall within the jurisdiction of the district health authority (under powers delegated by the Secretary of State under the National Health Service Act 1977, ss.13, 14 and 17) and are governed by Part II of the Act; dual registration is, however, possible, and some social services and health authorities are coming together to establish joint inspection units for administrative purposes.

RESIDENTIAL CARE HOMES — DEFINITION

Section 1(1) of the Registered Homes Act 1984 requires registration:

> "in respect of any establishment which provides, or is intended to provide, whether for reward or not, residential accommodation with both board and personal care for persons in need of personal care by reasons of old age, disablement, past or present dependence on alcohol or drugs, or past or present mental disorder."

A wide range of establishments is thus included within the definition, with the unifying factor that both board and "personal care" must be provided. The whole of the establishment is registrable, even if only four residents are in receipt of "personal care" (s.4). "Personal care" includes counselling and other types of therapy, as well as physical care. Establishments providing holiday board and care on a regular basis are also registrable, even if they hold themselves out to be "hotels". "Core and cluster" homes where a central residential unit provides staffing and support services for a number of smaller units pose particular problems. Usually only the central residential unit will be registrable. The effect of this is that residents in the smaller, more independent, units will be treated as "householders" and not "residents" for benefit purposes.[1]

Some residential homes provide day care as well as full residential facilities. Day patients in a registered residential home are not however resident there as defined in section 5(3) of the Registered Homes Act 1984: *Cotgreave v. Cheshire County Council.*[2] On the other hand, residents who are enjoying respite or short term care are counted in full. In *Swindells v. Cheshire County Council*[3] the proprietor of a residential home was convicted in the magistrates' court of exceeding the number of residents which was a condition of her registration. She appealed by way of case stated, but was unsuccessful in her appeal. It was held that although in other statutes the word "resident" involved some degree of continuity or permanence, continuity had no relevance to the Registered Homes Act 1984 which was concerned with the safety, health and care of those who were in residential homes, and the application of the Act could not vary according to the intention of the occupant.

REGISTRATION

An application for registration in respect of a residential care home must contain the information specified in Schedule 1 to the Residential Care Homes Regulations 1984,[4] "and any such information as the registration authority may reasonably require" (reg. 2). This information covers personal details, details of professional qualifications, staffing arrangements, charges, and arrangements for the handling of medicines, as well as details about the home itself.

If the person in control of the home and the person who is manager of the home are different people, both must be registered, as both are treated by section 3 of the 1984 Act as "carrying on" the home. Any person who "carries on" a residential care home without being registered in respect of it is guilty of an offence under section 2.

The local authority may register the applicant subject to conditions (relating to the numbers, ages, sex and category of persons to be accommodated within the home), or may refuse the application on one of the three grounds set out in section 9 of the Act:

(i)   that the applicant is not a "fit person";
(ii) that the premises are not "fit"; or
(iii) that the services or facilities provided are not reasonably required.

[1] Social Security Decision No. (15)2/92.
[2] (1992) 156 J.P.N. 762.
[3] *The Times*, February 18, 1993, D.C.
[4] S.I. 1984 No. 1345.

The registration authority must give the applicant notice of a proposal to refuse application, and the reasons for it (s.12(3) and (5)). The applicant has the right to make representations (s.13), and a right of appeal to a registered homes tribunal.

Schedule 3 to the Residential Care Homes Regulations 1984[5] requires authorities to keep a register of homes, which is open to public inspection (s.7). Circular No. LAC (84)15 deals generally with the registration of residential care homes and registered homes tribunals. Registration cannot be granted in advance of the actual facilities being made available.

REGISTRATION REQUIREMENTS

Local authorities will place registered homes in categories according to the types of resident which they will accommodate, for example, the elderly mentally infirm, or persons with a physical disability. Paragraphs 18 and 19 of Circular No. LAC (86)6 advise local authorities that these categories should be subject to annual review. Since it is the proprietor and manager, and not the premises, which are registered, registration cannot be transferred and re-registration is necessary when the proprietor or manager changes. However, section 6 of the Registered Homes Act 1984 permits personal representatives or relatives (s.19) to continue the running of the home for up to four weeks, or as long a period as the registration authority may allow.

By section 5(3) and (4) the registration authority may vary the conditions of registration from time to time, or impose additional conditions. No fee is chargeable for varying the conditions of registration. However, the local authority is not bound to accede to a request to vary the conditions of registration, and its decision to treat such an application as a new registration, for which the full fee is payable, is not subject to appeal to a registered homes tribunal.[6]

The "fit person" test

The "fit person" test, though fundamental to the working of the Act is not statutorily defined. It has, however, been interpreted as relating not only to the character of the applicant, but also to the standard of care that he can provide, and to his willingness to co-operate with the registration authority. Annex A to Circular No. LAC (91)4 enables police checks to be made on applicants for registration, who are also subject to the operation of the Rehabilitation of Offenders Act (Exceptions) Order 1975[7]; a national list is also kept of cancelled and refused registrations. A criminal conviction, even for an offence under the Registered Homes Act itself, is

---

[5] ibid.
[6] See Coombs v. Hertfordshire County Council, (1991) 89 L.G.R. 774.
[7] S.I. 1975 No. 1023.

not an automatic barrier to registration: see Registered Homes Tribunal Decision No. 88, *Love v. Wiltshire County Council*, where the former matron of a residential care home with convictions for dishonesty in the handling of residents' money was described nevertheless as a "caring and compassionate person". On the other hand, there is no need to establish a connection between the offence and the care of residents as in Decision No. 76, *Azzapardi v. London Borough of Havering*, where the conviction was for the possession of cannabis.

In Decision No. 62, *Pollard v. Dudley Metropolitan Borough Council*, failure to co-operate with the local authority, as evidenced by referring all correspondence to a solicitor, was evidence of "unfitness". Some evidence of professional and managerial expertise may be required prior to registration; financial viability will also be important as registration authorities will seek assurance that standards can be maintained. Guidance on the compilation of registration accounts is contained in Circular No. LAC (89)14.

Suitability of premises

The premises must also be fit for the purpose of a residential care home. Location may be important, neither too isolated, nor too prominent. In Decision No. 5, *Langford v. Devon County Council*, the registered homes tribunal upheld the local authority's decision to refuse registration for a residential care home on the edge of Dartmoor, which had no outlook, and where access to local facilities was difficult. Particular difficulties may arise with regard to the interpretation of regulation 10 of the Residential Care Homes Regulations 1984.[8] Regulation 10 covers the provision of facilities and services, such as accommodation space, laundry facilities, heating, cleanliness and recreational facilities, which having regard to the number, age, sex and condition of the residents are "adequate", "reasonable" and "suitable". Obviously there is wide scope for interpretation here, and local authorities will develop their own guidelines on what is suitable. In Decision No. 56, *Beck v. City of Birmingham*, such policy guidance (on single rooms) was described by the tribunal as only "a standard" which must not harden into a fixed rule, or even a rule from which the Sub-Committee will only depart in exceptional circumstances; this was despite evidence that several other local authorities imposed similar standards. Similar disputes may arise over staffing levels, particularly over the employment of night staff. Though regulation 10(1)(*a*) merely specifies that the person registered shall "employ by day, and where necessary, by night suitably qualified and competent staff in numbers which are adequate for the well-being of residents", decisions of the required registered homes tribunals have

---

[8] S.I. 1984 No. 1345.

consistently said that night staff should always be employed where there are elderly residents.

SETTING STANDARDS

Advising proprietors of residential care homes and their residents which conditions of registration are legally enforceable and which are simply advisory is a complex business. According to the judgment in *Warwickshire County Council v. McSweeney*,[9] only conditions of the nature specified in section 5(3) of the Act, *i.e.* those relating to the numbers, ages, sex and category of persons to be accommodated, may be made a condition of registration. This is important because breach of these conditions is a criminal offence (s.5(5)). However, breach of the Residential Care Homes Regulations may also be an offence, if so specified in those regulations. A clear distinction should be drawn between the criteria in section 9 of the Act for refusing registration, and the power to impose conditions subsequent to registration in section 5(3).[9a] Any general policy in relation to registration must be publicly stated, but may not be applied as a matter of routine without considering the circumstances of each individual case.[9b]

In an effort to raise standards and promulgate good practice, local registration authorities may seek to impose their own interpretation of quality upon home owners and managers. The Code of Practice known as *Home Life*[10] has long been regarded as a model for good practice in residential care. Its legal status is that of guidance issued under section 7 of the Local Authority Social Services Act 1970. More recently, the Social Services Inspectorate has produced a number of what it called "standards documents" under the general title of *Inspecting for Quality*.[11] These guides may well be used by registered homes inspectors when assessing standards; they cover such matters as the maintenance of individual care plans, the management of medication, and the creation of a safe but stimulating environment. Emphasis is placed on these and other matters as indicators of the six basic values of privacy, dignity, independence, choice, rights and fulfilment, flagged up in the Social Services Inspectorate's document *Homes are for Living In*.[12] These documents, however, are examples of good practice, and not legal standards.

---

[9] Unreported, December 8, 1988; see *Encyclopedia of Social Services and Child Care Law* (Sweet & Maxwell), paras. D5–004 *et seq.*
[9a] *Isle of Wight County Council v. Humphreys* (1992) 90 L.G.R. 186.
[9b] *ibid.* p. 198.
[10] *Home Life* (Centre for Policy on Ageing, 1984).
[11] The standards documents include: *Guidance on Standards for Residential Care of Elderly People* (H.M.S.O., 1990); and *Standards for the Residential Care of Elderly People with Mental Disorders* (H.M.S.O., 1993).
[12] *Homes are for Living In* (H.M.S.O., 1989).

However, regulations do set legal standards. Regulation 9 of the Residential Care Homes Regulations 1984[13] requires the person registered to arrange for the home to be conducted so as to make proper provision for the welfare, care and, where appropriate, treatment and supervision of all residents. Furthermore in reaching any decision relating to a resident the person registered first shall give consideration to the need to safeguard and promote the welfare of the resident and shall, so far as is practicable, ascertain the wishes and feelings of the resident and give them consideration as is reasonable having regard to the resident's age and understanding (reg. 9(2)).

Every resident shall be informed in writing (reg. 17) of the person to whom and the manner in which any request or complaint relating to the home may be made and the person registered shall ensure that any complaint made by a resident or a person acting on his behalf is fully investigated. The General Note (Preamble) to the Residential Care Homes Regulations 1984[14] makes it clear that the residents of a residential care home cannot by agreement relieve the registered person or the registration authority of their statutory duties (a similar provision exists in the case of nursing homes).

INSPECTION

Registered homes inspectors have the power to enter premises at any time (s.17), not just at "any reasonable time" in order to carry out an inspection. They may interview residents and inspect documentation. This power extends also to premises which are "believed to be used for the purposes of a residential care home."

Regulation 18 of the Residential Care Homes Regulations 1984[15] requires the registration authority to carry out an inspection not less than twice in any period of 12 months, and Circular No. LAC (88)15 advises that local authorities should carry out at least one inspection a year without prior notice.

Following a formal inspection, a report should be sent to the proprietor and the manager of the home, and to the local authority's Social Services Committee. Their role, however, is to advise and assist as well as to inspect. This role is reflected in regulation 20 of the Registered Care Homes Regulations 1984,[16] allowing up to three months' notice to be given to remedy a breach of the registration conditions.

The existing sanctions are either de-registration or prosecution for breaches of the Act or Regulations or both. A breach of the conditions of

---

[13] S.I. 1984 No. 1345.
[14] ibid.
[15] ibid.
[16] ibid.

registration does not however impose a duty upon the local authority to cancel registration: *Harrison v. Cornwall County Council.*[17]

OFFENCES UNDER THE REGISTERED HOMES ACT

Part IV of the Registered Homes Act specifies a number of offences which may be committed by any person, owner or manager, registered in respect of the home. These are:

(a) failure to register (s.2);
(b) failure to affix "in a conspicuous place" the certificate of registration (s.5(6));
(c) breach of any condition as to registration (s.5(5)); and
(d) obstructing the exercise of the power of entry and inspection (s.17(6)).

In addition, the local authority has power under section 53(2) of the Act to institute proceedings for offences under section 35(5) which relate to refusal to allow the inspection of premises or interviewing of residents or obstructing an authorised person in the exercise of his functions, and for offences under section 35(6) in insisting on being present during an interview or examination from which he is requested to withdraw.

Officers of a limited company may be jointly liable for offences committed by the company.[18]

REGISTERED HOMES TRIBUNALS

Appeals against the refusal of or cancellation of registration are dealt with by registered homes tribunals.[19] A registered homes tribunal shall consist of a chairman (appointed by the Lord Chancellor), and two other "expert" members (s.41); however, appeals relating solely to registration under Part II of the Act (which deals with nursing homes) shall include a registered medical practitioner and a qualified nurse or midwife. The burden of proof, on the balance of probabilities, lies on the registration authority.

---

[17] (1992) 90 L.G.R. 81.
[18] Registered Homes Act 1984, s.52.
[19] Registered Homes Act 1984, Pt. III.

An appeal on a point of law against a decision of a registered homes tribunal may be made to the High Court under the Tribunals and Inquiries Act 1992, s.11 and R.S.C., Ord. 94, rr. 8 and 9.

A registered homes tribunal has no power to award costs but has a duty to give reasons for its decisions under the Tribunals and Inquiries Act 1992, s.10. It has power either to confirm the decision or order appealed against, or to confirm that it shall not have effect. It also has the power to cancel, vary or impose conditions. Registered homes tribunals have been criticised for having limited powers, and making conflicting decisions on the operation of the Act.[20]

One particular area of controversy has been the extent of the tribunal's power to impose "any such condition as it thinks fit [. . .] in respect of the home"; a power which it is given by virtue of section 15(6)(c) of the Registered Homes Act. In *Warwickshire County Council v. McSweeney*, the High Court held that a tribunal could not have any wider powers than registration authorities had under section 5(3); that is the power to impose conditions relating to the number, category and sex of residents. Thus the tribunal had no power to impose a condition that Mr. McSweeney, the applicant's husband who had convictions for dishonesty, assault and unlawful wounding, have nothing to do with the running of the home.[21]

CANCELLATION OF REGISTRATION

Cancellation of registration may be based upon any of the grounds upon which registration may be refused in the first place (s.10), or upon conviction for an offence under the Registered Homes Act or for non-compliance with any condition of registration. However, a conviction for an offence under the Act will not automatically lead to a cancellation of registration.

The procedure is that the local authority will serve notice of its intention to cancel the registration, and the persons registered in respect of the home will be invited to make representations (s.13). Commonly, this procedure will be protracted over at least a three-month period and possibly up to 18 months. Section 11 of the Registered Homes Act 1984, therefore, provides for an emergency procedure whereby the local authority may apply for an order from the magistrates' court, or a single justice, for the immediate cancellation of registration. The application

---

[20] Harman and Harman, *No Place Like Home: A Report of the First Ninety-Six Cases of the Registered Homes Tribunal* (NALGO, 1989).
[21] Unreported, December 8, 1988; see *Encyclopedia of Social Services and Child Care Law* (Sweet & Maxwell), paras. D5–004 *et seq.*

may be made *ex parte*. The two procedures may often run side by side: *Lyons v. East Sussex County Council*, 86 L.G.R. 369, C.A.

NURSING HOMES

Section 21 of the Registered Homes Act 1984 defines a "nursing home" as:

(a) any premises used, or intended to be used, for the reception of, and the provision of nursing for, persons suffering from any sickness, injury or infirmity;

(b) any premises used, or intended to be used, for the reception of pregnant women, or of women immediately after childbirth (in this Act referred to as a "maternity home"); and

(c) any premises not falling within either of the preceding paragraphs which are used, or intended to be used, for the provision of all or any of the following services, namely:

    (i) the carrying out of surgical procedures under anaesthesia;
    (ii) the termination of pregnancies;
    (iii) endoscopy;
    (iv) haemodialysis or peritoneal dialysis;
    (v) treatment by "specially controlled techniques", specified by regulations under sub-section 4; for example, cosmetic surgery.

In practice, particularly if reliance is placed on the definition in section 21(1)(a), it can be very difficult to distinguish between what is properly to be classified as a nursing home, and what is a residential care home for very dependent elderly people. The difference is often one of personnel. A nursing home must have a registered medical practitioner, or a qualified nurse, or, in the case of a maternity home, a registered midwife, as the person in charge of the nursing home (s.25(1)(f)). The registration authority for residential care homes cannot, in comparison, specify the qualifications to be held by either the owner or by the person in charge. It is an offence by the Registered Homes Act, s.24, for any person, with intent to deceive, to apply any name to premises in England and Wales, or in any way describe such premises or hold them out as to indicate, or what could reasonably be understood as to indicate, that the premises are a nursing home, or a maternity home, or a mental nursing home. There is no parallel offence in relation to residential care homes; the section therefore seems to be directed at proprietors of residential care homes who hold them out to be nursing homes. However, dual registration of premises with mixed accommodation, as both nursing homes and residential care homes, is possible under sections 1 and 23(2), but it is not possible to register both as a nursing home and a mental nursing home.

A health authority is not liable in negligence for an alleged lack of care in the inspection of a nursing home which leads to an application being made for the cancellation of registration: *Martine v. South East Kent Health Authority.*[22]

STANDARDS OF CARE

Regulation 12 of the Nursing Homes and Mental Nursing Homes Regulations 1984,[23] requires there to be "adequate arrangements for patients in the home to receive medical and nursing services." Circular No. LAC (92)24 governs the provision of community health services for residents of residential care homes and nursing homes placed there by local authorities. Paragraph 2 of Circular No. LAC (92)24 in particular asks local authorities:

> "to ensure that the nursing home that is funded by them includes the provision of all general nursing care services (including incontinence services and aids)."

Specialist nursing and other community health services, for example, stoma care, physiotherapy, speech therapy and chiropody may, however, be provided by agreement between the local authority and the National Health Service.

By section 29 of the Registered Homes Act 1984 a condition may be imposed on the registration as to the number of nurses to be on duty in the nursing home at a time. Apart from this, the only legally enforceable standards are those set out in the regulations which require that facilities, services and staffing are "adequate": what is adequate will vary with the degree of dependency of the residents.

Guidance on the inspection of nursing homes is given in paragraphs 19 and 20 of Health Circular No. HC (84)21. The National Association of Health Authorities has also provided a *Handbook for Health Authorities on the Registration and Inspection of Nursing Homes*. By regulation 11 of the 1984 Regulations, the frequency of inspection must be not less than twice in any period of 12 months.

MENTAL NURSING HOMES

Special provisions relating to mental nursing homes are contained in sections 35 and 36 of the Registered Homes Act. A mental nursing home is defined in section 22(1) as:

---

[22] *The Times*, March 8, 1993.
[23] S.I. 1984 No. 1578.

"any premises used, or intended to be used, for the reception of, and the provision of nursing or other medical treatment (including care, habilitation and rehabilitation under medical supervision) for one or more mentally disordered patients (meaning persons suffering, or appearing to be suffering from mental disorder), whether exclusively or in common with other persons."

Thus registration is required if only one person suffering from mental disorder is provided with accommodation. An entry on a special part of the register is required under section 25(5)(*b*) if the home is to be registered to receive persons detained under the Mental Health Act 1983. Under section 145(1) of the Mental Health Act 1983 the person or persons registered in respect of a nursing home take on the functions of the "managers" of the home for the purposes of that Act.

"SMALL HOMES" AND THE REGISTERED HOMES (AMENDMENT) ACT 1991

The Registered Homes (Amendment) Act 1991 amends section 1(4) of the Registered Homes Act 1984 which excluded from the requirement of registration any establishment providing personal care for fewer than four persons. Now the only exemption (contained in the new section 1(4A) of the Registered Homes Act 1984) is where those persons are actually engaged in carrying on the home, or are employed there, or are relatives of persons carrying on the home or employed there. Some adult placement schemes on the "fostering" model may thus be caught by these new provisions.

The registration formalities are, however, less stringent for "small homes". In particular, the only grounds upon which registration may be refused is the "fit person" ground (s.1(7)); the local authority may waive the whole or part of its initial registration fee or annual fee (s.1(4) and (5)), and the certificate need not be on public display (s.1(4)). Failure to complete annual financial returns and send them to the local authority is however a ground on which registration may be cancelled (s.1(6) and (8)).

Local authorities have no duty to inspect (as opposed to register) small homes. Paragraphs 3 to 5 of Annex A to Department of Health Circular No. LAC (92)10 explains modifications made to the Residential Care Homes Regulations 1984 by the Residential Care Homes (Amendment) Regulations 1992,[24] in that small homes are exempt from the requirement to undertake fire precautions or fire drills, and to consult with the environmental health officer with regard to matters of hygiene.

---

[24] S.I. 1992 No. 2241.

IMPACT OF THE NATIONAL HEALTH SERVICE AND COMMUNITY CARE ACT 1990

Section 42(2) of the National Health Service and Community Care Act 1990 enables local authorities to make arrangements with voluntary or registered residential homes or nursing homes, in order to fulfil their statutory obligation to provide care under Part III of the National Assistance Act 1948. Section 42(10), however, expressly forbids the local authority to enter into such arrangements with any person who has been convicted of an offence under any provision of the Registered Homes Act 1984 or Regulations. Premises registered under the Registered Homes Act 1984 are excluded from the definition of premises providing community care services which are subject to inspection under section 48(1) of the National Health Service and Community Care Act. Nevertheless, the local authority may wish to make periodic visits in order to confirm that contract specifications are being adhered to. Such visits should be clearly distinguished from inspection visits under the Registered Homes Act.

The local authority may furthermore wish to impose contractual conditions which are more stringent than the basic registration requirements. It is clear that they are able to do this provided they are not *ultra vires* the National Assistance Act 1948 (as amended) and provided they are not unreasonable: *R. v. Newcastle upon Tyne City Council, ex p. Dixon*.[25]

QUALITY ASSURANCE AND QUALITY CONTROL

Quality assurance and quality control are important means by which standards are set and maintained. Quality assurance is used to refer to those processes which aim to ensure that concern for quality is designed and built into services; quality control refers to processes of verification and will include systematic monitoring, audit and inspection designed to establish whether standards are being achieved; total quality management describes an approach to quality assurance which stresses the importance of creating a culture in which concern for quality is an integral part of service delivery.[26]

These principles are designed to apply equally to social services departments internally, as well as to external providers of services.

---

[25] *The Times*, October 26, 1993.
[26] See *Committed to Quality: Quality Assurance in Social Services Departments* (H.M.S.O., 1992) and *Purchase of Service: Practice Guidance and Practice Materials for Social Services Departments and Other Agencies* (H.M.S.O., 1991).

BRITISH STANDARDS

The British Standards Institute has approved BS 5750, a quality assurance system for manufacturing industries. Some local authorities, most notably Gloucestershire and Norfolk, have adapted the concepts of "fitness for purpose" and "safety in use" contained therein, to the needs of social care agencies. The British Quality Association, Social Care Agencies Sector Committee, have produced *Guidance on the Interpretation of BS 5750 with reference to Social Care Agencies.*[27] The same organisation has also produced *Notes for the Application of BS 5750 to the Continuing Nursing Care Sector.*[28] The latter provides guidance on how companies can establish, document and maintain quality planning and quality control as well as review, with procedures, record keeping and training needs.

INSPECTION UNITS

The *Policy Guidance* (H.M.S.O., 1990) required local authorities to set up inspection units with responsibility for the inspection of residential care homes by April 1, 1991 (para. 5.5). These units are to be "free standing", that is separate from line management, in order that they can also assume responsibility for inspecting the local authority's own services. The intention is that the inspection of residential care in the public, private and voluntary sectors should be placed on a common footing (para. 5.1). The Director of Social Services is responsible to the Social Services Committee for the performance of the unit and the action taken within the department in response to its findings, even if the unit is located elsewhere than in the Social Services Department (para. 5.8). In particular, a registration authority may not delegate to another agency its power to approve, withdraw or alter the terms of registration of a home.

In the case of local authority homes, there may be additional scrutiny by the Social Services Inspectorate using the powers under section 48 of the National Health Service and Community Care Act 1990 to enter and inspect premises used for the provision of community care services. The Policy Guidance anticipates that the Inspectorate will pay particular attention to cases where local authorities fail to act on inspection reports on their own homes (para. 5.17).

An annual report of the work of the Inspection Unit should be presented to the Social Services Committee. There should be public access to these reports, as well as to reports on individual homes or

---

[27] British Quality Association (1987).
[28] British Quality Association (1994).

services, which should not be anonymised (subject to legal advice to the contrary (para. 5.19)).

Advisory Committees

The work of inspection units will be supported by the setting up of an "Advisory Committee" in each authority. A model format is provided in Annex B to the Policy Guidance. Such committees should not however be constituted as sub-committees of the local authority under section 4(2) of the Local Authority Social Services Act 1970.[29] Users and carers may be represented on advisory committees, as well as registered home owners. Advisory committees will not have executive powers but may "serve as a forum for the exchange of views between the (Registration) Authority, its officers and service providers".[30] Thus, they may be a first stage in the resolution of disputes.

Lay Assessors

Circular No. LAC (94)16, *Inspecting Social Services*, seeks to apply the principles of openness and accessibility set out in the Citizens' Charter[31] to the work of local authority inspection units, by requiring local authorities to appoint "lay assessors" to complement the work of professional inspectors (para. 11). Lay assessors should take part in all full inspections of residential homes for adults with high levels of dependency and disability, and in annual inspections of homes directly managed by the local authority.

[29] Circular No. LAC (94)16, para. 20.
[30] Para. 4(1) of the Inspection Units Directions 1994, contained in Annex A to D.O.H. Circular No. LAC (94)16.
[31] See Chap. 7—Complaints Procedures, p. 94.

Chapter 7
Complaints Procedures

THE NATIONAL HEALTH SERVICE

The Patient's Charter

The Patient's Charter, setting out standards of care for the National Health Service, came into effect on April 1, 1992. Local charter standards devised by particular units or trusts within the National Health Service supplement national standards.

The national "Patient's Charter" sets out a number of "rights" of patients, supplemented by standards of service, which the National Health Service expects to provide. Some are existing rights—others are new.

The Patient's Charter—Seven existing rights

(1) To receive health care on the basis of clinical need, regardless of the ability to pay.
(2) To be registered with a general practitioner.
(3) To receive emergency medical care at any time, through the general practitioner or the emergency ambulance service and hospital accident and emergency departments.
(4) To be referred to a consultant, acceptable to you, when the general practitioner thinks it necessary, and to be referred for a second opinion if you and the general practitioner agree this is desirable.
(5) To be given a clear explanation of any treatment proposal, including any risks and alternatives, before agreement is given to treatment.
(6) To have access to health records, and to know that the contents of those records will be kept confidential.
(7) To choose whether or not to take part in any medical research or medical student training.

The Patient's Charter—Three new rights from April 1, 1992

(1) To be given detailed information on local health services, including quality standards and maximum waiting times.

(2) To be guaranteed admission for virtually all treatments by a specific date no later than 18 months from the day when your consultant places you on a waiting list.
(3) To have any complaint about the services of the National Health Service—whoever provides them—investigated, and to receive a full and prompt written reply.

Legal issues around the provision of National Health Service services are discussed in Chapter 4—The Provision of National Health Services.

The Patient's Charter—Standards of service

(1) Respect for privacy, dignity and religious or cultural beliefs.
(2) Arrangements to ensure everyone, including people with special needs, can use the services.
(3) Information to be given to relatives and friends about the progress of treatment, subject to the patient's wishes.
(4) An emergency ambulance should arrive within 14 minutes in an urban area, or 19 minutes in a rural area.
(5) When attending an accident or emergency department, the patient should be seen immediately and their need for treatment assessed.
(6) Specific appointments should be given at out-patients clinics, and the patient should be seen within 30 minutes of that time.
(7) An operation should not be cancelled on the day you arrive in hospital, unless an emergency occurs. If an operation has to be postponed, you will be admitted within one month of the cancelled operation.
(8) A named, qualified nurse, midwife, or health visitor will be responsible for your nursing or midwifery care.
(9) A decision should be made about any continuing health or social care needs prior to discharge from hospital.

The system for monitoring the implementation of the Charter rights and standards is contained in HSG (92)36, *The Patient's Charter: Monitoring and Publishing Information on Performance*.

COMPLAINTS AGAINST NATIONAL HEALTH SERVICE PRACTITIONERS

Complaints concerning National Health Service practitioners (general practitioners, dentists, pharmacists and opticians) are dealt with by the Family Health Services Authority for that area in accordance with the National Health Service (Service Committees and Tribunal) Regulations

1992.[1] The primary concern of the Family Health Services Authority in investigating a complaint is to ascertain whether the terms of its agreement with the family practitioner have been broken; this may be a somewhat different focus from that of the complainant. The complaint must be put to the general manager of the Family Health Services Authority no later than 13 weeks after the event (or in the case of dental treatment within six months of the course of treatment being completed).

The first stage of the complaints procedure is informal, and involves the appointment of a lay conciliator. The second stage is a formal investigation by a service committee made up of equal numbers of lay people and professionals, with a lay chairman. The service committee itself decides whether it will deal with the matter by way of written submissions, or whether it will proceed to a full oral hearing. There will be no legal representation at this hearing although the Secretary of the Community Health Council may present the complainant's case. A complaint may be made on behalf of a person who is incapable of making the complaint himself by reason of old age, sickness or another infirmity.[2]

If the practitioner is found to have broken his terms of service he may be given a warning, or money may be withheld from his renumeration: *R. v. Secretary of State for Health, ex p. Hickey*.[3] Such a payment is not, however, made to the complainant; a legal claim in negligence (if appropriate) is the only way of receiving monetary compensation. Appeal is to the Secretary of State for Health, and legal representation is available at this inquiry.

PROFESSIONAL MISCONDUCT

Complaints of professional misconduct will be dealt with by the relevant professional body concerned with the maintenance of standards in the profession. For doctors, whether employed by the National Health Service or in private practice, it is the General Medical Council which performs this function under the Medical Act 1978, and the General Medical Council Preliminary Proceedings Committee and Professional Conduct Committee (Procedure) Rules Order of Council 1980.[4] A complaint must allege serious professional misconduct, which has been interpreted to include inappropriate standards of personal behaviour as well as dereliction of duty in the care and treatment of patients. The ultimate sanction is removal of the doctor's name from the list of registered medical practitioners.

---

[1] S.I. 1992 No. 664, as amended by the National Health Service (Service Committees and Tribunal) Amendment Regulations 1994 (S.I. 1994 No. 634).
[2] *ibid*. reg. 6(*b*)(ii).
[3] [1993] 4 Med. L.R. 94.
[4] S.I. 1980 No. 858.

The Nurses, Midwives and Health Visitors Act 1992 restructures the professional organisations concerned with nursing, midwifery and health visiting. The United Kingdom Central Council now has responsibility, transferred from the National Boards, for preliminary investigations into allegations of professional misconduct or unfitness to practice, as well as responsibility for holding full hearings in these matters (s.5(4)). Sections 7 and 9 of the Act also clarify the power to suspend and caution practitioners for whom the ultimate sanction is removal from the nursing register. The meaning, in this context, of "professional misconduct" was clarified in *Dennis v. U.K. Central Council for Nursing, Midwifery and Health Visiting*[5] to include crimes of violence, sexual misconduct "of a grave nature" and also road traffic convictions for offences involving alcohol.

COMPLAINTS CONCERNING HOSPITALS

The Hospital Complaints Procedure Act 1985 imposes a duty upon the Secretary of State for Health to give directions to health authorities under section 17 of the National Health Service Act 1977 to establish a complaints procedure for persons who are or have been patients at each hospital for which the authority is responsible. This section was brought into force on July 11, 1989, by the Hospital Complaints Procedure Act 1985 (Commencement) Order 1989[6] and its operation is extended to any National Health Service Trust which is responsible for the management of a hospital by paragraph 6(2)(e) of Schedule 2 to the National Health Service and Community Care Act 1990. Directions are contained in HC (88)37 and WHC (88)36.

Arrangements must be made for staff to deal informally with complaints. Such complaints need not be made in writing, but should be noted.

A designated officer must be appointed to receive and be accountable for all formal complaints made by or on behalf of a patient. Complaints should be in writing, and be made within three months of the event. Formal complaints should result in a report detailing the results of an investigation into the case, and should contain an apology, where appropriate, and an explanation of why things went wrong, and what will be done to put them right in the future. If the complainant remains dissatisfied, he or she should be advised to refer the matter to the Health Service Commissioner if the complaint is within his jurisdiction.[7]

The designated officer will not deal with matters involving clinical judgement which cannot be resolved by discussion; the separate procedure for these is discussed below. Nor should he deal with

---

[5] [1993] 4 Med. L.R. 252.
[6] S.I. 1989 No. 1191.
[7] See Health Service Commissioners Act 1993, s.3, discussed at p. 90.

disciplinary matters, or matters of a criminal nature which may require investigation by the police.

All necessary steps should be taken to ensure that patients, visitors and staff, and the local Community Health Council are informed about the arrangements made to deal with complaints within the authority's own area. This may include the use of admissions booklets and informative leaflets.

COMPLAINTS ABOUT MEDICAL JUDGMENT

Complaints against hospital consultants and the staff for whom they are responsible in respect of matters involving clinical judgement are outside the statutory hospital complaints procedure. An agreed procedure does however exist for dealing with these matters on an intra-professional basis.[7a]

The first stage is referral of the complaint to the consultant concerned who will take responsibility for discussing the case with any other staff concerned and formulating a reply which normally the district general manager will forward on behalf of the authority. If the complainant is dissatisfied with the response thus received, the regional medical officer will become involved and he may, if he thinks the matter sufficiently serious, refer it for independent professional review by two consultants working in the same specialism, one of whom is from another region. If the independent professional review upholds the complaint, the district general manager must write to the patient giving an assurance that remedial action has been taken designed to ensure that the same problem will not arise again.

However, this procedure will not be followed if legal action is threatened at any stage.[7b]

ACTIONS IN TORT AGAINST MEDICAL PERSONNEL

The appropriate course of action against an individual medical practitioner for breach of a duty of care owed to the patient is an action in negligence. In *Bolam v. Friern Hospital Management Committee*,[8] the "standards of reasonably competent medical men at the time" were used as a quantifier for the level of care thus owed. Of course, it will be necessary to show that it was a breach of the duty of care which actually

---

[7a] Circular HC (50)37.

[7b] See R. v. Canterbury and Thanet District Health Authority; South East Thames Regional Health Authority, ex p. F. and W. [1994] 5 Med. L.R. 132.

[8] [1957] 1 All E.R. 118.

caused the damage which was suffered, and that such harm was foreseeable. The fact that a decision can be shown to be mistaken does not prove causation, as in *Hughes v. Waltham Forest Health Authority*,[9] where it was argued that the patient was discharged prematurely without all available tests having been carried out. As long as the clinical decision made was not one which no competent surgeon exercising reasonable care and skill would have made, the fact that others might disagree was seen to be irrelevant.

The principle of vicarious liability will operate to extend liability to the employing authority, though this will not be possible where the tortfeasor is an independent contractor, such as a family practitioner or a doctor in private practice: *Cassidy v. Ministry of Health*[10]; *Roe v. Ministry of Health*.[11] Where the parties are in a contractual, professional relationship, for example where care is privately purchased, a potential plaintiff is not thereby limited to an action in contract; the appropriate course of action is still an action in negligence for breach of a duty of care, though the express and implied terms of that contract will regulate the extent of that duty: *Lancashire and Cheshire Association of Baptist Churches Inc. v. Howard and Seddon Partnership*.[12]

Where it is alleged that medical treatment was given without the consent of the patient, the appropriate action in tort will be trespass to the person. An action may also arise for false imprisonment if the patient is unlawfully restrained, or prevented from leaving hospital when he wishes to do so.

THE HEALTH SERVICE COMMISSIONER

The Health Service Commissioner (or Ombudsman) provides a further opportunity for the investigation of complaints against regional health authorities, district health authorities, special health authorities, National Health Service Trusts and Family Health Services Authorities. The Health Service Commissioners Act 1993 is a consolidation Act which reconstitutes separate Health Service Commissioners for England, Wales and Scotland, and defines their jurisdiction and powers. A complainant may allege that he has sustained injustice or hardship in consequence of either a failure in a service provided by a health service body; a failure of such a body to provide a service which it was a function of the body to provide; or maladministration connected with any other action taken by or on behalf of such a body (s.3). Nothing in the Act authorises or requires a Commissioner to question the merits of a decision taken without maladministration in the exercise of a discretion (s.3(4)). As only "health

---

[9] [1991] 2 Med. L.R. 155.
[10] [1951] 2 K.B. 343.
[11] [1954] 2 All E.R. 131.
[12] [1993] 2 All E.R. 467.

service bodies" are subject to investigation (s.2), complaints about services provided by "family practitioners", that is general practitioners, dentists, opticians and pharmacists, are outside the Health Service Commissioner's remit.

Nor can the Health Service Commissioner investigate matters which come within the jurisdiction of the courts or a tribunal, unless he considers it unreasonable to expect the complainant to make use of such remedies (s.4). Matters of clinical judgment concerned with the diagnosis of illness, or the care and treatment of a patient are also outside his jurisdiction (s.5), as is "action taken in connection with any general medical services under the National Health Service Act 1977" (s.6). Matters arising from National Health Service contracts and service provision agreements are, however, within his jurisdiction (s.7).[13]

A complaint should be made in writing, and should normally be made within one year from the date when the matter first came to the notice of the complainant. A complaint may be made where the patient has died, or is unable to act for himself, by either his personal representative, or a member of his family, or some body or individual suitable to represent him (which may itself be a health services body) (s.9).

The investigation is conducted in private, and will involve interviewing relevant personnel and scrutinising documents. A written report is sent to the complainant and to the relevant body, together with a statement as to whether the authority has agreed to remedy any injustice or hardship found to be caused. The power of the Ombudsman is, however, purely persuasive, he cannot compel the making of an apology or changes in policy or procedures; what he can do, however, is publicise shortcomings and make recommendations.

PUBLIC INQUIRIES

Section 84 of the National Health Service Act 1977 enables the Secretary of State to cause an inquiry to be held in any case in which he deems it advisable "in connection with any matter arising under this Act". A well-known example of such an inquiry is that into allegations of ill-treatment and neglect at Whittingham Hospital known as the *Payne Report* of 1992.

JUDICIAL REVIEW AND ACTIONS FOR BREACH OF STATUTORY DUTY

The National Health Service Act 1977 is quite explicit about the duties which are imposed upon the Secretary of State. These are as follows:

---

[13] See p. 37.

"to continue the promotion in England and Wales of a comprehensive health service designed to secure improvement—
  (a) in the physical and mental health of the people of those countries, and
  (b) in the prevention, diagnosis and treatment of illness,
and for these purposes to provide or secure the effective provision of services in accordance with this Act" (s.1).

"to provide throughout England and Wales, to such extent as he considers necessary to meet all reasonable requirements—
  [. . .]
  (e) such facilities for the prevention of illness, the care of persons suffering from illness and the aftercare of persons who have suffered from illness as he considers are appropriate as part of the health service"(s.3).

Any attempt by an individual actually to enforce sections 1 or 3(c) by way of an action for breach of statutory duty would however meet the same barriers as an attempt to enforce the performance of statutory duties by local authorities.[14] The subjective wording of the duty, the availability of alternative remedies, and the difficulties in showing that the duty was owed to an individual complainant as opposed to the public at large, would all militate against successful action.

In *R. v. Secretary of State for Social Services, ex p. Hincks*[15] the applicants were orthopaedic patients at a hospital in Birmingham who brought an action for breach of statutory duty under the 1977 Act, ss.1 and 3, for failing to provide adequate facilities for their operations to be carried out within a reasonable time. Building a new treatment facility for orthopaedic patients had been shelved owing to financial difficulties. The Court of Appeal would not intervene by way of declaration against the Secretary of State because the subjective wording of the statute gave him a discretion as to the allocation of financial resources. The only possible grounds for intervention would be if the Secretary of State had acted in this way to frustrate the policy of the Act, or if no reasonable Minister could have acted in that way. Moreover, the court considered itself unable to grant mandamus or a declaration against the health authorities concerned because specific remedies were available against them under Part V of the Act, and in particular section 85 (the default power). No relief by way of damages would in any case be available to the plaintiffs since the duties created by sections 1 and 3 were public law duties and did not confer rights upon individuals affected by their breach. It is worth noting here that section 6 of the Health Service Commissioners Act 1993 specifically excludes "action taken in connection with any medical services under the National Health Service Act 1977", from the jurisdiction of the Health Service Commissioners.

A less limited interpretation of health authorities' statutory duties, and their enforcement was, however, made by Orton J. in *R. v. Ealing District*

---

[14] See p. 99.
[15] (1979) 123 S.J. 436.

Health Authority, ex p. Fox.[16] An order of certiorari was granted against the health authority which had refused to appoint a responsible medical officer to carry out the decision of a mental health review tribunal to discharge a detained patient under section 73 of the Mental Health Act 1983. The court also granted a declaration that the authority was in breach of its statutory duty under section 117 of the Mental Health Act 1983 in failing to provide aftercare facilities for a patient detained under section 3. Orton J., however, referred not only to section 117 as the source of the health authority's duty to provide services, but also to the "general statutory framework" to provide a comprehensive range of hospital and psychiatric and community services. Not only did this general duty exist; it was a continuing duty *to the patient.* The door is therefore open in future cases for individual patients to argue that such a general statutory framework is not only enforceable in public law, but that it also creates individual rights enforceable by private action.

Even if a health authority is found to be in breach of its public law duty, a remedy may be refused on the basis that it would not directly benefit the complainant especially if he could receive treatment elsewhere. Thus, in *R. v. North West Thames Regional Health Authority and Secretary of State for Health, ex p. Daniels,*[16a] the running down and closure of a regional transplant unit had already taken place, notwithstanding a breach by the regional health authority of its statutory duty to consult with the local community health council. A remedy was refused as the potential patient was already receiving treatment elsewhere and there were no longer proper facilities or personnel available to treat him in his own locality. The case illustrates how powerless individuals (and the courts) are to intervene when decisions concerning the allocation of resources are involved. Responsibility for such decisions, the court acknowledged, lay with the Secretary of State, who would ultimately not have been prevented by an order of the court from moving the unit elsewhere.

ACTIONS AGAINST PUBLIC AUTHORITIES

"Our law in relation to claims for damages for administrative wrongdo-ing is notoriously unsatisfactory from the claimant's point of view. Thus it comes about, I suspect, that the claim is put in a number of different ways—in contract, in tort, and under statute . . . " *per* Schiemann J. in *R. v. Knowsley Borough Council, ex p. Maguire.*[17] The case concerned alleged maladministration in changing the criteria for the issue of taxi-cab licences, and failed on all three counts: in contract, because a letter to taxi-

---

[16] [1993] 1 W.L.R. 373.
[16a] [1993] 4 Med. L.R. 364.
[17] (1992) 142 New L.J. 1375 at 1375.

cab owners outlining council policy did not constitute an offer that could be accepted; in negligence, because there was no evidence of breach of a duty of care in this case, though the court left open the question of whether a possible duty of care did exist; and for breach of statutory duty, because there was no indication that the statute was passed for the benefit of would-be cab drivers rather than the public at large. A further claim based on estoppel failed because there was no evidence that the council ever represented that it considered a claim for a licence as a contractual claim.

The claim encapsulates the difficulties that those who deal with local authorities will face when seeking to hold those authorities to statements made in policy documents. It has particular implications for providers of care services. There are, however, administrative as well as legal remedies available.

THE CITIZEN'S CHARTER

The Citizen's Charter, launched in 1991, is in fact a White Paper the principles of which are intended to apply to all public services.[18] According to the Foreword, the aim of the Charter is "To make public services answer better to the wishes of their users, and to raise their quality overall." This is to be done through the six key principles of the so-called Charter Standard:

(1) Publications of the standards of service that the customer can reasonably expect, and of performance against those standards.
(2) Evidence that the views of those who use the service have been taken into account in setting standards.
(3) Clear information about the range of services provided in plain language.
(4) Courteous and efficient customer service.
(5) Well signposted avenues of complaint, with some means of independent review wherever possible.
(6) Independent validation of performance against standards and a clear commitment to improving value for money.

The Charter Standard may thus be invoked when negotiating concerning acceptable levels of service; it will also be reflected in future legislation and guidance pertaining to the public sector.

---

[18] *Citizen's Charter*, Cm. 1599 (1991).

LOCAL AUTHORITY COMPLAINTS PROCEDURES IN RESPECT OF SOCIAL SERVICES FUNCTIONS

Section 50 of the National Health Service and Community Care Act 1990 inserts a new section 7B into the Local Authority Social Services Act 1970, requiring local authorities to set up representations and complaints procedures which will operate in respect of matters arising after April 1, 1991 (the appointed day). The format which the procedures are to follow is laid down in the Complaints Procedure Directions 1990.

Complaints must be made by and in respect of a "qualifying individual". A person is a qualifying individual if:

(1) a local authority has a power or a duty to provide, or to secure the provision of, a social service for him; and
(2) his need or possible need for such a service has (by whatever means) come to the attention of the local authority.

It will be open to local authorities, at their discretion to deal with complaints or representations falling outside these parameters.

> "Complaints can result from an unresolved problem or from a measure of dissatisfaction or disquiet about the organisation, about the implementation of decisions, about the quality and appropriateness of services, or about their delivery or non-delivery.[19]"

Authorities' complaints procedures should be kept separate from grievance procedures and disciplinary procedures which concern internal staffing matters.

The Complaints Procedure Directions require local authorities to:

(1) designate an officer to assist in the co-ordination of representations and complaints procedure;
(2) ensure familiarity with procedures by all members or officers involved; and
(3) monitor the operation of the procedures.

THE PROCEDURES

The procedures are in three stages:

(1) an informal stage;
(2) a formal "registered complaint" stage; and
(3) a review stage at which an independent element is introduced.

---

[19] *Policy Guidance* (H.M.S.O., 1990), para. 6.7.

They thus differ from complaints procedures under section 26(3) of the Children Act 1989 which require an independent element at the second stage as well.

The informal stage

Paragraph 5(1) of the Directions requires that where the local authority receives representations from any complainant, they shall attempt to resolve the matter informally. If this cannot be done to the satisfaction of the complainant, he will be invited to submit a written representation (para. 5(2)), and will be given assistance and guidance in the use of the formal procedure, or advice on where he may obtain it (para. 5(3)).

The formal stage

A formal written complaint becomes a "registered" complaint which the authority should respond to within 28 days (para. 6(1)). Alternatively, the local authority should explain why a response within that time is not possible and advise the complainant when he can expect a response, which in any case should be given with three months (para. 6(1)).

The review panel stage

If the complainant informs the authority in writing within 28 days of notification of the outcome of the complaint that he is still dissatisfied and wishes the matter to be referred to a panel for review, the authority is required to convene a panel (para. 7(2)).

The panel must meet within 28 days of the request and must record its decision in writing within 24 hours. This decision is in the form of a recommendation to the Director of Social Services, and the Social Services Committee; it is not binding on them. The process is, however, amenable to judicial review.

The review panel should be made up of three people, one of whom should be independent of the local authority. Ten days' notice should be given, during which written submissions may be made. There is a right to an oral hearing, and a right to be accompanied by or represented by some other person at the hearing, though legal representation is excluded. The procedure is informal, though the complainant (or his representative) should be given the opportunity to make an oral submission before the authority's representative does.

Complaints concerning voluntary and private sector provision

"Wherever possible, the service provider should handle complaints about care services provided in the voluntary sector with financial support from the local authority" (*Policy Guidance*, para. 31). Complainants who are dissatisfied with the response they receive, or who do not wish to complain to the service provider may choose to refer the matter to

the Social Services Department; complaints received in those circumstances should be treated as "registered complaints". There should be
formal procedures for dealing with complaints concerning nursing home
care, which will involve the forwarding of a copy of the complaint to the
health authority responsible for inspection of the home (*Policy Guidance*,
para. 6.32).

Judicial review of the complaints procedure

Local authority complaints procedures are themselves subject to judicial
review. The process was examined by Henry J. in *R. v. Avon County
Council, ex p. Mark Hazell*[20] A review panel recommended that Mark, a
young man of 22 years with learning difficulties, should be given his
preferred choice of accommodation which was a placement with the
Home Farm Trust, rather than alternative residential accommodation
favoured by the local authority. The finding of the review panel was that
only the Home Farm Trust placement could fully meet Mark's needs
including those that were psychological. Henry J. held that the Social
Services Committee could not overrule the review panel's recommendation without substantial reason, and without having given that recommendation the weight it required because of its status within the
statutory process as "the obvious and intended forum for a detailed
examination of the facts". The decision of the Social Services Committee
was thus *"Wednesbury"*[20a] unreasonable, either because there was
unintentional perversity in the decision, or there was a failure to take all
relevant matters into account properly, or there was an implicit error in
law not giving those recommendations sufficient weight. The same
conclusions could thus be argued for on a number of grounds.

Complaints procedures and the commissioner for local administration

The incorrect operation of complaints procedures may also amount to
maladministration within the jurisdiction of the Commissioner for Local
Administration. See the report on investigation No. 92/A/3725, against
the London Borough of Haringey, and investigation No. 92/C/1042, into a
complaint against Cleveland County Council. In both cases compensation was recommended, and in the former case a review of the
procedures was recommended so as to ensure that proper investigations
were carried out when complaints were made against a senior officer of
the authority.

---

[20] Unreported, July 5, 1993; see Parsloe, in *Community Care*, p. 16, August 5, 1993.
[20a] [1948] 1 K.B. 223 and below, p. 102.

The Commissioner for Local Administration

The Commissioner for Local Administration (or Ombudsman) may investigate allegations of injustice caused by maladministration in the performance of its functions by a local authority. Maladministration is generally taken to mean those matters contained in the so-called Crossman catalogue: "bias, neglect, inattention, delay, incompetence, ineptitude, arbitrariness and the like".[21]

There is no power to question the merits of a decision where there is no maladministration: *R. v. Local Commissioner for Administration, ex p. Bradford Metropolitan County Council*.[22] The complainant will usually apply in person, but where he is unable to do so, "some body or individual suitable to represent him" may apply on his behalf (Local Government Act 1974, s.27(2)). Complaints must be made within 12 months, and alternative rights or remedies must already have been exhausted unless the Commissioner feels that it is not reasonable to expect the complainant to use these rights (s.26(6)). An attempt is usually made to achieve a settlement without a formal investigation. Payments towards legal costs will, however, be considered in exceptional cases. A copy of the final report will be sent to all the parties, and if the local authority does not act upon his recommendations, the Ombudsman may publish a further report leading to a statement in an agreed form which must be published in the local press. Local authorities also have the power to pay compensation to those found to have suffered injustice as a consequence of maladministration (Local Government and Housing Act 1989, s.31(3)).

Complaints of delay in responding to requests for assessment or in the delivery of services are frequently made. Examples are investigations Nos. 92/A/4108 and 92/A/1173 into delays (of 18 months and three years respectively) in providing occupational therapy assessments in the London Borough of Redbridge. Investigation No. 92/C/1042 into a complaint against Cleveland County Council, led to a recommendation for a review of the care facilities following the death of a disabled resident in one of the authority's homes. Failure to implement a proper care programme for residents and determining the appropriate level of supervision required was clearly maladministration.

The Parliamentary Commissioner

The Parliamentary Commissioner for Administration investigates complaints against government departments and certain non-departmental

---

[21] H.C.Deb., Col. 51, October 18, 1966.
[22] [1979] 2 All E.R. 88.

public bodies. The system was set up by the Parliamentary Commissioner Act 1967. Members of Parliament are used as the filter to refer complaints onto the Parliamentary Commissioner for Administration. Certain matters are excluded from this brief which include:

(i) personnel matters in the public service and armed forces;
(ii) the investigation of crime; and
(iii) the conduct of proceedings by government departments.

Complaints about government policy and the content of legislation are for Parliament itself to decide. Proceedings, which may involve the investigation of government files and papers and the consideration of oral evidence, are held in private. A report will be sent to the Member of Parliament who referred the case and the complainant. There is no power to compel any body to comply with the Parliamentary Commissioner for Administration's findings, but he may report the matter to Parliament. Compensation may be paid on an *ex gratia* basis. A majority of complaints involve the Department of Social Security and the Inland Revenue. The jurisdiction of the Parliamentary Commissioner is extended to include actions taken by the administrative staff of relevant tribunals by the Parliamentary Commissioner Act 1994.

Actions of the Parliamentary Commissioner for Administration are within the scope of judicial review: *R. v. Parliamentary Commissioner for Administration, ex p. Dyer.*[23]

ACTIONS FOR BREACH OF STATUTORY DUTY

In dealing with actions for breach of statutory duty brought against local authorities in respect of their social services functions, the courts have been reluctant to concede that public law duties can give rise to rights in private law. The leading case is *Wyatt v. Hillingdon London Borough Council,*[24] in which an elderly woman who was disabled sought to bring an action against the local authority for breach of the statutory duty under section 2 of the Chronically Sick and Disabled Persons Act 1970 to provide services to meet an assessed need; the dispute in this case was over the number of home help hours to be allocated properly. The procedure for enforcing such a duty was held to be use of the default powers of the Secretary of State under the National Assistance Act 1948, s.36, which the plaintiff had not considered. Furthermore, since the discretion within the Act was so subjectively worded, the court was reluctant to interfere in a decision which it saw as clearly delegated by Parliament to the authority concerned.

---

[23] *The Times*, October 27, 1993.
[24] (1978) 76 L.G.R. 727.

In *R. v. Ealing London Borough Council, ex p. Leaman*[25] the court again took the view that it had no power to award damages for a breach of section 2 of the 1970 Act, though it did grant a declaration in public law that the local authority's refusal to sponsor privately arranged holidays as well as holidays provided by itself was an error in law.

Whether or not a public law duty is enforceable in private law depends upon the nature of the duty sought to be enforced: *Southwark London Borough Council v. Williams.*[26] Many of the reported cases have been concerned with the proper interpretations of the homeless persons legislation. Judicial interest has focused not on the "executive" function of matching people to resources, but on the decision-making function as to eligibility which logically precedes it. Though the executive function might not give rise to a right of action for breach of statutory duty, this does not necessarily mean that there is no remedy. The appropriate remedy would be an application for judicial review of the decision-making function: *Cocks v. Thanet District Council.*[27]

A number of recent cases involving local authorities' duties to house homeless persons have, however, been successful in acknowledging that public law decisions can give rise to private law rights: see, for example, *R. v. Tower Hamlets London Borough Council, ex p. Ali (Mohib); R. v. same, ex p. Uddin (Ain).*[28] A continued failure on the part of a local authority to discharge its statutory duty to house may result in damages: *R. v. Lambeth London Borough Council, ex p. Barnes (Olive),*[29] once the duty to house has been acknowledged.

JUDICIAL REVIEW

Scope of judicial review

Judicial review, as a remedy, is limited to public bodies performing public law functions. The procedure is governed by the Supreme Court Act 1981, s.31 and R.S.C., Ord. 53. Leave must first be applied for and may be refused either if the applicant does not have a sufficient interest in the proceedings, or if an alternative remedy is available. In some instances, however, "public interest" challenges have been allowed where the decision impugned affects an identifiable class of persons as litigant: see for example, *R. v. Secretary of State for the Environment, ex p. Rose Theatre Trust Co.*[30]; *R. v. Secretary of State for Social Services, ex p. Child Poverty Action Group.*[31] Judicial review may be refused if alternative remedies exist,

---

[25] *The Times*, February 10, 1984.
[26] [1971] Ch. 734.
[27] [1983] 2 A.C. 286.
[28] (1993) 25 H.L.R. 218.
[29] (1992) 25 H.L.R. 140.
[30] [1990] 1 Q.B. 504.
[31] [1990] 2 Q.B. 540.

whether judicial or administrative: *ex p. Waldron*[32]; *R. v. Epping and Harlow General Commissioners, ex p. Goldstraw*.[33] The issue decided may, however, be deemed "particularly suitable" for judicial review, as in *R. v. Devon County Council, ex p. Baker; R. v. Durham County Council, ex p. Curtis*[34]; cases concerned with the adequacy of consultation of residents prior to the closure of residential homes for the elderly owned by the local authority. The availability of an application to the Secretary of State to use his default powers did not preclude the applicants from seeking judicial review. This may be contrasted with the decision in *Wyatt v. Hillingdon London Borough Council*[35] where the availability of default powers precluded an action for breach of statutory duty.

Given the three-month time-limit in R.S.C., Ord. 53, r.4(1), it may be appropriate to seek leave to apply for judicial review, and then request an adjournment pending determination, for example, of the local authority complaints procedure. In any event, a letter before action should be seen as a pre-requisite.[35a]

Grounds for intervention

Judicial review is not concerned with the merits of the decision, but with the process by which that decision is reached. The decision may be:

(1) *ultra vires*: that is, outside the statutory powers of the body making the decision, or a failure to exercise powers given by statute;
(2) based on a misinterpretation of the law;
(3) procedurally incorrect;
(4) contrary to the rules of natural justice, or otherwise procedurally "unfair";
(5) unreasonable or irrational.

Examples from the law on welfare issues may illustrate the points made above. In *R. v. Secretary of State for Social Services, ex p. Hincks*,[36] judicial review was seen as the appropriate course of action for challenging the Secretary of State's failure to provide a comprehensive National Health Service as required by the National Health Service Act 1977. If a public body misinterprets the extent of the obligation placed on it, that decision is available to judicial review, as in *R. v. Secretary of State for Social Services, ex p. Association of Metropolitan Authorities*,[37] where the Secretary of State misinterpreted the obligation to consult prior to amending housing benefit regulations, by regarding it as directory rather than mandatory. Failure to follow an established procedure in assessing

---

[32] [1986] Q.B. 824.
[33] [1983] 3 All E.R. 257.
[34] (1993) 91 L.G.R. 479.
[35] (1978) 122 S.J. 349.
[35a] McCarthy, R., "What to do before starting judicial review", S.J., March 4, 1994.
[36] (1979) 123 S.J. 436. See p. 92.
[37] [1986] 1 All E.R. 164.

the need for community care services or changing the basis of eligibility may constitute a breach of a legitimate expectation that a particular procedure would be followed: in *Council of Civil Service Unions v. Minister for the Civil Service,*[38] Lord Diplock upheld a challenge based upon a "well established practice" that important alterations to the terms and conditions of civil servants' conditions of service would be subject to prior consultation. The procedure complained of, however, must be a matter of public law, and the fact that it is carried out by a public body does not necessarily make it so. Thus, in *R. v. Lord Chancellor, ex p. Hibbitt,*[39] where the process of tendering for court reporting services was challenged as unfair, this was held to be an example purely of a common law right to contract, which was not subject to a duty of fairness. What was lacking was a sufficient public law element to be susceptible to judicial review.

Bodies exercising quasi-judicial functions are required to act in accordance with the rules of natural justice: *Ridge v. Baldwin,*[40] where disciplinary proceedings were being taken against a Chief Constable, is a prime example. Administrative bodies which make decisions affecting individual rights are also under an obligation to act fairly, provided the apparent purpose of the legislation is not thereby frustrated: *Wiseman v. Borneman.*[41] Local authorities in the child care field have been obliged to extend the "right to be heard" to parents and others involved in child protection procedures where the consequences of their decision-making are sufficiently serious to warrant it: *R. v. Norfolk County Council, ex p. M.*[42]

In *R. v. Devon County Council, ex p. Baker; R. v. Durham County Council, ex p. Curtis,*[43] a general right for residents to be consulted prior to the closure of their homes was upheld, though this did not amount to a requirement that every individual resident should be consulted by an officer or councillor of the local authority. A decision based on adequate consultation is less likely to fail the classic tests of "illegality" and "unreasonableness" laid down by Lord Greene M.R. in *Associated Provincial Picture Houses Ltd. v. Wednesbury Corporation.*[44] If the local authority has taken into account matters which they ought not to take into account, and have refused to take into account matters which they ought to take into account, they will be acting "illegality". Even if the decision thus made comes within the "four corners" of the Act, it may still nevertheless be so unreasonable that no reasonable authority could have come to it, and therefore subject to judicial review on that ground alone. This is commonly referred to as the "*Wednesbury* unreasonableness" test.

[38] [1985] A.C. 374.
[39] *The Independent*, March 16, 1993.
[40] [1964] A.C. 40.
[41] [1971] A.C. 297.
[42] [1989] Q.B. 619.
[43] (1993) 91 L.G.R. 479.
[44] [1948] 1 K.B. 223 at 234.

The *Mark Hazell* case[45] is a prime example of local authorities acting unreasonably in disregard of their own procedures, in dealing with complaints.

Judicial review therefore potentially offers a wide scope for challenging decisions made by local authorities and by health authorities in the provision of services. There are two major limitations, however, based on the failure of the courts to impose a general duty to give reasons for administrative decisions, and the failure to address the problem of limited financial resources. The giving of adequate reasons for decisions is very often the key to a successful challenge, but although the 1993 White Paper on Open Government[46] has recommended that reasons should be given for all administrative decisions except where there is statutory authority or established convention to the contrary, this is not reflected in the current legal position.[47] Whether or not there is a duty to give reasons will be inferred from the characteristics of the particular decision and the general demands of fairness, though the House of Lords in *Doody v. Secretary of State for the Home Department*,[48] a case concerned with disparities between the Home Secretary and the trial judge in the sentencing of mandatory life prisoners, considered that the failure to give reasons should be "exceptional".

The extent to which lack of resources can be successfully pleaded by an authority is, however, a major barrier to judicial review. Either the statute itself is subjectively worded so as to impose a duty to provide services only to the extent considered necessary (as in *R. v. Secretary of State for Social Services, ex p. Hincks*[49]), or the court refuses to become involved in disputes about allocations devolved by Parliament to a minister (as in the "*Daniels*" case[50]). Where the reason given for the non-provision of service is inadequate staffing levels, Richard Gordon suggests that breach of the Local Authority Social Services Act 1970, s.6(6), should always be pleaded.[51] Section 6(6) states that:

> "a local authority which [has] appointed, or concerned in the appointment of a Director of Social Services, shall secure the provision of adequate staff for assisting him in the exercise of his functions."

Delays in assessment or the provision of services may, of course, amount to maladministration and may be subject to a referral to the Ombudsman (see p. 98).

Where there is competition for scarce resources a remedy may be denied on the grounds of distributive justice. In *R. v. Bristol Corporation, ex*

---

[45] See *Community Care*, July 15, 1993, pp. 18–19.
[46] Cm. 2290 (1993).
[47] Cragg and Ashiagbor, "A Duty to give reasons?", New L.J., February 25, 1994.
[48] [1993] 3 All E.R. 92.
[49] (1979) 123 S.J. 436.
[50] *R. v. North West Thames Regional Health Authority and Secretary of State for Health, ex p. Daniels* [1993] 4 Med. L.R. 364.
[51] Gordon, "The Challenge to Community Care", [1993] L.S.Gaz, January 27.

p. Hendy,[52] Lord Scarman, in refusing to make an order of mandamus, was quite clear that the courts would not make an order requiring a local authority to do:

> "that which it cannot do or which can it only do at the expense of other persons not before the court who may have equal rights with the applicant and some of whom would certainly have equal moral claims."

AVAILABLE REMEDIES

The following final forms of relief are available on judicial review under R.S.C., Ord. 53, r.1: the prerogative orders of certiorari, prohibition and mandamus, a declaration, or injunction. However, all of these remedies are discretionary: relief may even be refused if it is "administratively inconvenient" (*R. v. Secretary of State for Social Services, ex p. Cotton*).[53] An application for relief shall be made "promptly" and in any event within three months of the date when grounds for the application first arose, unless the Court considers that there is good reason for extending the period within which the application shall be made."[54] Judicial review is also available for the purpose of securing a declaration that certain U.K. primary legislation is incompatible with European Law; see *R. v. Secretary of State for Employment, ex p. Equal Opportunities Commission*.[54a]

INTERIM RELIEF

Interim relief may be given by way of injunction, for example, to maintain service provision, but only if a strong prima facie case is made out: *R. v. Kensington and Chelsea Royal Borough Council, ex p. Hammell*.[55] Interim injunctive relief is available against the Crown: *M. v. Home Office*.[56] The factors to be taken into account when the court is considering whether or not to grant interim injunctive relief were explored in *American Cyanamid Co. v. Ethicon Ltd.*[57] The strongest consideration is whether or not a remedy in damages would be sufficient relief in a final action; if there is any doubt about this, then the status quo should be preserved by the granting of an interim injunction. Interim declaratory relief is not, however, known to English law: *Riverside Mental Health National Health Service Trust v. Fox*.[58]

---

[52] [1974] 1 W.L.R. 498 at 503.
[53] *The Times*, December 14, 1985.
[54] See R.S.C., Ord. 53, r.4(1).
[54a] [1994] 2 W.L.R. 409, H.L.
[55] [1989] Q.B. 518.
[56] [1993] 3 W.L.R. 433.
[57] [1975] A.C. 396.
[58] *The Times*, October 28, 1993.

Chapter 8
Compulsory Intervention

The receipt of health care and social services is in the vast majority of cases entirely voluntary. No service can be imposed without the consent of the would-be recipient of those services. The only exceptions to this general principle are contained in the provisions of the Mental Health Act 1983 and section 47 of the National Assistance Act 1948. In these instances for those who are deemed to be "at risk" in the community either because of their own actions or those of others, the function of the law is not enabling or normative, but protective. Moreover, both pieces of legislation also provide for compulsory intervention for the protection of other persons.

SECTION 47 OF THE NATIONAL ASSISTANCE ACT 1948

Section 47(1) of the National Assistance Act 1948 provides for the compulsory removal from home "for the purposes of securing the necessary care and attention" of persons who:

(a) are suffering from grave chronic disease or, being aged, infirm or physically incapacitated, are living in insanitary conditions; and
(b) are unable to devote themselves, and are not receiving from other persons, proper care and attention.

The procedure is for the "proper officer" (s.47(2)), formerly the Medical Officer of Health (now Community Physician), to certify in writing to the local authority that:

> "he is satisfied after thorough inquiry and consideration that in the interests of any such person as aforesaid residing in the area of the authority, or for preventing injury to the health of, or serious nuisance to, other persons, it is necessary to remove any such person as aforesaid from the premises in which he is residing."

The section is designed to deal with two different situations: where a person's condition has deteriorated over a period of time, or where a patient has become seriously ill and a crisis has arisen. In the latter instance, although removal may be to "a suitable hospital or other place in, or within convenient distance of, the area of the appropriate authority" (s.47(3)), there is no provision for medical treatment to be given without consent.

Application is to the magistrates' court for the place where the premises are situated. Seven days' notice is required of the proposed application (s.47(7)) and the maximum initial duration of the order is three months, renewable for further periods of up to three months indefinitely (s.47(4)). An application for revocation may be made only after the expiry of six clear weeks (s.47(6)). The court must be satisfied on oral evidence of the allegations in the certificate (s.47(3)), but there is no requirement that the person who is the subject of the allegations should be brought before the court. Legal aid is not available.

An emergency procedure under the National Assistance (Amendment) Act 1951, s.1, allows applications to be made *ex parte* and, with the agreement of the local authority, directly by the Community Physician (s.1(3)). The application must however be supported by two medical recommendations that it is in the person's interest to be removed "without delay", and the period of removal is then three weeks, renewable up to a maximum of three months.

There is wide geographical variation in the interpretation of section 47 and in the frequency of its use, with an estimated 200 cases each year in England and Wales as a whole. The emergency procedure is in fact used in the vast majority of cases. Possibly 50 per cent of those removed from home under section 47 are suffering from mental disorder and ought properly to have been admitted under mental health legislation which contains greater procedural safeguards, but is a non-judicial process. The distinction to be drawn in the legislation between those physically at risk who are covered by section 47 of the National Assistance Act and those who are mentally disordered who are dealt with under the Mental Health Act 1983 may not therefore hold up so clearly in practice.

Section 47 has been much criticised as an ageist piece of legislation which betrays its roots in pre-war public health and slum clearance measures, and which fits uneasily into the welfare legislation of the post-war period. Being "aged", living in insanitary conditions, and being unable to care for oneself are sufficient criteria for removal under the Act. The British Association of Social Workers stated in 1977 that the section should not be used unless the patient's functioning, whether physical, psychological or emotional, would be improved by compulsory action. Local authorities have their own procedures for deciding whether or not to use the section; most involve the convening of a case conference or equivalent. Only a small minority of those removed under section 47 ever return to their own homes; careful attention therefore needs to be paid to the quality of life that can be offered elsewhere. For a discussion of the application of the legislation see Tregaskis B. and Mayberry J., "The Anniversary of Section 47 of the National Assistance Act 1948".[1]

PUBLIC HEALTH ACT 1936

The cleansing and disinfecting of premises and persons is governed by the Public Health Act 1936, often used as a corollary to removal under the National Assistance Act 1948, s.47.

Section 84(1) of the Public Health Act 1936 states that "upon the application of any person, a county council or a local authority may take such measures as are, in their opinion, necessary to free him or his clothing from vermin." Sub-section (2) provides that in the absence of consent, an application may be made by the medical officer of health (now Community Physician) or a sanitary inspector to the magistrates' court.

Section 83 of the Act further provides for the cleansing of premises "in such a filthy or unwholesome condition as to be prejudicial to health" or verminous. The primary responsibility is that of the owner or occupier of the premises, on whom the local authority may serve an enforcement notice. The local authority has default powers when the work is not carried out. Section 287 of the Public Health Act 1936 gives the local authority power of entry to ascertain whether there has been a breach of the Act or bye-laws, and for the purposes of enforcement under the Act. Twenty-four hours' notice must be given. If entry is refused, or refusal is apprehended, a warrant may be obtained from a magistrates' court which permits entry by an "authorised officer", "if need be by force" (s.287(2)(b)).

THE MENTAL HEALTH ACT 1983

Mental Illness in Older People

The elderly mentally infirm pose particular problems of assessment, intervention and treatment, and are in fact the largest sector of the population with a need for psychiatric services. Dementia, particularly of the Alzheimer's type, is seen as the "classic" mental illness of old age, with an incidence of about 5 per cent in the total population over 65, but of up to 20 per cent in the population over 80.[1a] Dementia is a progressive illness, and legal mechanisms therefore need to be sensitive to the different needs of people at varying stages of their illness. Of greater numerical significance even than dementia is depression amongst

---

[1] J.P., April 23, 1994.
[1a] Brayne and Ames, "The Epidemiology of Mental Disorders in Old Age" in *Mental Health Problems in Old Age* (Gearing *et al.*, 1988).

elderly people, and there is a significant risk of successful suicide; between 25 and 30 per cent of those who commit suicide each year are over 65 years old.[2]

Support in the community for the elderly mental infirm is provided both by the health authority and by the local authority (see Chapter 2 — The Delivery of Social Services and Chapter 4 — The Provision of National Health Services). In an acute situation, or where there is a marked deterioration in functioning, admission to hospital may have to be considered.

Admission under the Mental Health Act 1983

Although the Mental Health Act 1983 regulates compulsory admission to psychiatric hospitals, section 131 of the Act makes it clear that informal admission should be the norm. Though the vast majority of elderly patients in hospital are informal patients, the Mental Health Act Commission has drawn attention to the fact that many are *de facto* detained, being unable to exercise any genuine choice or express any effective dissent.[3] Informal admission therefore is not the same as voluntary admission; not expressing an objection to detention is not the same as voluntarily agreeing to accept it, but it is only the former that the law requires.

For the minority of patients who do not accept informal admission, or for whom it is not appropriate, the provisions of the Mental Health Act 1983 define the circumstances in which compulsory admission to hospital can take place, and treatment can be provided. The Act is drafted so as to give a wide scope for professional discretion, particularly on the grounds for admission. Though the Act is also concerned with mentally disordered offenders, only those subject to civil powers will be discussed here.

APPLICATION OF THE MENTAL HEALTH ACT 1983

By section 1(1) of the Mental Health Act 1983:

> "the provisions of this Act shall have effect with respect to the reception, care and treatment of mentally disordered patients, the management of their property and other related matters."

The Act is divided into 10 parts as follows.

    Part 1.   The definition of mental disorder.
    Part 2.   Compulsory admission to hospital and guardianship.

---

[2] *ibid.*
[3] *Mental Health Act Commission 3rd Biennial Report* (1987–1989).

Part 3.   Patients concerned in criminal proceedings or under sentence.

Part 4.   Consent to treatment.

Part 5.   Mental health review tribunals.

Part 6.   Removal and return of patients within the United Kingdom.

Part 7.   Management of property and affairs of patients.

Part 8.   Functions of local authorities and the Secretary of State.

Part 9.   Offences.

Part 10. Miscellaneous and supplementary.

Section 12(1) of the Act gives statutory definition to the Mental Health Act Commission which is a general watchdog body for the Act; its members include lay people as well as mental health professionals. The Mental Health Act Commission (Establishment and Constitution) Order[4] defines the functions of the Mental Health Act Commission. These include a visiting and inspection function in respect of detained patients, the setting up of a complaints procedure, and the monitoring of compulsory treatment under the Act. The Commission has a legal officer, though his role is not to give advice in individual cases.

The Mental Health Act Commission also gives advice to the Secretary of State on the drawing up of a Code of Practice under section 118 of the Act. Though primarily aimed as a commentary on the needs, rights and entitlements of detained patients, the Code of Practice also has much to say about good practice with informal patients. However, it is of persuasive value only. Relevant regulations are the Mental Health (Hospitals, Guardianship and Consent to Treatment) Regulations 1983[5] and the Mental Health Review Tribunal Rules 1983.[6]

Compulsory admissions under the Mental Health Act are by the process known as "sectioning". Persons involved in the process of admission and detention are the nearest relative, the approved social worker, the hospital managers, and the responsible medical officer. These terms must first be defined.

The nearest relative

Modern mental health legislation has retained an important role for the nearest relative of the patient in the process of admission and detention.

Section 26 of the Act defines "relative" and "nearest relative" to mean any one of the following persons:

(*a*) husband or wife;

(*b*) son or daughter;

(*c*) father or mother;

(*d*) brother or sister;

---

[4] S.I. 1983 No. 892.
[5] S.I. 1983 No. 893.
[6] S.I. 1983 No. 942.

(e) grandparent;
(f) grandchild;
(g) uncle or aunt;
(h) nephew or niece.

An illegitimate person is treated as the child of his mother, and also of his father, if the father has parental responsibility for him within the meaning of section 3 of the Children Act 1989.

The "nearest relative" (s.26(3)) is the person first described in subsection (1); relations of the whole blood being preferred to relatives of the same description of the half blood, and the elder being preferred to others in the same category, regardless of sex. It is the existence of the blood tie which counts, not the quality of the social relationship. An exception which may be important in the case of elderly people is subsection (4) which states that:

> "subject to the provisions of this section and to the following provisions of the part of this Act, where the patient ordinarily resides with or is cared for by one or more of his relatives (or, if he is for the time being an in-patient in a hospital, he last ordinarily resided with or was cared for by one or more of his relatives) his nearest relatives shall be determined:
>
> (a) by giving preference to that relative or those relatives over the others; and
>
> (b) as between two or more such relatives in accordance with sub-section three above."

A "substantial and sustained" contact between relative and patient would probably be required for sub-section (4) to come into operation; a relative who made infrequent calls to "keep an eye" on the patient would not qualify under this section.

A relative who is not resident in the United Kingdom cannot be the nearest relative (s.26(5)(a)); nor can a spouse who is in desertion or permanently separated (whether legally separated or not). Cohabitees of not less than six months duration will be considered to be the "husband" or "wife" of the patient.

A person, other than a relative, with whom the patient ordinarily resides, and with whom he has been ordinarily residing for a period of not less than five years, is to be treated as a relative, last in line for consideration as the nearest relative after the persons listed in subsection (1) (s.26(7)). Thus, a fellow resident of a nursing home or residential home may fall to be regarded as a "nearest relative" for the purposes of the Mental Health Act.

Regulation 14 of the Mental Health (Hospital, Guardianship and Consent to Treatment) Regulations 1983[7] provides that the nearest relative may authorise in writing any other person, not otherwise disqualified, to perform the functions of the nearest relative under Part II of the Act.

---

[7] S.I. 1983 No. 893.

Functions of the nearest relative

The nearest relative may be the applicant under sections 2, 3 or 4 of the Mental Health Act 1983 for admission of the patient to hospital. In contrast to the constraints imposed on approved social workers' applications for admission, the nearest relative need not give reasons for wishing the admission to take place. In fact only 1 to 2 per cent of all admissions are by the nearest relative.

The nearest relative has the right to be informed (not necessarily before the event) of an application by an approved social worker under section 2 or section 4 (s.11(3)), and to be consulted about an application under section 3 (see below). The nearest relative has the power to bar an application under this section, or for guardianship in which case displacing the nearest relative under section 29 of the Act may have to be considered.

The nearest relative can discharge the patient from his section (s.23) or from guardianship (s.26). In the case of guardianship the discharge is absolute, but in other cases the responsible medical officer can bar the nearest relative's application under section 25 if he considers that the patient would, if discharged, be likely to act in a manner dangerous to other persons or to himself. The nearest relative can then apply to a mental health review tribunal to decide the issue of dangerousness (s.66(1)(g), (2)(d)).

Appointment by the Court of acting nearest relative

There are three situations in which an acting nearest relative may be appointed, two of which are in effect displacement of the actual nearest relative. The procedure is contained in section 29 of the Mental Health Act 1983 and involves application to the County Court by (a) any relative of the patient, (b) any other person with whom the patient is residing (without qualification of time), or (c) an approved social worker (s.29(2)).

An application for an order under this section may be made upon any of the following grounds:

(a) that the patient has no nearest relative, or that it is not reasonably practicable to ascertain whether he has such a relative, or who that relative is;

(b) that the nearest relative of the patient is incapable of acting as such by reason of mental disorder or other illness;

(c) that the nearest relative of the patient unreasonably objects to the making of an application for admission for treatment or a guardianship application in respect of the patient (s.29(3)).

The court may appoint the applicant, or any other person specified in the application who, in the opinion of the court, is a proper person to act as the patient's nearest relative and is willing to do so (s.29(3)). If a local authority is appointed it assumes visiting and welfare responsibilities towards the patient (s.116) similar to guardianship.

The procedure to be followed, as identified by section 31, is that laid down in the County Court Rules, Ord. 49, r.12.[8]

The test of reasonableness is an objective one, and was explored by the Court of Appeal in *W. v. L.*[9] There, the wife objected to the making of an application for her husband's detention despite his past history of violent and aggressive acts and the threat to their unborn child. Lord Denning M.R. put the point succinctly: "looking at it objectively, what would a reasonable woman in her place do when faced with this wife's problems?" He decided that her decision was unreasonable, and that she should be displaced.

A nearest relative who has been displaced by an order under this section can apply to a mental health review tribunal under section 66(1)(*h*) or section 66(2)(*g*) for reinstatement.

The approved social worker

The approved social worker introduces a social element into the assessment for compulsory admission. In the vast majority of cases it will be the approved social worker and not the nearest relative who is the applicant. Indeed, the *Code of Practice* states a clear preference for approved social worker applications:

> "The approved social worker is usually the right applicant, bearing in mind professional training, knowledge of the legislation and of local resources, together with the potential adverse effect that a nearest relative application might have on the relationship with the patient. The doctor should advise the nearest relative that it is preferable for an Approved Social Worker to make an assessment of the need for a patient to be admitted under the Act."[10]

It is nevertheless still open to the nearest relative to make an application (provided it is supported by the requisite medical recommendations) if the approved social worker in the exercise of professional judgment decides not to apply. However, in such cases section 14 of the Act requires the local authority as soon as is practicable to arrange for a social worker (not necessarily an approved social worker) to interview the patient with a view to producing a report on his social circumstances.

It is incumbent upon the local authority to appoint a sufficient number of approved social workers for their area (s.114), though this authority to act extends outside his own local area (s.13(3)). Qualification as an approved social worker involves a specialist period of study further to a Diploma in Social Work qualification. The liability of the approved social worker for negligent performance of their duties under the Act is personal, though the doctrine of vicarious liability will apply. Section 139 moreover restricts liability, whether civil or criminal, or any persons

---

[8] S.I. 1981 No. 1687.
[9] [1974] Q.B. 711.
[10] *Mental Health Act 1983 — Code of Practice* (H.M.S.O., 1983), para. 2.30, hereafter known as *Code of Practice.*

carrying out functions under the Act to acts done in bad faith or without reasonable care. Civil proceedings require the leave of the High Court, whilst criminal proceedings require the consent of the Director of Public Prosecutions (s.139(2)). In *Buxton v. Jayne*,[11] an authorised officer of the local authority under the Lunacy Act 1890 was held to owe a duty of care to the patient, on the ground that detention under section 20 of the Act was dependent upon the duly authorised officer having reasonable grounds for believing that person to be of unsound mind, and, it was submitted there was no evidence upon which to found that belief.

The duties of the approved social worker
The duties of the approved social worker are set out in section 13 of the Mental Health Act 1983. Section 13(4) places a duty on the local social services authority, if so required by the nearest relative of a patient residing in their area, to direct an approved social worker to take the patient's case into consideration under sub-section (1). If in any case the approved social worker decides not to make an application he shall inform the nearest relative of his reasons in writing. In the vast majority of cases, however, the request comes not from the nearest relative, but from a medical representative. A medical recommendation, however, is not sufficient authority for detention under the Act; the patient may be suffering from a mental disorder which warrants detention in hospital, but it is the further responsibility of the approved social worker to:

> "satisfy himself that detention in a hospital is in all the circumstances of the case the most appropriate way of providing the care and medical treatment of which the patient stands in need" (s.13(2)).

The approved social worker, therefore, should consider whether treatment in the community or as an out-patient would be a more suitable alternative to detention in hospital. There is, however, nothing in the Mental Health Act itself which requires health authorities to devise and implement alternatives to hospital care. Much will depend therefore on the range of discretionary resources available locally.

The quality of assessment is crucial. Though their roles are different, joint assessment by doctors and approved social workers are to be preferred (*Code of Practice*, para. 2.2). There is a statutory duty upon the approved social worker to interview the patient in a "suitable manner" before making an application (s.13(2)). So what of the patient who is deaf, or does not speak English, or who refuses or is unable to speak? The *Code of Practice* makes it clear that where there is a language or a communication barrier, an interpreter should be used, but that the duty to "interview" is not absolute:

---

[11] [1960] 1 W.L.R. 783.

"where the patient is still unable or unwilling to speak to the Approved Social Worker the assessment will have to be based on whatever information the Approved Social Worker can obtain from all reliable sources" (para. 2.11).

Gaining entry where admission is being refused is discussed below.

Factors to be taken into account at assessment are not only the health and safety of the patient, but also the patient's wishes and opinions as to his own needs; his social and family circumstances; his cultural background; the nature of his illness and associated behaviour; the impact that compulsory detention would have on the patient's life after discharge; the burden on those close to the patient of a decision not to admit under the Act; and the appropriateness of guardianship (*Code of Practice*, para. 2.6). Also relevant is the likelihood that the patient would change his mind about informal admission (para. 2.7). The revised *Code of Practice* emphasises that admission is not limited to circumstances where there is a risk to the patient's safety or that of other people, but is also available in the interests of the patient's own health. This new emphasis arises from the finding that the "criteria for admission under the Act have not been correctly understood by all professionals."[12]

The role of the approved social worker is, however, confined to the question of whether or not to admit to hospital; he has no legal voice in the treatment of the patient whilst he is in hospital, or in whether the patient is ready to be discharged, except that he may have a consultative role in decisions concerning compulsory treatment under Part IV of the Act.

As an applicant for admission of the patient, the approved social worker has the authority "to take the patient and convey him to hospital" (s.61(1)). He may authorise any other person to do this on his behalf, for example, the ambulance service or the police. There is no authority to convey the patient to any hospital other than that named in the application for admission. An approved social worker also has the authority to take into custody and return to hospital any patient absent without leave or in breach of his conditions of leave (s.18(1)).

The doctors

The giving of medical recommendations under the Mental Health Act is designed to ensure a balance between expertise and familiarity with the patient. Where two medical recommendations are required (that is in every case except for admission in an emergency under section 4) the general rule in section 12(2) applies; *i.e.* that one of the recommendations shall be given by a practitioner approved by the Secretary of State as having special experience in the diagnosis and treatment of mental disorder, and unless that practitioner has previous acquaintance with the patient, the other recommendation shall, if practicable, be given by a registered medical practitioner who has such previous acquaintance. The

---

[12] *Code of Practice*, p. iii.

usual combination is consultant psychiatrist and general practitioner. Strict rules against complicity apply: doctors who are related to the patient or to each other cannot give recommendations (s.12(5)); nor can staff both employed at the same hospital, unless one is employed on less than a half-time basis (s.12(4)), and in the case of private hospitals, a doctor cannot make a recommendation for the accommodation of a patient who would be fee paying (s.12(3) and para. 14, Sched. 2 to the National Health Service and Community Care Act 1990). However, if the hospital is a National Health Service hospital (or trust) not a private hospital, the *Code of Practice* merely states that it is "undesirable" for a doctor to provide a recommendation for a person who will become a private patient of his (para. 4.3).

Section 12(1) does not define what form the medical examination should take, but paragraph 2.21 of the *Code of Practice* says that those making the medical recommendations for admission should always discuss the case with one another, and preferably with the applicant (para. 2.22).

A medical practitioner carrying out functions under the mental health legislation was held to owe a duty of care to the patient in *Harnett v. Fisher*.[13] The gist of the action was seen by Viscount Sumner (at p. 584) as being not the signing of the prescribed form of certificate but the lack of care in looking into the appellant's mental state and in forming an adverse opinion about it. Thus, the proper form of action was not an action for breach of statutory duty, but an action on the case for negligence; the appellant was therefore unsuccessful in his claim because the Limitation Act pleaded by the defendant did not apply to the former, but did apply to the latter.

The requirement of "bad faith or lack of reasonable care" that is the prerequisite of an action for negligence against a medical officer or approved social worker, does not apply to an application for *habeas corpus*, which is the preferred remedy when legality of detention is questioned.

A further term of art used in the Act is the "Responsible Medical Officer" (s.34). He is the doctor who is in charge of the patient's treatment. He can discharge the patient (s.23); bar the discharge of the nearest relative (s.25); and extend the authority of the patient's detention.

The hospital managers

It is the job of the hospital managers to scrutinise applications for admission for their legality. This means compliance not only with the Mental Health Act 1983, but also with the Mental Health (Hospital, Guardianship and Consent to Treatment) Regulations 1983,[14] which provide forms in Schedule 1 for use in connection with applications

---

[13] [1927] A.C. 573.
[14] S.I. 1983 No. 893.

under the Act. The hospital managers are in fact the formal detaining authority under the Act to whom application should be made. There is freedom of movement, without need for further formality, between hospitals, whether psychiatric or general hospitals, which have the same managers.

Mental nursing homes, by section 34(2) of the Mental Health Act 1983, are "hospitals" for the purposes of Part II of the Act, and their managers are the persons registered in pursuance of the Registered Homes Act 1984 (s.145(c)). The directors of National Health Service Trusts are not however designated managers.[15] No hospital is under any legal duty to accept a patient unless it has agreed to do so. Section 140 of the Mental Health Act 1983, however, obliges every regional health authority to notify all social services departments in its region of arrangements to receive patients in cases of "special urgency".

Scrutiny of documents
Rectification of documents for errors on their face is in fact possible under the Mental Health Act, s.15. The time limit is 14 days (s.15(1)). An insufficient medical recommendation may be rectified using the provision of section 15(2). Loopholes may be filled thus.

The Act is silent as to the power or duty of managers to allow the relevant documents to be examined by the patient or his representative for the purpose of establishing their legal sufficiency. The duty on the managers to maintain records of admissions is governed by regulation 4(3) of the 1983 Regulations. A registered medical practitioner, however, does have the power to inspect documentation relating to detention or treatment in two circumstances:

(i)   when authorised by the nearest relative seeking to exercise his power of discharge (s.24(1)); and
(ii) when authorised by the patient for the purpose of furnishing information for a tribunal (s.68(3)).

Duty to Give Information
A major function of the hospital managers is to take all practical steps to ensure that all detained patients are given and understand specific information about which provisions of the Act have been used to authorise their detention and the effect of those provisions, including any right of application to a mental health review tribunal (s.132). Information should be given both orally and in writing (s.132(3)), and written information should also be given to the nearest relative, except where the patient otherwise requests (s.132(4)). The Department of Health publishes leaflets about the information required to be given under section 132.

---

[15] s.1 of the Mental Health (Amendment) Act 1994, amending National Health Service and Community Care Act 1990, Sched. 9, para. 24(a).

Discharges

The hospital managers may exercise their power under section 23 to discharge the patient; this is so, even if grounds for detention still exist (*Kynaston v. Secretary of State for Home Affairs*[16]). There are no statutory criteria governing the exercise of this power. However, paragraph 24.12 of the Code of Practice advises hospital managers to ensure that reviews of the patient's detention take place not only at the time stipulated for review by the responsible medical officer in section 20 of the Act.

The hospital managers have a further important role in relation to mental health review tribunals. They should ensure that any patient who wishes to apply to a mental health review tribunal is given all necessary assistance.[17] In addition, they are obliged to make automatic referral of certain patients detained under Part II of the Act.

Part 1 of the Mental Health Act—The definition of mental disorder

The definition of mental disorder is central to the working of the Act. The definition is contained in section 1(2): "mental disorder" means mental illness, arrested or incomplete development of mind, psychopathic disorder and any other disorder or disability of mind.

For some sections of the Act[18] a general diagnosis of "mental disorder" as above is sufficient. Thus under these sections a person suffering from "arrested or incomplete development of mind", *i.e.* that which was previously known as mental handicap, may be detained, as may a person suffering from "any other disorder or disability of mind", generally considered to be the minor forms of mental disorder referred to as neuroses, as opposed to the "major" forms of mental disorder or psychoses, for example, depression, schizophrenia, dementia.

Other sections of the Act however require evidence of one of the four major forms of mental disorder, *i.e.* mental illness, severe mental impairment, mental impairment, or psychopathic disorder.[19] Mental illness is not defined anywhere in the Act; its meaning therefore is a matter for psychiatric practice. In *W. v. L.*,[20] Lawton L.J. resisted imposing a legal definition on the term "mental illness":

> "The words are ordinary words of the English language. They have no particular medical significance. They have no particular legal significance. How should the court construe them? The answer in my judgement is to be found in the advice which Lord Reid . . . gave in *Brutus v. Cozens* [1972] 3 W.L.R. 521, namely that ordinary words of the English language should be construed in the way that ordinary sensible people would construe them. That being, in my judgment, the right test, then I ask myself, what would the ordinary sensible person have said. 'Well the fellow is obviously mentally ill'."

---

[16] (1981) 73 Cr.App.R. 281.
[17] *Code of Practice*, para. 24.16.
[18] ss.2.4.5, 135 and 136.
[19] See ss.3 and 7, for example.
[20] [1974] 1 Q.B. 711.

The consequence of the Court of Appeal's judgement in *W. v. L.* is that there is no precise legal (or medical) definition of the point at which compulsory admission to hospital is permissible.

Excluded from the definition of mental disorder is behaviour due solely to "promiscuity or immoral conduct, sexual deviancy or dependence on alcohol or drugs" (s.1(3)), though of course, any of these may be a contributory factor to, or a cause of, mental disorder. The Percy Commission made it clear that "mental infirmity of old age" (as they referred to it) would be included as a form of mental disorder.[21]

Section 2: Admission for assessment

Admission for assessment may take place under section 2 of the Act or (more rarely) under section 4 (which governs admission for assessment in an emergency).

Section 2(2) of the Mental Health Act 1983 states that:

"An application for admission for assessment may be made in respect of a patient on the grounds that —

(a) he is suffering from mental disorder of a nature or degree which warrants the detention of the patient in a hospital for assessment (or for assessment followed by medical treatment) for at least a limited period; and
(b) he ought to be so detained in the interests of his own health or safety or with a view to the protection of other persons."

Note that both grounds (a) and (b) must be satisfied, though as paragraph 2.6 of the *Code of Practice* emphasises, it is a misconstruction of subsection 2(b) to limit its use to situations of risk and to exclude considerations relating solely to the patient's own health. The application is to be founded upon the written recommendations of two registered medical practitioners, one of whom must be a specialist in mental disorder.

The medical recommendations need not agree on the precise form of mental disorder from which the patient is suffering.

The maximum period of detention is 28 days beginning with the day on which the patient is admitted (s.2(4)), see *Hare v. Gocher*.[22] This period will, however, be extended if an application to displace the nearest relative is pending (s.29(4)(a)), or such an order has been made, in which case the period of extension is seven days (s.29(4)(b)).

No renewal of a section 2 application is possible; if the patient remains in hospital he must do so as an informal patient or under section 3 of the Act (admission for treatment). The nearest relative cannot bar an

[21] *Report of the Royal Commission on the Law relating to Mental Illness and Mental Deficiency (the Percy Commission)*, Cmnd. 169 (1959), para. 17(a).
[22] [1962] 2 Q.B. 641.

application under section 2. There are between four and five times as many admissions for assessment, as there are for treatment.

Section 4: Admission for Assessment in an Emergency

In some circumstances, it may not be possible to comply with the procedures for admission for assessment under section 2. Section 4 of the Act therefore makes provision for an "emergency application" (s.4(1)) to be made. Every such application shall include a statement that it is of "urgent necessity" for the patient to be admitted and detained under section 2, and that compliance with the provisions of the Act relating to applications under that section would involve undesirable delay (s.4(2)).

The difference is that only one medical recommendation is required for an admission under section 4, but this should be given "if practicable, by a practitioner who has previous acquaintance with the patient" (s.4(1)). Therefore a general practitioner who is approved under section 12 of the Act as having special experience in the diagnosis of mental disorder, may provide the sole medical recommendation required.

The nearest relative should be informed of an application under section 4 if practicable to do so.

The *Code of Practice* (para. 6.3) makes it clear that to be satisfied that an emergency has arisen there must be evidence of:

(i)   the existence of significant risk of mental or physical harm to the patient or to others; and/or
(ii) the danger of serious harm to property; and/or
(iii) the need for physical restraint of the patient.

An application under section 4 ceases to have an effect on the expiration of a period of 72 hours from the time when the patient was admitted to hospital (s.4(4)). During this time, only the responsible medical officer and the hospital managers have the power of discharge (s.23). No application to a medical health review tribunal is possible, and an application for discharge by the nearest relative under section 25 is not possible because the required period of notice for such an application is itself 72 hours (s.25(1)). Patients admitted under section 4 are not subject to the consent to treatment provisions in Part IV of the Act, and are therefore informal patients as far as consent to treatment is concerned. If a patient is admitted under section 4, then an appropriate second doctor should examine him as soon as possible after admission to decide whether the power given by section 11(3) to "convert" the section 4 into a section 2 should be used.

Section 3: Admission for Treatment

An application for admission for treatment (s.3) may be made only in respect of persons suffering from the four specific forms of mental disorder set out in section 1 of the Act, *i.e.* mental illness, severe mental impairment, psychopathic disorder or mental impairment. "Arrested or incomplete development of mind" or "any other disorder or disability of mind" are not included: therefore, although a person suffering from these disorders may be detained for assessment under section 2 or section 4, he may not be subjected to the more draconian power of detention for treatment under section 3. The mental disorder must, moreover, be of a "nature or degree which makes it appropriate for him to receive medical treatment in a hospital" (s.3(2)(a)); in the case of psychopathic disorder or mental impairment, there is a further "treatability" test; such treatment should be likely to alleviate or prevent a deterioration in his condition (s.3(2)(b)). It must be necessary for the health or safety of the patient or for the protection of other persons that he receive such treatment which cannot be provided unless he is detained under this section (s.3(2)(c)).

An application must be founded on the written recommendation of two registered medical practitioners (s.3(3)), who must specify whether other methods of dealing with the patient are available, and, if so, why they are not appropriate (s.3(3)(b)). By section 11(6), in an application for a section 3 admission, both doctors must agree that the patient is suffering from one particular form of mental disorder, whether or not he is also described in either of those recommendations as suffering from another.

Whereas, a section 2 application cannot be renewed, a section 3 application may be renewed, by report of the responsible medical officer or for a further six months, followed by successive periods of one year (s.20(2)). A treatability test now applies on renewal to patients suffering from any of the specified forms of mental disorder in section 1 (s.3(4)(b)). In the case of mental illness or severe mental impairment, however, the "treatability" test may be substituted by a finding that the patient, if discharged, would be unlikely to be able to care for himself, or to obtain the care which he needs, or to guard himself against serious exploitation (s.20(4)(c)). An elderly person suffering from mental illness or severe mental impairment may thus be subject to continuing detention when his social competency is in doubt.

The *Code of Practice* gives pointers (para. 5.3) as to when a section 2 or a section 3 application is more appropriate. Indications for the latter are where a patient has had previous admissions for a known disorder and where he is unwilling to remain in hospital informally beyond the 28 days of section 2. Section 2 is indicated where there have been qualitative changes following previous admission, or where a judgment has to be made as to whether a particular treatment proposal would be effective.

The Mental Health Act Commission reviewed the operation of section 3 in relation to elderly people.[23] It noted that it could in fact be to the detriment of an elderly person not to be admitted compulsorily in some situations where his competence to give consent to treatment was in doubt, the danger being that he might be denied treatment which could

---

[23] *Mental Health Act Commission 2nd Biennial Report* (1985–1987), para. 17.7.

be beneficial to him. Note, however, that the treatment permitted under Part V of the Act is solely for psychiatric (not physical) disorder.

Powers of Entry

One practical difficulty which precedes the decision compulsorily to admit, is that of securing entry to premises when admission, for whatever reason, is refused. The duty placed upon the approved social worker to interview the patient "in a suitable manner" (s.13(2)) compounds the problem, for the *Code of Practice* at paragraph 2.11 states that it is not desirable for a patient to be interviewed through a closed door or window except where there is a serious risk to other people.

The police may be able to assist by using their powers under section 17(5) and (6) of the Police and Criminal Evidence Act 1984 to enter premises to save life or limb or to prevent serious damage to property, for example where a person is in a deteriorated condition and is unable to summon assistance, or where violence is being threatened. Section 17(5) and (6) also retain the common law power to enter premises without warrant where a serious breach of the peace is being committed. Otherwise, two particular sections of the Mental Health Act 1983 may be of assistance (ss.115 and 135).

Section 115 of the Mental Health Act 1983
Section 115 of the Mental Health Act authorises an approved social worker to enter and inspect any premises, which are not a hospital and in which a mentally disordered person is living, if he has reasonable cause to believe that the patient is not under proper care. This section does not permit him to gain entry by force. If he is acting within his powers, however, it is an offence for anyone to obstruct him without reasonable cause (s.129). Section 115 is potentially useful in cases where abuse or neglect is suspected, though the power that it gives is purely investigative. Section 115 contains no power of removal; for that a warrant under section 135 would be required.

The use of reasonable force in self defence to repulse a person, who is a trespasser in the legal sense, even though he may be a doctor or police officer, was sanctioned in *Townley v. Rushworth*.[24] In that case the defendant's wife signed an emergency application order under what now would be section 4 of the Mental Health Act, prior to the doctor's arrival at the house with the defendant's brother-in-law and two policemen. They were all told to leave by the defendant. The doctor then referred to the application and left to prepare an injection. The defendant struck one of the constables whom he believed to be making a move towards him. The doctor returned, injected the defendant and signed the form of medical recommendation. In the judgment of Lord Parker C.J., since the application was not at the relevant time "duly completed" by

---

[24] (1963) 107 S.J. 1004.

the giving of the medical recommendation, all those refused entry were trespassers and reasonable force was permitted to eject them. Presumably a civil action could have been brought against the doctor as well for assault in these circumstances.

Where property is jointly owned, by a husband and wife, the wife, for example, could presumably give consent to the entry. Similarly, a landlord could permit entry where premises were rented, or the patient was a licensee. Otherwise a warrant under section 135(1) should be sought.

Section 135(1) of the Mental Health Act 1983
Under section 135(1) an approved social worker may lay information before a magistrate that:

> "there is reasonable cause to suspect a person believed to be suffering from mental disorder
>
> (a) has been, or is being, ill-treated, neglected or kept otherwise than under proper control, in any place within the jurisdiction of the justice, or
> (b) being unable to care for himself, is living alone in any such place."

The magistrate may then issue a warrant authorising a police constable to enter, by force if need be, the premises specified in the warrant, and if thought fit, to remove the person to a place of safety, with a view to the making of an application under Part II of the Act, or of other arrangements for his treatment or care. Section 134(4) specifies that in executing the warrant, the police constable must take with him an approved social worker (not necessarily the informant) and a doctor. Since section 135(3) authorises detention for up to 72 hours, there is no need to further "section" the patient once entry to the premises has been gained, even if he is reluctant to go to hospital. A "place of safety" is defined for purposes of this section (and for s.136) to include residential accommodation whether private or local authority, a hospital (as defined in s.145 of the Act), a police station, or "any other suitable place the occupier of which is willing temporarily to receive the patient" (s.135(6)).

Section 136 of the Mental Health Act 1983
Sections 115 and 135 deal with persons found on private premises. Section 136 is the section that applies to mentally disordered persons found in places "to which the public have access" (s.136(1)), and who appear to be suffering from mental disorder and to be in immediate need of care or control. If it is in the interest of that person, or necessary for the protection of other people, a police constable may effect their removal to a place of safety.

Authority for the detention lapses once the purpose of the section "enabling him to be examined by a registered medical practitioner and interviewed by an approved social worker, and making any necessary arrangements for his treatment or care" has been fulfilled (s.136(2)).

There should be a locally agreed policy between the police, the social services authority, and the district health authority for the implementation of section 136.[25] Detention under section 136 is an "arrest", therefore relevant sections of the Police and Criminal Evidence Act 1984 apply, in particular, the right to have one person of one's choice informed of one's arrest and whereabouts (s.56) and the right of access to legal advice if the place of safety used is a police station (s.58).

Where detention is in a place of safety other than a police station access to legal advice should still be facilitated whenever it is requested.[26]

Though a hospital may be the preferred place of safety, there is no legal obligation upon the hospital managers to admit a patient detained under section 136.[27] Regulation 7 of the Mental Health (Hospital, Guardianship and Consent to Treatment) Regulations 1983[28] does not permit transfer between hospitals for patients subject to this section.

Section 136 enables the police, who are often the first professionals to be alerted to the situation, to deal with the distress of mentally disordered elderly people found wandering or disorientated in public places. Its use, however, is controversial, with scope for much subjectivity in the phrase "appears to be suffering from mental disorder". If the person is taken directly to hospital by the police, section 136 may be a *de facto* admission section, avoiding the formalities of a section 2 or section 4 assessment. However, any action for false imprisonment based on the misuse of section 136 is subject to the requirements of section 139 of the Act; that an applicant must show "substantial grounds" for the contention that the person to be proceeded against had acted in bad faith and without reasonable cause.

In the Hospital

Treatment and care

It is the responsibility of the responsible medical officer or doctor in charge of treatment to ensure that the provisions of the Mental Health Act relating to medical treatment are complied with. In the particular circumstances of detained patients these are contained in Part IV of the Act; otherwise common law principles apply and continue to govern non-detained patients. Consideration may have to be given to the position of patients who are incapacitated and unable to make a decision about their medical treatment (see Chapter 4 — The Provision of National Health Services).

---

[25] *Code of Practice*, para. 10.1.
[26] *ibid.* para. 10.9.
[27] *Carter v. Metropolitan Police Commissioner* [1975] 1 W.L.R. 507.
[28] S.I. 1983 No. 893.

For the purposes of this Act, medical treatment includes nursing, and also includes "care, habilitation and rehabilitation under medical supervision" (s.145). Therapeutic regimes come within the ambit of "treatment".[29] Counselling, behaviour modification and cognitive therapies are all methods of "treatment" which could be employed, instead of or as well as the prescribing of medication.

Good practice would dictate the drawing up of treatment plans with clearly stated goals and regular reviews. Wherever possible the plan should be discussed with the patient and "appropriate relatives" (if the patient consents to this).[30] The plan should be recorded in the patient's clinical notes (para. 15.5).

Before an individual can be given medical treatment his valid consent is required except where the law (either the common law or statute law) provides lawful authority to treat the patient without consent. Part IV of the Mental Health Act provides specific statutory authority for forms of treatment for mental disorder to be given to most patients liable to be detained without their consent, but contains particular safeguards relating to certain types of treatment deemed to be the most intrusive.

All proposals for treatment must first of all be discussed with the patient for his agreement and consent, even though that treatment could be given without his consent.

Part IV of the Act divides treatment into four distinct categories:

(1) Treatments requiring the patient's consent and a second opinion (s.57).
(2) Treatments requiring the patient's consent or a second opinion (s.58).
(3) Treatments that do not require the patient's consent (s.63).
(4) Urgent treatment (s.62).

(1) Treatments requiring the patient's consent and a second opinion (s.57)
The provisions of section 57 of the Act apply to both detained and informal patients.

Section 57 applies to the following forms of medical treatment:

"(*a*) any surgical operation for destroying brain tissue or for destroying the functions of brain tissue (*i.e.* psychosurgery); and
(*b*) such other forms of treatment as may be specified for the purposes of this section by regulations made by the Secretary of State."

To date, the only treatment specified in regulations is surgical implantation of hormones for the purpose of reducing male sex drive.[31]

Subject to section 62 (which relates to emergencies) treatment cannot be given unless (i) there is a certificate in writing that the patient is

---

[29] *Re H. (Mental Patient: Diagnosis), The Times,* July 17, 1992.
[30] *Code of Practice,* para. 15.7.
[31] Mental Health (Hospital, Guardianship and Consent to Treatment) Regulations 1983 (S.I. 1983 No. 893), reg. 16.

capable of understanding the nature, purpose and likely effects of the treatment, *i.e.* that he possesses competency in this regard, and (ii) an independent doctor has certified the appropriateness of the treatment for alleviating or preventing deterioration in the patient's condition. The use of section 57 will be closely monitored by the Mental Health Act Commission, which must agree procedures with the hospitals concerned (*Code of Practice*, para. 16.6).

(2) Treatments requiring the patient's consent or a second opinion (s.58)
Section 58 of the Mental Health Act applies to all patients liable to be detained under sections 2 or 3. Those who are not subject to its provisions are those detained under sections 4, 5(2) or 5(4) (doctor or nurse's holding power, see below), and sections 135 and 136. The scope of section 58 is as follows:

(*a*) Such forms of treatment as may be specified for the purposes of this section by regulations made by the Secretary of State.
(*b*) The administration of medicine to a patient by any means (not being a form of treatment specified under paragraph (*a*) above or section 57 above) at any time during the period for which he is likely to be detained as a patient to whom this part of the Act applies if three months or more have elapsed since the first occasion in that period when medicine was administered to him by any means for his mental disorder.

The only treatment currently specified for the purposes of section 58(1)(*a*) is electro-convulsive therapy (E.C.T.).[32] Section 58(1)(*b*) in effect allows drug therapy to be given without consent for a maximum of three months from the beginning of the detention with either consent or a second opinion being required thereafter.

Procedure if consent is given
If the patient consents to treatment, the responsible medical officer or a registered medical practitioner approved for the purposes of Part IV of the Act must certify (on Form 38 of Schedule 1 to the 1983 regulations) that the patient is capable of understanding the nature, purpose and likely effects of the treatment and has consented to it.

Competency to give consent is discussed in Chapter 4—The Provision of National Health Services, though the law generally does not require that consent to be an "informed consent": *Sidaway v. Board of Governors of the Bethlem Royal Hospital and Maudsley Hospital*.[33] The wording of section 58(3)(*a*) "capable of understanding its nature, purpose and likely effects", appears explicitly to impose a duty of care upon the responsible doctor to discuss the procedure involved and any side-effects with the patient.

---

[32] *ibid*. reg. 16(2).
[33] [1985] A.C. 871.

The standard of care required, however, might not be higher than that set by the House of Lords in *Bolam v. Friern Hospital Management Committee*,[34] that is, that a doctor is not negligent if he has acted in accordance with a practice accepted as proper by a responsible body of medical opinion within that particular speciality. Even though the use of E.C.T. in particular is controversial, the giving of a second medical opinion would appear to confirm professional legitimacy rather than patient-centred concern as the appropriate test to be applied if any action in negligence is to be pursued.

Paragraph 16.11 of the Code of Practice clarifies the meaning of the "three-month rule" in section 58(1)(*b*). The three-month period is inextricably linked to the patient's liability to be detained so that a course of medication begun earlier when the patient was an informal patient would not count towards the three-month period. On the other hand, the three-month period is not prolonged by renewal of the detention order or presumably its change (for example, from s.2 to s.3), by temporary withdrawal of consent or discontinuance of the treatment or by a period of home leave; in other words, time does not continue to run against the patient every time there is a change in his circumstances.

Procedure where consent is not given
When consent to treatment is not given, or is withdrawn, the procedure in section 58(3)(*b*) may be invoked. A Second Opinion Appointed Doctor (S.O.A.D.) must then certify in writing either that the patient is not capable of understanding the nature, purpose and likely effects of the treatment; or has not consented to it, but that, having regard to the likelihood of its alleviating or preventing deterioration of his condition, that treatment should be given.

Non-competent patients for whom E.C.T. or prolonged drug therapy is recommended, therefore, have the benefit under this section of a second opinion concerning their treatment, as do competent but non-consenting patients.

The S.O.A.D. must be a registered medical practitioner appointed by, or a member of, the Mental Health Act Commission (s.121(2)). Before certifying his opinion in writing (on Form 39) the S.O.A.D. must consult with two other persons who have been professionally concerned with the patient's medical treatment.

Section 58 in law allows the issuing of a certificate from the S.O.A.D. without limit of time, though good practice would dictate that the certificate is in fact time-limited.

Treatment by medication of mental disorder in elderly people is by no means straightforward. There is as yet no known cause for dementia. All that doctors can do at the moment is treat some of the symptoms. An excellent and easily readable guide by a psychogeriatrician to the assessment and treatment of mental disorder in old age is given by Elaine

---

[34] [1957] 1 W.L.R. 582.

Murphy.[35] Relevant to a discussion of section 58 is Murphy's emphasis on the importance of careful prescribing:

> "elderly people are often extra sensitive to the effects of drugs and tend to suffer more than younger people from these unwanted effects which are present to some degree in all medicine."[36]

Long term use of medication can moreover have its own deleterious effects.

Urgent treatment

Section 62(1) of the Mental Health Act provides that:

> "Sections 57 and 58 shall not apply to any treatment—
>
> (a) which is immediately necessary to save the patient's life; or
> (b) which (not being irreversible) is immediately necessary to prevent a serious deterioration of his condition.
> (c) which (not being irreversible or hazardous) is immediately necessary to alleviate serious suffering by the patient; or
> (d) which (not being irreversible or hazardous) is immediately necessary and represents the minimum interference necessary to prevent the patient from behaving violently or being a danger to himself or others."

For the purposes of this section treatment is irreversible if it has unfavourable irreversible physical or psychological consequences; it is hazardous if it entails significant physical hazard (s.62(3)). The reasoning is somewhat tautologous.

The scope of emergency provisions in section 62 is wider than that of the doctrine of necessity in common law. It is therefore important to recognise that section 62 only modifies sections 57 and 58 and applies to no other section. Furthermore treatment under section 62 cannot be justified once the emergency has passed and only operates where treatment is urgently necessary. Unfortunately the Mental Health Act Commission has not detailed which conditions should be considered "irreversible" or "hazardous": but it is considered that the former would include psychosurgery, and the latter, unmodified E.C.T.

Section 63 of the Mental Health Act: the general power to treat without consent

Section 63 reads: "The consent of a patient shall not be required for any medical treatment given to him for the mental disorder from which he is suffering, not being treatment falling within section 57 or 58 above, if the treatment is given by or under the direction of the Responsible Medical Officer."

---

[35] Murphy, *Dementia and Mental Illness in Older People: a Practical Guide* (1993).
[36] *ibid.* p. 74.

Section 63 thus states the "usual" situation, with regard to detained patients; any medical treatment for mental disorder may be given without consent. It should be noted, however, that section 63 applies only to treatment for mental disorders; treatment for physical disorders will require actual consent, unless the treatment being refused, for example feeding by naso-gastric tube of a patient with anorexia, is related to the mental illness: *Re K.B. (Adult) (Mental Patient: Medical Treatment)*.[36a]

Preventing the patient leaving hospital

There may be some situations where a patient is attempting to leave hospital and this, although lawful, is deemed detrimental to his own safety, or such a risk to other persons that he ought to be detained. The Mental Health Act 1983 provides for such detention in section 5(2) and (4): doctor's holding power, and nurse's holding power.

Doctor's holding power
Section 5(2) provides that:

> "If in the case of a patient who is an in-patient in a hospital, it appears to the registered medical practitioner in charge of the treatment of the patient that an application ought to be made under this part of the Act for an admission of the patient to hospital, he may furnish to the managers a report in writing to that effect; and in any such case the patient may be detained in the hospital for a period of 72 hours from the time when the report is so furnished."

Section 5(2) applies to any patient in any hospital, general or psychiatric. However, where a report under section 5(2) is provided by a consultant other than a psychiatrist, for example a geriatrician, the doctor invoking the power should make immediate contact with a psychiatrist (*Code of Practice*, para. 8.5).

Part IV of the Act relating to treatment without consent for mental disorder does not apply to a patient detained under section 5 (s.56(1)(*b*)). Any patient detained under section 5(2) should be discharged from the order immediately an assessment for admission is carried out or the doctor decides that no assessment for possible admission needs to be carried out. The power cannot be renewed but may be used more than once. The managers must furthermore ensure that the requirements of section 132 (information) are fulfilled.

The patient's doctor, or nominated deputy (s.5(3)), must only use the power immediately after having personally examined the patient. Section 5(2) should only be invoked if the use of sections 2, 3 or 4 is not practicable or safe. No doctor should complete a section 5(2) form and leave it on the ward with instructions to other staff to forward it to the manager if, in their opinion, the patient is about to leave. Nor should this section be used to prolong detention when another section is about to expire (s.5(6)).

[36a] (1994) 19 B.M.L.R. 144. See also *B. v. Croydon Health Authority, The Times*, December 1, 1994.

Section 5(2) and (4) (below) are available only in respect of informal hospital in-patients, *i.e.* those who have completed and co-operated in the admission procedure. The section cannot therefore be used for an out-patient or for a patient attending a day hospital; this is because section 5 is a holding section. A patient detained under this section cannot be transferred to another hospital under the provisions of regulation 7 of the 1983 Regulations, because he is not in hospital by virtue of an application under this part of the Act (s.19(1)(*a*), 2(*a*)). The Mental Health Act Commission has encountered many difficulties caused by this restriction on transfer.[37]

Nurse's holding power (s.5(4))
This section applies only to informal patients who are receiving treatment for mental disorder. It authorises detention for up to six hours, or until a doctor arrives, whichever is earlier.

The decision to detain can only be taken by a nurse of the prescribed class (s.5(4)), that is a senior nurse who is a specialist in mental illness or mental handicap as described by the Mental Health (Nurses) Order 1983,[38] and is personal to him/her.

It must appear to that nurse:

(*a*) that the patient is suffering from mental disorder to such a degree that it is necessary for his health or safety or for the protection of others for him to be immediately restrained from leaving the hospital; and

(*b*) that it is not practicable to secure the immediate attendance of a practitioner for the purpose of furnishing a report under subsection (2) above.

A nurse invoking section 5(4) is entitled to use the minimum force necessary to prevent the patient leaving hospital. The nurse in charge of the ward should explain in private to the patient the need for using section 5(4) and, when it occurs, the need to lock the ward door (*Code of Practice*, paras. 9.6, 9.7).

Restraint

The Mental Health Act Commission in its third Biennial Report 1987 to 1989 expressed concern over the use of restraint in the management of patients; and in particular in the case of psychogeriatric patients, the locking of ward doors on open wards. In *Pountney v. Griffiths*,[39] it was accepted that psychiatric hospitals have powers of control and discipline over their patients, but how far does this go?

---

[37] *Mental Health Act Commission 4th Biennial Report* (1989–1991).
[38] S.I. 1983 No. 891. See also the Mental Health (Nurses) Amendment Order 1993 (S.I. 1993 No. 2155).
[39] [1976] A.C. 314.

It is acknowledged that some patients with challenging behaviour pose particular problems of management for staff (*Code of Practice*, paras. 18.2, 18.30).

Lawful justification would have to be sought for any act which was technically an assault or battery. Consent, of course, would be a defence to an action in tort; and in addition to expressing consent verbally or in writing, the absence of any resistance to an act ordinarily expected in the course of a professional/patient relationship could be construed as consent. The effect of institutional pressure upon the patient to give consent is likely to be disregarded: *Freeman v. Home Office*.[40] The doctrine of necessity might also be pleaded as a defence, and would provide a justification for acting where the patient is incapable of giving consent. Thus restraint designed to prevent the patient from causing himself physical harm would be permissible.

Restraint for the prevention of crime, for example, an assault upon another patient, would be justified by section 3(1) of the Criminal Law Act 1967, but only in circumstances where a crime is being or is about to be committed. The force used however must be both necessary and proportionate to the harm to be avoided. A nurse, or any other person present, would also have the right to use reasonable force against any person who is breaching or threatening to breach the peace under section 2(7) of the Criminal Law Act 1967; this is wide enough to cover threatening behaviour or language without the use of actual violence.

Two situations give rise to concern: the administration of medication, and the use of confinement. The use of medication to calm a threatening or abusive patient may be justified on the grounds discussed above, but there may also become a point where long-term administration of medication which began as therapeutic may become a method not of treatment but of restraint. The *Code of Practice* recommends that each individual case should be reviewed and a decision made whether if medication had to be administered by force, it would be lawful and therapeutic in the longer term (para. 18.14).

The use of seclusion, or the locking of doors, may amount to false imprisonment, as would the confining of a person once the authority for detention has expired. The remedy would lie in tort or in an action for *habeas corpus*. In *Herring v. Boyle*,[41] it was held not to be false imprisonment if the person did not know that he was being detained, though the case is a weak authority as there was no evidence of actual restraint. Atkin L.J. in *Meering v. Grahame White Aviation Co.*,[42] however, did accept that a person could be imprisoned whilst he was asleep, in a state of drunkenness, unconscious, and "whilst he was a lunatic". This is an important decision for those who may not have the mental faculty to

---

[40] [1984] 1 All E.R. 1036.
[41] [1834] 1 Cr. M. & R. 377.
[42] (1919) 122 T.L.R. 44 at 53–54.

know that they are being restrained, for example, the elderly mentally infirm.

There are two types of ward regime used in relation to persons who are mentally ill which may potentially amount to a false imprisonment. One is the use of seclusion, and the other is the use of locked wards. Seclusion is defined in the *Code of Practice* as "the supervised confinement of a patient alone in a room which may be locked for the protection of others" (para. 18.15). Although it falls technically within the definition of treatment in section 145, seclusion is not, according to paragraph 18.15, a treatment technique and should not feature as part of any treatment programme.

Health Authorities should have clear written guidelines on the use of seclusion (para. 18.5) and of restraint (para. 18.13). In addition the Authority should appoint a senior manager who should be informed of any patient who is subjected to any form of restraint for more than two hours (para. 18.12). He should, as soon as is practicable, see the patient to ascertain if he has any complaints and follow this up with visits at regular intervals.

The maintenance of locked wards in psychiatric units is not *per se* rejected by the *Code of Practice*. Indeed for detained patients professional judgment may be seen as dictating physical security as a prerequisite to treatment (para. 18.28). For non-detained patients, at liberty to leave the hospital, the emphasis is on the maintenance of a safe environment (para. 18.25). Thus it might be justifiable to lock the ward door if patients are likely to wander out of the hospital and on to the road. It must be borne in mind however that physical restraint should not be used as a substitute for adequate staffing levels. What should also be avoided is the stereotyping of elderly people without an individualised assessment of the actual risks involved, for example, in leaving hospital and walking into the town. It may be that individual patients would have sufficient road sense and knowledge of their locality to lessen risks in their particular case; the psychological harm of close confinement would also need to be weighed in the balance. To refuse all patients exit from the ward may in some cases amount to a false imprisonment. The 1993 Code of Practice is more explicit than its 1986 predecessor in distinguishing between those patients who may wander off the ward occasionally and those who evidence a clear intention to leave. The guidance in paragraph 18.27 is that:

"Combination locks and double handled doors to prevent mentally frail elderly people or people with learning disabilities (mental handicap) from wandering out should be used as little as possible and only in units where there is a regular and significant risk of patients wandering off accidentally and, as a result, being at risk of harm. There should be clear unit policies on the use of locks and other devices and a mechanism for reviewing decisions. Every patient should have an individual care plan which states explicitly why and when he will be prevented from leaving the ward. Patients who are not deliberately trying to leave the ward, but who may wander out accidentally may legitimately be deterred from leaving the ward by those devices. In the case of patients who persistently and purposely attempt to leave a ward or nursing home, whether or not they understand the risk involved, consideration must be given to assessing whether they would more appropriately be formally detained under the Act in the hospital or a registered mental nursing home rather than remain as informal patients."

Discharge from detention

Apart from the provisions of the Mental Health Act for discharge by a mental health review tribunal, section 23 provides generally for the discharge of patients liable to be detained under the Act: informal patients may discharge themselves with or without the consent of the responsible medical officer. Detained patients may be discharged by the responsible medical officer; the nearest relative (unless barred by the responsible medical officer); the hospital managers; or in the case of a guardianship patient, the local social services authority. Section 23 however, contains no guidance on how the discretion to discharge should be exercised[42a] and a patient may be discharged even though the statutory grounds for detention still exist: *Kynaston v. Secretary of State for Home Affairs.*[43] The *Code of Practice* recommends that the hospital manager should carry out periodic reviews of detained patients: though such a review may operate in effect as an appeal against the decision of the responsible medical officer, it is exceedingly rare for the hospital managers to exercise their power in this way (para. 24.10).

Leave of absence

As a half-way house between detention and discharge, leave of absence may be granted by the responsible medical officer "subject to such conditions (if any) as that officer considers necessary in the interests of the patient or for the protection of other persons" (s.171(1)). The view of the Mental Health Act Commission[44] that it was unlawful to use leave of absence, subject to recall, as a "long leash" to achieve compulsory treatment in the community, was confirmed by the Court of Appeal in *R. v. Hallstrom, ex p. W.*[45] There, the patient, refusing to take medication, was admitted to hospital under section 3, but remained there for only one night before being given leave of absence. Not only was this an unlawful use of section 3 for which the need for treatment in hospital is a prerequisite, but had the responsible medical officer succeeded in his strategy, the patient would in effect have been subject to a compulsory treatment order in the community.

Whether or not such an order should be introduced is a matter of continuing controversy. As early as 1977, the British Association of Social Workers proposed the idea of a "community care order", but this was not

---

[42a] General guidance to Health Authorities on the discharge of mentally disordered people is given in HSG (94)27. See p. 136.
[43] (1981) 73 Cr.App.R. 281.
[44] *Mental Health Act Commission 1st Biennial Report* (1983–1985), at pp. 25–27.
[45] [1986] Q.B. 1090.

incorporated into what became the 1983 Act. The responsible medical officer's power to extend treatment into the community is thus at present limited to circumstances where genuine leave of absence is given.

Aftercare

Final discharge of long stay patients in particular into the community, ought to be given careful planning to ensure that adequate support systems are in place. In fact the reality is often very different, with legal and administrative requirements often not being adhered to. For general discussion of available services in the community see Chapter 2 — The Delivery of Social Services.

There is only one section in which the Mental Health Act explicitly requires aftercare services to be provided, and that is the discharge of a person who was liable to be detained under section 3. Section 117(2) of the Act states: "It shall be the duty of the District Health Authority and of the local social services authority to provide, in co-operation with relevant voluntary agencies, aftercare services for any person to whom this section applies until such time as the district health authority and the local social services authority are satisfied that the person concerned is no longer in need of such services." Section 117 does not define the type or quality of aftercare services to be provided, and their duration is left to the separate discretions of the health authority and the social services authority.

In R. v. Ealing District Health Authority ex p. Fox,[46] a mental health review tribunal used its power under section 73(2) and (7) of the Mental Health Act 1983 to defer the patient's discharge until appropriate after-care arrangements had been made, namely the appointment of a responsible medical officer to provide out-patient care. As the health authority disagreed with the decision of the tribunal, it did not appoint a responsible medical officer as directed, and so the patient remained in hospital. In an action seeking an order of certiorari and a declaration, Orton J. held that the authority had erred in law in not attempting with all reasonable expedition and diligence to make arrangements to enable the applicant to comply with the conditions laid down by the mental health review tribunal. Furthermore, the duty to provide aftercare was not limited to the operation of section 117, but was part of the general statutory framework which required the health authority to provide a comprehensive range of hospital and psychiatric and community services. This raises the question of whether the "continuing duty to the patient" thus disclosed could form the basis of an action in tort for breach of statutory duty. Under section 117 the duty is owed to an individual patient, whereas the duty to provide a comprehensive health care service

---

[46] [1993] 1 W.L.R. 373.

under section 3(1)(*e*) of the National Health Service Act 1977 is a public duty. It could well be then that an action for breach of statutory duty is available, if at all, only to those who are within section 117 of the Act.

The care programme approach for people with a mental illness

The care programme approach for people with a mental illness referred to the specialist psychiatric services is outlined in HC (88)43, HC (90)23 / LASSL (90) and HC (90)24 / LAC (90)10. It requires district health authorities, the Bethlem and Maudsley Special Health Authority and the Special Hospitals Service Authority to take particular action in order to implement the care programme approach for all new patients accepted by the specialist psychiatric services whilst living in the community, and all in-patients returned to the community upon discharge from hospital. People with dementia are specifically referred to as coming within the definition of mental illness for this purpose. The action that health authorities are required to take is to draw up local care programme policies in consultation and agreement with social services authorities, by a final date of April 1, 1991. Where a district health authority purchases psychiatric services from a self-governing trust or elsewhere, the contractual arrangements should require those bodies to have themselves adopted the care programme approach. The intention is clearly that people in the community with mental illness should have their needs addressed. There is no new requirement, however, to provide services. The guidance concerns predominantly procedural matters, though it does contain reference to the mental illness specific grant, payable from the beginning of the financial year 1991 to 1992.

The care programme approach is being developed to ensure that in the future patients treated in the community receive the health and social care they need, by:

(1) Introducing more systematic arrangements for deciding whether a patient referred to the specialist psychiatric services can, in the light of available resources and the views of the patient and, where appropriate, his/her carers, realistically be treated in the community.
(2) Ensuring proper arrangements are then made for the continuing health and social care of those patients who can be treated in the community. This will include an assessment and review of both health care and social care needs, and checking that such services are in fact being provided by a monitoring system involving key workers.

The system thus predates, and is narrower than the concept of care management discussed in Chapter 3—Community Care.

Insofar as discharge from hospital is concerned, the care programme approach supplements the guidance given in the general circular on hospital discharges HC (89)5.[47] The Code of Practice under the Mental Health Act 1983 replicates the care programme approach by providing for a multi-disciplinary discussion which leads to the establishment of a care plan and the appointment of a key worker (para. 27.9). The plan should be recorded in writing (para. 27.10), and should be regularly reviewed (para. 27.11). The patient and his nearest relative should be fully involved and their wishes taken into account.

The care programme approach, though it is concerned in guidance, is not statutory. Section 7 of the Disabled Persons (Services, Consultation and Representation) Act 1986 would have imposed a duty upon health authorities to give social services authorities notice of discharge in respect of any patient who had remained in hospital (whatever his legal status) for more than six months. The section was never implemented. And although section 133(1) of the Mental Health Act 1983 requires the hospital managers to give seven days' notice to the nearest relative that the patient is to be discharged from detention, that duty does not extend to informing the nearest relative of his discharge from hospital.

The mental illness specific grant

Section 50 of the National Health Service and Community Care Act 1990 introduces a new section 7E into the Local Authority Social Services Act 1970, providing for the payment of a mental illness specific grant. The grant is available for locally relevant packages of social care for two different classes of people: those whose illness is so severe that they have been accepted for treatment by the specialist psychiatric services; and those who need assistance in making contact with such services.[48] The grant is a recurrent annual contribution (initially for three years, but now extended to 1997) to social services authorities' revenue spending. It should not be used as a substitute source of finance for care already provided: the intention is that it should be used imaginatively to fund new projects. The bulk of the grant is allocated to a formula of 50/50, for the under- and over-65s.

Services in the Community

Community care services (see Chapter 3—Community Care) will be available generally to people with a mental illness living in the community. Day care and out-patient services, and community psychiatric nursing services may also be provided by the health authority, as part of its duty to provide a comprehensive health care service under section 3 of the National Health Service Act 1977. It is also worth noting that people suffering from mental disorder are "disabled" for the purposes of the Chronically Sick and Disabled Persons Act 1970, and are thus entitled to a

---

[47] See p. 48.
[48] See Circular No. HC (90)24 / LAC (90)10.

range of services which, once need is established, are mandatory (see Chapter 2—The Delivery of Social Services).

Supervision registers and supervised discharge

General guidance to health authorities on the discharge of mentally disordered people and their continuing care in the community is provided by HSCT (94)27.[48a] The criteria for discharge are as follows:

(1) whether with adequate medication, care and supervision in the community the patient could still present any serious risk to him or herself or to others;
(2) whether his or her needs for therapy, supervision, sanctuary or security require continuing inpatient treatment;
(3) whether he or she could be cared for effectively or safely in the community.

The guidance is clearly directed at limiting the discretion of the responsible medical officer to discharge patients who may be considered "dangerous" in the community. It will also be relevant to the needs of vulnerable elderly people who are more of a risk to themselves than to others. The difficulty lies in applying such guidance to mentally ill people who are refusing to agree to a post-discharge treatment plan in the community. It is arguable that such people can legally no longer be detained in hospital if they satisfy, in all other respects, the criteria for discharge by a mental health review tribunal under section 72 of the Mental Health Act 1983. There is thus an incongruence between community care guidance and the legislation, though this may be less marked in the case of elderly people where a tribunal has discretion to substitute a "viability" test for a treatability test.[48b]

The concern that patients who pose the greatest risk to themselves or others should be identified and monitored has led to the introduction of supervision registers, first introduced in April 1994, with a target date for full implementation of October 1, 1994.[48c] The idea of supervision registers has met with a mixed response, and no coherent pattern seems to have emerged for deciding who should be on the register and what (if any) additional services they should receive in consequence. Patients should be told that they are on a register, unless to do so would cause serious harm to their physical or mental health. Reviews should be held at six-monthly intervals, and the patient, or someone on his behalf, may request removal from the register. If this request is rejected, there is a right to a second medical opinion. The introduction of supervision registers has not required legislation. Legislation would, however, be

---

[48a] *Guidance on the Discharge of Mentally Disordered People and their Continuing Care in the Community*, HSG (94)27.
[48b] See p. 142.
[48c] *The Supervision Register*, HSG (94)5.

required to implement a power of supervised discharge as is currently under discussion. Proposals have been put forward by both the Royal College of Psychiatrists and the Department of Health.[48d]

Mental health review tribunals

Mental health review tribunals perform a continuing quasi-judicial function within the scheme of compulsory intervention, following the ending of judicial commitment with the Mental Health Act 1959.

The mental health review tribunals for England and Wales correspond with the boundaries of regional health authorities and their constitution and powers are set out in Part V of the Mental Health Act 1983. There is a legally qualified chairman, a medical member and a lay member of the tribunal. The tribunal is not concerned with whether the patient should have been admitted to hospital in the first place; that decision may be challenged by an application for *habeas corpus* or judicial review in accordance with the principles set out in *Ex p. Waldron*[49]: that is that the admission process was *ultra vires* or discloses an error on its face. The tribunal is concerned only to answer the question; should the patient continue to be detained? Though aspects of the patient's treatment and care will be relevant to this decision, the tribunal is not concerned to explore the patient's grievances about how they are being treated in hospital.

Applications and referrals
Applications may be made by patients compulsorily detained, and (in some cases) by their nearest relative. There are also automatic referrals by the hospital managers of some long stay patients. The various methods of making an application or referral are as follows:

(1) A patient admitted for assessment may apply within 14 days of the day of admission (s.66(1)(a) and (2)(a)).
(2) Patients admitted for treatment, transferred from guardianship or received into guardianship may apply within the first six months (s.66(1) and (2)), and once within each period for which their detention is renewed (s.66(1)(f) and (2)(f)).
(3) Any patient whose category of mental disorder is reclassified under section 16 may apply within 28 days of being informed of this (s.66(1)(d)).
(4) The nearest relative may also apply within 28 days of being told that the patient's disorder has been reclassified (s.66(1)(i)).

[48d] *Community Supervision Orders* (Royal College of Psychiatrists, 1993); *Legal Powers on the Care of Mentally Ill People in the Community. Report of the Internal Review* (Department of Health, 1993).
[49] [1986] Q.B. 824.

(5) The nearest relative may apply within 28 days of his power of discharge of a patient detained under section 3 being blocked by a responsible medical officer's report (s.66(1)(g)).

(6) The nearest relative may also apply to the tribunal against an order taking away his rights as a nearest relative; application may be made within the first 12 months and once in every 12-month period after that (s.66(1)(h) and (2)(g)).

(7) The hospital managers must refer any patient admitted for treatment under civil powers (including one transferred from guardianship) who has not exercised his right to apply during the first six months of his section (s.69(1)), or whose application was withdrawn before it was heard.

(8) The managers must also refer any patient whose detention is renewed under section 20 after a period of three years has elapsed without his being considered by a tribunal. The review is of their legal status, and not necessarily their treatment plan.

The application
Section 132(1)(b) of the Mental Health Act requires the hospital managers to inform any detained patient of his right to apply to a mental health review tribunal.

The patient, or any other person entitled to make an application may arrange for an independent medical examination of the patient in private (s.76(1)(a)): this right extends to the production of and inspection of any documents relating to his detention and treatment (s.76(1)(b)). Section 68(3) makes similar provision on a hospital manager's reference. There are, however, limits to confidentiality; an independent doctor may disclose information to the tribunal without consent if he fears that otherwise decisions may be made on the basis of inadequate information and with a real risk of danger to the public.[50]

Parties to the application are the patient, the applicant, the responsible authority, anyone notified under rule 7 or rule 31 of the Mental Health Review Tribunal Rules 1983,[51] and anyone added as a party under rule 29.

Applications relating to patients admitted for assessment under section 2 or 4 must be heard no later than seven days from the making of an application (to the local office of the tribunal). There is no application form as such, but all applications should conform to rule 3 of the Mental Health Review Tribunal Regulations 1983[52]: names and addresses of the patient, the nearest relative, and the authorised representative and the section in the Act under which the patient is detained. No evidence in support of the application is required at this stage. The hospital must supply the tribunal with a copy of the admission documents and such

---

[50] See *W. v. Edgell* [1990] 1 All E.R. 835.
[51] S.I. 1983 No. 942.
[52] *ibid.*

information and reports as would be required by Schedule 1 that can reasonably be provided in the time available.

Applications in other cases will attract a hearing within three weeks. The responsible authority must send a "rule 6 statement" to the tribunal with the information required by Part A of Schedule 1 to the rules. As well as the personal details, including the name and address of the nearest relative or any other person who takes a close interest in the patient, previous tribunal applications and decisions should be included, as well as details of any Court of Protection proceedings and of any receivership order made in respect of the patient.

In addition the authority must provide an up-to-date medical report, prepared for the tribunal, including the relevant medical history and a full report on the patient's medical condition as required by paragraph 1 of Part B of Schedule 1. There must also be an up-to-date social circumstances report (para. 2) including reports on:

(a) the patient's home and family circumstances, including the attitude of the patient's nearest relative or person so acting;
(b) the opportunities for employment or occupation and the housing facilities which would be available to the patient if discharged;
(c) the availability of community support and relevant medical facilities; and
(d) the financial circumstances of the patient.

This report will be prepared by a social worker either from within the hospital or in the community, though not necessarily an approved social worker.

Finally the views of the authority on the suitability of the patient for discharge (para. 3), and any other information or observations on the application which the authority wishes to make should be submitted to the tribunal.

Once these statements have been received, the tribunal must give notice of proceedings to the nearest relative (unless he is the applicant); any private guardian; the registration authority of any private nursing home in which the patient is liable to be maintained; any health authority which has the right to discharge the patient under section 23(2) of the parent Act; to the Court of Protection where the patient's financial affairs are under its control and to any other person who, in the opinion of the tribunal, should have an opportunity of being heard (r.7). Though the period of notice required to the parties is four days, it is unlikely that the hearing will take place even within the Council on Tribunal's target time of eight weeks.

Legal aid provisions
Assistance by way of legal representation is available for appearance before mental health review tribunals. The means test for assistance by way of representation in proceedings before a mental health review

tribunal was abolished from April 11, 1994.[52a] In 1992 to 1993 there were 4,680 bills paid for representation before mental health review tribunals. This was a growth of 30.8 per cent over the previous year.[53]

The hearing
The hospital and responsible medical officer do not normally employ advocates, but patients are entitled to have anyone, except a fellow patient, represent them. The tribunal may itself appoint a person to act for the patient as his "authorised representative" (r.10(3)). Authorised representatives who are barristers or solicitors or registered medical practitioners, or "in the opinion of the tribunal, a suitable person by virtue of his experience or professional qualification" (r.12(3)) may not be excluded from the hearing even if the patient is asked to withdraw whilst certain evidence is heard (r.21(4)); nor may they be denied disclosure of any document not given to the patient on the grounds that disclosure would adversely affect the health or welfare of the patient or others (r.12(3)).

The tribunal may hear evidence on oath and may *subpoena* witnesses to appear (r.14), but may also act inquisitorially and call "for such further information or reports as it may think desirable" (r.15). Under rule 11 the medical member of the tribunal must examine the patient before the hearing; even though the results of this examination are strictly speaking not part of the evidence before the tribunal, natural justice requires that his opinion is disclosed and is open to challenge: *R. v. Mental Health Review Tribunal, ex p. Clatworthy*.[54]

Hearings almost always take place in hospital, and are in private unless the patient requests otherwise, which request can be refused if it is deemed contrary to his interests (r.21). The tribunal can however admit anyone it likes on such terms as it thinks appropriate, for example, a relative or a friend (r.21(3)). The hearing may be conducted in whatsoever manner appears appropriate but avoiding formality (r.21(3)). However, the law of contempt applies but only to prevent publication of the evidence heard and of any conditions imposed by the tribunal on the patient's discharge: *Pickering v. Liverpool Daily Post and Echo Newspaper*.[55] The tribunal must interview the patient without anyone else present if he asks for this (r.22(2)).

The decision
The powers of the tribunal on the determination of an application are set out in section 72 of the Mental Health Act 1983. In assessment applications the tribunal's powers are limited to ordering the discharge of the patient: in other cases, the tribunal may order discharge or delayed

---

[52a] See the Legal Advice and Assistance (Amendment) Regulations 1994 (S.I. 1994 No. 805).
[53] *Legal Aid Board Annual Report* (1992–1993).
[54] [1985] 3 All E.R. 699.
[55] [1991] 1 All E.R. 622, H.L., interpreting r.21(5) of the Mental Health Review Tribunal Rules 1983 (S.I. 1983 No. 942).

discharge, or make recommendations for transfer, leave of absence, or reclassification.

The decision may be made by a majority vote, must be recorded in writing (r.23(2)), and must be given within seven days of the hearing (r.24(1)).

Section 72 makes it clear that discharge of a patient by a tribunal may either be discretionary or mandatory. It is discretionary in the sense that even if the statutory criteria for discharge are not met, nevertheless, the tribunal has a general discretion to discharge the patient (s.72(1)). On the other hand, the statute makes discharge mandatory where the tribunal finds that certain criteria are met. In assessment cases, these are either that he is then not suffering from mental disorder at all; the disorder is not of a nature or degree to warrant his detention in hospital for assessment; or his detention is not justified in the interests of his own health or safety or with a view to the protection of others (s.72(1)(a)). In other words, if the patient would no longer meet the criteria for admission under section 2 then he must be discharged.

In the case of patients admitted for treatment under section 3, the tribunal must order discharge if satisfied (s.72(1)(b)) that:

(a) the patient is not then suffering from one of the four specific forms of mental disorder; or

(b) that it is not necessary for his health or safety or the protection of others that he should receive treatment in hospital; or

(c) in the case of an application under section 66(1)(g) by the nearest relative following the barring of a discharge order, that the patient is not dangerous.

By contrast to section 2 applications, the general discretion of the tribunal to order discharge even if the statutory criteria are not met, is structured for section 3 patients. The tribunal must have regard to the following criteria (s.72(2)):

(a) the likelihood of medical treatment alleviating or preventing deterioration of the patient's condition; and

(b) in the case of mental illness or severe mental impairment, the likelihood that if discharged he will be unable to care for himself, obtain the care he needs, or guard against serious exploitation.

If the patient is not "treatable" as in section 72(2)(a) then the tribunal should seriously consider his discharge, as the responsible medical officer will in any case have to discharge him at his next renewal date because section 20(3) states that for all of the four specific forms of mental disorder "treatability" is a criterion for renewal. For the purposes of the "treatability" test medical treatment should not be narrowly construed and can, for example, include group therapy. A patient is not to be considered untreatable merely because he or she refuses to co-operate: *R. v. Canons Park Mental Health Review Tribunal, ex p. A.*[55a] Both the responsible medical officer at the renewal and the tribunal in exercising its discretion, however, can override the "treatability" test with the "viability" test, that the patient would not be able to care for himself outside the hospital; note, however, that in both instances the viability test applies only to people suffering from mental illness and severe mental impairment. Much would of course depend upon the resources in the community and the willingness of the person to accept the alternative care offered; there is always the possibility in these circumstances of the tribunal transferring the patient into guardianship with a view to facilitating his discharge at a future date (s.72(3)(*a*)).

In the case of applications relating to guardianship patients the tribunal has a general discretion to discharge any patient subject to guardianship (s.72(4)). It must discharge the patient if it is satisfied (s.72(4)) that:

(*a*) he is not suffering from one of the four major forms of mental disorder (in whatever degree); or

(*b*) it is not necessarily in the interests of his welfare or the protection of others that he should remain under guardianship.

"Welfare" here is wider than the concept of health and safety applied to hospital patients, and is more akin to a "viability" test but is not restricted (as is that test) to those suffering from mental illness or severe mental impairment. It could include factors such as a person's inability to resist exploitation or abuse, or more controversially to display competence in decision-making according to a "best interests" formulation.

Remedies
Those aggrieved by any aspect of the decision of a mental health review tribunal would appear to have two remedies at law, through judicial review, and by way of case stated.

Judicial review
An application under R.S.C., Ord. 53, may be based on the grounds that:

(*a*) the decision of the tribunal was *ultra vires*;

(*b*) there was an error of law on the face of the record;

(*c*) the decision was so unreasonable that no reasonable tribunal could have come to that decision;

(*d*) there was a breach of the tribunal's own rules or the rules of natural justice.

[55a] [1994] 2 All E.R. 659, C.A.

Case Stated

> "A Mental Health Review Tribunal may, and if so required by the High Court, shall state in the form of a special case for determination by the High Court any question of law which may arise before them" (s.78(8)).

R.S.C., Ord. 56, rr. 7–12, lays down the procedure to be followed. Twenty-one days are allowed after the decision of the tribunal is communicated to the parties. The High Court can then give any direction the tribunal itself could have given; a more satisfactory remedy therefore than an order for certiorari in judicial review.

There is no provision for appeal against the decision of a mental health review tribunal. Nor is there any provision for amendment or revocation of its decision; the decision of a mental health review tribunal is a final order[56] (*R. v. Ealing District Health Authority, ex p. Fox*) and the tribunal has no power to adjourn to monitor progress. The fact that a mental health review tribunal has previously discharged the patient, does not prevent an immediate application for readmission under section 3: *R. v. South Western Hospital Managers, ex p. M.*[57] If the application appears to be duly made, any argument that there was a bar to its operation will be by way of judicial review, not *habeas corpus*.

Guardianship

Incidence

In a situation where admission to hospital is inappropriate, but a degree of control over the autonomy of a mentally disordered person in the community is thought to be desirable, guardianship is available as an option to be considered. In practice, it is very rarely used, there are only 200 or so applications each year. Guardianship is an administrative process, under the control of the local authority.

In contrast to the Mental Health Act 1959 which gave the guardian all the powers that a parent has over a child under the age of 14 years, guardianship under the Mental Health Act 1983 is a limited "essential powers" order which limits the powers of the guardian to three particular instances:

(*a*) to require the patient to reside at a place specified by the guardian;
(*b*) to require the patient to attend at times and places specified for the purposes of medical treatment, occupation, education or training; and
(*c*) to require access to the patient to be given to any doctor, approved social worker, or any person similarly specified (s.8(2)).

It is the lack of any sanctions for its breach which is the main reason for the unpopularity of guardianship. The only real sanction is threat of

---

[56] [1993] 3 All E.R. 170.
[57] [1994] 1 All E.R. 161.

admission to hospital, or the criminal sanction in section 129 for refusing entry to a person authorised under section 8(2).

The *Code of Practice* is, however, enthusiastic about the potential for guardianship:

> "Approved Social Workers and registered medical practitioners should consider guardianship as a positive alternative when making decisions about a patient's treatment and welfare. In particular it should be actively considered as an alternative both to admission to hospital and to continuing hospital care" (para. 13.2).

The Mental Health Act Commission has also consistently lamented the little use made of guardianship.

Grounds

The grounds for guardianship are similar to those for admission for treatment under section 3 and are contained in section 7(1) of the Mental Health Act. The patient must be suffering from mental illness, psychopathic disorder, severe mental impairment, or mental impairment of a nature or degree which warrants his reception into guardianship, and it is necessary in the interests of the welfare of the patient or for the protection of other persons that the patient should be so received (s.7(2)(b)). People with a mental handicap (or learning disability) are, for the most part therefore, excluded from guardianship. There is no "treatability" test, and the section 7 criterion is "welfare" not "health or safety" as in section 3.

A private individual may be appointed guardian, but he must have the approval of his local social services authority so to act (s.7(5)); in the vast majority of cases it will be the local authority that is appointed guardian. The local authority cannot be compelled to use its guardianship powers, but once guardianship is accepted, Part III of the Mental Health (Hospital, Guardianship and Consent to Treatment) Regulations[58] imposes minimum visiting requirements, similar to the Boarding Out Regulations[59] for children looked after by a local authority; for example, regulation 13 requires visits to take place (not necessarily by an approved social worker) at not less than three-monthly intervals, and also provides for an annual visit by an approved doctor. However, as a patient under guardianship is not liable to be detained under section 56(1) he is not subject to the consent to treatment provisions in Part IV of the Act. It is an offence to neglect or ill-treat a patient under one's guardianship (s.127(2)).

The nearest relative can bar an application for guardianship (s.11(4)). As the responsible medical officer cannot use his powers under section

---

[58] S.I. 1983 No. 893.
[59] The Arrangements for Placement of Children (General) Regulations 1991 (S.I. 1991 No. 890).

25 to prevent the nearest relative discharging the patient from guardian-ship, an application under section 29(3)(*d*) will be necessary for the appointment of an acting nearest relative.

The local authority may call for reports from a private guardian under regulation 12 and may furthermore make application to the county court for the transfer of the guardianship to them if the private guardian has performed his functions negligently or in a manner contrary to the interests of the welfare of the patient (s.10(3)). A mental health review tribunal may also order the discharge of a patient from guardianship (s.66(1)). The initial duration of a guardianship order is six months, but this may be extended by a further six months, and then for periods of one year at a time (s.20(1)). A guardianship order remains in force if the patient is admitted to hospital under section 2 or 4 of the Mental Health Act, but not under section 3. Transfers are possible under section 19 of the Mental Health Act and regulations 7 to 9 of the Mental Health (Hospital, Guardianship and Consent to Treatment) Regulations 1983.[60]

Uses of guardianship
The positive use of guardianship within the framework of community care is acknowledged in the *Code of Practice* (para. 13.1); guardianship is seen as a legitimate means to enable patients to receive community care services where it cannot be provided without the use of compulsory powers. It enables the establishment of an authoritative framework for working with a patient with a minimum of constraint to achieve as independent a life as possible within the community. Guardianship, however, should only be used as part of a comprehensive care plan, and is inappropriate if no such power is needed to achieve any part of that plan; in other words the case for compulsion must be clearly established (para. 13.4). As well as carrying out his protective functions, the guardian should also act as advocate in securing necessary services for his client (para. 13.5). This advocacy aspect of guardianship is certainly one which could be further developed. Guardianship imposes no power of compul-sory treatment, it must therefore be clearly distinguished from any community treatment order. Guardianship does give the guardian the power to say where the patient should reside (s.8(1)(*a*)). The question then arises, could it be used to transfer an unwilling person to residential care? The *Code of Practice* (para. 13.9) is clear that guardianship should never be used solely for the purpose of transferring an unwilling person into residential care (and indeed there is no power in the guardian to remove or convey persons subject to his guardianship to the premises specified); however, paragraph 13.9 of the *Code of Practice* also says that:

"where an adult is assessed as requiring residential care but due to mental incapacity is unable to make a decision as to whether he wishes to be placed in residential care, those responsible for his care should consider the

---

[60] S.I. 1983 No. 893.

applicability and appropriateness of guardianship for providing a framework within which decisions about his current and future care can be
planned."

Guardianship may also play a role as a legal source of authority for
constraints upon elderly people already in residential care, who are
seeking to exercise their right to leave; it would thus legitimise what is
often at present *de facto* control, and through the mechanisms of the
Mental Health Act 1983 give access to review processes and tribunals.

Reform of the law of guardianship was proposed by the Law
Commission in its discussion papers on *Mentally Incapacitated Adults and
Decision Making*.[61] The chief criticism of the present law of guardianship is
that it does not permit intervention in areas which may be appropriate
because of the limited nature of its powers, whilst at the same time
limiting decision-making in areas in which the person subject to
guardianship may be competent. Furthermore there is no provision to
deal with financial affairs under guardianship. For this a separate
application to the Court of Protection must be made.[62] The Law
Commission's proposals for the appointment of personal and financial
managers would seek to address these difficulties in a private law context
making guardianship under the Mental Health Act an exclusively public
law institution (perhaps exercisable also by health authorities). Furthermore, the Law Commission proposed that the powers of the Mental
Health Act Commission should extend to guardianship.

---

[61] *Mentally Incapacitated Adults and Decision Making* (H.M.S.O., 1993). Consultation Papers
Nos. 128 and 130.
[62] See Chap. 12—Delegation of Financial Responsibility, at p. 227.

Chapter 9
Abuse of the Elderly

Recognition that elderly people may be subjected to abuse and neglect within their families as well as by outsiders dates from the mid 1980s. The seminal work is by Mervyn Eastman.[1] The Law Commission in their consultation paper *Mentally Incapacitated and Other Vulnerable Adults: Public Law Protection*,[2] adopted Eastman's definition of abuse as:

> "the systematic maltreatment, physical, emotional or financial of an elderly person . . . this may take the form of physical assault, threatening behaviour, neglect and abandonment or sexual assault."[3]

Situations may range from the deliberate infliction of physical harm, through sexual and financial exploitation, to a failure to provide sufficient care to prevent physical and mental deterioration, or emotional abuse by persistent criticism or ridicule. The difficulty for the lawyer is that not all of these situations fit neatly into existing legal categories. There are, of course, fundamental difficulties in transferring a concept such as abuse, developed in relation to children, into an adult context. Issues of vulnerability may be similar, but it cannot be assumed that similar rights and duties exist, nor that remedies which are appropriate in a child care context can easily be applied to individuals who otherwise have full legal rights.

PHYSICAL ABUSE

The criminal law

Physical abuse may involve consideration of both the civil and criminal law. A criminal prosecution under the Offences Against the Person Act 1861 would most likely be causing grievous bodily harm with intent (s.18), assault occasioning actual bodily harm (s.47), or unlawful and malicious wounding or inflicting grievous bodily harm (s.20). The House

---

[1] Eastman, *Old Age Abuse* (1984).
[2] *Mentally Incapacitated and Other Vulnerable Adults: Public Law Protection* (H.M.S.O., 1993).
[3] *ibid.* p. 37.

of Lords in *R. v. Savage; D.P.P. v. Parmenter*[4] confirmed that a verdict of guilty of assault occasioning actual bodily harm under section 47 was a permissible alternative verdict on a count alleging unlawful wounding contrary to section 20.

Intent

In order to establish the offence under section 20 the Crown must prove that the defendant either intended or foresaw that his act would either cause harm, or was reckless as to whether it would do so. For section 47, however, it is sufficient for the Crown to show that the defendant committed an assault and that actual bodily harm was occasioned by the assault; it is not necessary to prove that the defendant intended to cause some actual bodily harm, or was reckless as to whether such harm could be caused. However, the physical harm which the defendant must have intended or foreseen in section 20 need only have been "of a minor character" and not of the gravity of that described in the offence itself, *i.e.* either wounding or grievous bodily harm. Thus the throwing of a beer glass, intended to cause minor discomfort, could constitute the offence under section 20 when serious injury was caused by its accidental breakage. One consequence of *R. v. Savage; D.P.P. v. Parmenter*[5] is that the defendant must take his victim as he finds him in terms of frailty or unusual physical reactions, for example, in the administration of medication, or on the "eggshell skull" principle.

Assault

An assault includes, but is not limited to, an attempt to commit a battery, provided an apprehension of immediate and unlawful violence is present in the mind of the victim. In *Smith v. Superintendent Woking Police Station*,[6] the Divisional Court held that an assault was committed when S stared for three to four seconds through the bedroom window of an elderly woman dressed in her nightclothes. The intention to frighten together with the fear of some act of immediate violence was sufficient to amount to an assault.

An assault which causes a hysterical and nervous condition is an assault occasioning actual bodily harm: *R. v. Miller*.[7] Expert evidence of psychiatric injury will however need to be called: "mere emotion" such as fear, distress or panic is not sufficient (*R. v. Chan-Fook*[8]). Psychological harm does not come within the section 20 offence: Lord Roskill in *Wilson*[9] accepted the view of the Supreme Court of Victoria in *Salisbury*[10] that the

---

[4] [1992] 1 A.C. 699.
[5] *ibid.*
[6] (1983) 76 Cr.App.R. 234.
[7] [1954] 2 Q.B. 282.
[8] *The Times*, November 19, 1993, C.A.
[9] [1984] A.C. 242.
[10] [1976] V.R. 452.

word "inflicts" connotes an application of force to the body of the victim, and thus does not embrace the concept of psychological harm.

Death

When injuries result in death, subject to appropriate proof of causation, the law of homicide applies. Following the decision of the House of Lords in *Seymour*,[11] the concept of liability in manslaughter for foreseeable damage caused by one's gross negligence, has been extended by that of "risk" where liability extends even to consequences unforeseen by the defendant. Thus a person who unlawfully kills another is guilty of involuntary manslaughter if his conduct was attended by an obvious and serious risk of causing unlawful physical injury to that person and either he acts recklessly in that, having recognised that there was some risk involved, he nevertheless goes on to take it, or he acted without having given any thought to the possibility of there being any such risk. Protection is thus extended to those whose physical safety is completely disregarded in the actions of others or whose special vulnerability is unknown to the defendant.

Failure to act

A difficulty, however, arises in cases of neglect or failure to act to prevent a life-threatening deterioration in a person in need of care. Such situations are probably more likely than the overt infliction of physical harm upon a vulnerable elderly person. But the question then arises, who has a duty to intervene to provide a person, not otherwise able to cope for themselves, with the necessities of life such as food, heat or medical care? The same difficulty arises as in the civil law: first of all it is necessary to find a person who in law owes a duty to the elderly victim, and then to define the extent of that duty. In fact it appears that no personal relationship automatically infers a duty of support of this nature. It is arguable whether even the marital relationship by which spouses owe a duty of support to each other and by which they are deemed to be "liable relatives" in Social Security legislation[12] extends to a duty to provide care and assistance to each other. Moreover, although parents owe a duty to their infant children (enforceable in criminal proceedings under the Children and Young Persons Act 1933), children do not conversely owe a duty to their elderly parents. It is in the non-existence of familial duties towards elderly people that the distinction from child protection issues in cases of abuse becomes most apparent.

Duty of care

It is otherwise if a duty is voluntarily assumed; criminal liability may arise from the breach of that duty of care. In *Instan*[13] the defendant lived in her aunt's house and was provided with free board and lodging in return for

---

[11] [1983] 2 A.C. 493.
[12] See Social Security Administration Act 1992, s.106.
[13] [1893] 1 Q.B. 450.

looking after the aunt. The aunt contracted gangrene and the defendant did nothing to obtain medical help or to give assistance which certainly accelerated her aunt's death. The niece was found guilty of manslaughter on these facts. The court will look at the whole situation, and not just one aspect of it, in order to ascertain whether or not a duty does exist; if a duty of care is found to exist, then it is no defence for the defendant to say that he would have found it difficult because of his own limitations to discharge that duty properly.

The duty of care is quite high as was seen in the case of *Stone*.[14] The defendant took in his sister as a lodger. She became bedridden and anorexic and died in conditions of great squalor in her attic room. The family were all of low intelligence and although they made ineffectual attempts to get medical help they did not persist with these efforts. The defendant himself was unable to use the telephone. He argued that he owed no duty of care to his sister who was a free agent, but it was held that a duty had been assumed on the basis of the situation as a whole: the relationship; the awareness of her condition; the attempts to help that were actually made; and the past provision of food and care. According to the Australian case of *Taktak*,[15] an important factor is the extent to which the defendant's conduct has reduced the chances of others providing the help that the victim needed to stay alive; at the very minimum this would involve calling medical assistance. A particularly high duty of care would conversely be inferred in the case of patients who present special risks such as the elderly mentally infirm, and it was accepted in *Seymour* that failure to protect from obvious risks may itself form the offence.

Situations where death is caused by the negligent act of a professional person in breach of a duty of care owed to his patient or client were considered in *R. v. Adomako*.[15a] That case concerned the death of a patient following an operation when the anaesthetist, who should have been monitoring his patient's condition, failed to notice that the ventilator was disconnected. It was the extent to which the defendant's conduct departed from the standard of care incumbent upon him as a professional person in a situation in which there was a risk of death to the patient that marked the boundary between civil liability and criminal liability.

The civil law

Negligence
In the tort of negligence, acts of omission will cause the greatest difficulty. As discussed above, in relation to criminal liability, a duty of care cannot be assumed from family relationships alone, but must be proved. The standard of care required will moreover be an amalgam of

---

[14] [1977] 1 Q.B. 354.
[15] [1988] A. Crim. R. 334.
[15a] [1994] 5 Med. L.R. 277, H.L.

the likelihood and the gravity of the injury which may be caused if adequate safety precautions are not taken.

In the case of professional carers, the standard of care required is that of the ordinary skilled person exercising and professing to have that special skill: see *Roe v. Minister of Health*.[16] Vicarious liability will of course operate to extend liability, for example, to the registered owners of a residential home for the negligent activities of their staff. As to the adequacy of the quality of care required, general guidelines such as those in *Home Life: A Code of Practice for Residential Care*[17] may be used to set standards.

Psychological harm

Is the infliction of psychological harm, for example by being exposed to threats of abandonment, insults or belittling, actionable?

It is probable that the mere use of words would not constitute an assault, no matter how insulting or even menacing. Some sort of overt act is required: *Meade's and Belt's cases*.[18] In the civil law, the intentional infliction of emotional distress is a category of behaviour known to the law of tort since the case of *Wilkinson v. Downton*.[19] That case concerned a practical joke which misfired, the plaintiff being told that her husband had met with an accident on the way home from a race meeting and that she must go at once to bring him home. The "nervous shock" which resulted was held not to be too remote a consequence of the defendant's actions, to entitle her to recover damages for her loss.

Telling a person that they must go into a home, provided that that is calculated to cause distress would thus, it appears, form the basis of an action.[19a] The tort of "wrongful interference" is not, however, well developed. The leading case in the United States of America, where "dignity law" is well established, is *Nickerson v. Hodge*[20] where damages were awarded to a mentally infirm woman who had been subjected to unsolicited ridicule. No statutory sanctions exist for the use of ageist language or behaviour along the lines of the Race Relations Act 1976, though Article 14 of the European Convention on Human Rights refers to "birth or other status" as a ground upon which discrimination should not occur.

Limitations on the scope of the tort for reasons of public policy were made explicit in the judgment of Lord Keith in the "Hillsborough" case: *Alcock v. Chief Constable of South Yorkshire Police*.[21] According to Lord Keith three elements need to be considered in claims for damages for "what is

---

[16] [1954] 2 Q.B. 66.
[17] *Home Life: A Code of Practice for Residential Care* (Centre for Policy on Ageing, 1984).
[18] [1823] 1 Lew. 184.
[19] [1897] 2 Q.B. 57.
[19a] See *Khorasandjian v. Bush* [1993] Q.B. 727, where an injunction was granted preventing further harassment by telephone calls interfering with the recipient's ordinary and reasonable enjoyment of her property and thus constituting a private nuisance.
[20] 1920.
[21] *Sub nom. Jones v. Wright* [1992] 1 A.C. 310.

commonly known if inaccurately described as 'nervous shock' ".[22] These are:

(1) the class of persons whose claims should be recognised;
(2) the proximity of those persons to the incident in time and space; and
(3) the means by which the shock has been caused.

These cases were all concerned with liability to third parties for the consequences of an (admittedly) negligent act. Witnessing abuse inflicted on another for example in an institutional setting could therefore form the basis of an action by a witness who suffered "nervous shock" in consequence.

INSTITUTIONAL ABUSE

The extent of abuse in institutional care is not well researched. Avenues of complaint would include the use of local authorities' or health authorities' own complaints procedures, and ultimately the withdrawal of registration from private or voluntary homes. Failure by the local authority to respond to a complaint of abuse may come within the jurisdiction of the Commissioner for Local Administration. See Complaint 89/C 1320, in which the local authority was guilty of maladministration in failing to respond to the concerns of a relative about the welfare of a resident in a private home registered with that authority.

Mental Health Act 1983

Though there is a general absence of protective legislation, section 127(2) of the Mental Health Act 1983 provides that it is an offence wilfully to ill-treat or neglect any person suffering from mental disorder, in one's custody or care. Ill-treatment and neglect are two separate offences and should be charged as such. Guidance on the framing of the indictment and on directions to be given to the jury was delivered by Watkins L.J. in R. v. Newington[23]; a case involving the owner of a residential home for the elderly in Margate. Ill-treatment requires proof of intent or recklessness, and is deliberate conduct "which could properly be described as such whether or not it had caused or was likely to cause harm." Ill-treatment need not result in actual injury, it includes bullying and the use of harsh words. The presence of mental disorder in the victim does have to be specifically proved. By section 130 of the Mental Health Act 1983 local authorities can prosecute for offences under section 127, but require the consent of the Director of Public Prosecutions.

---

[22] ibid. pp. 392 et seq.
[23] (1990) 91 Cr.App.R. 247.

Officers on the staff of, or employed in, or managers of, any hospital or nursing home are specifically covered by the offence, under section 127(1), of ill-treating or wilfully neglecting an in-patient or out-patient of that hospital or nursing home.

DOMESTIC VIOLENCE

The legislation

The Domestic Violence and Matrimonial Proceedings Act 1976 and the Domestic Proceedings and Magistrates' Courts Act 1978, provide civil remedies for victims of domestic violence. Ouster orders (1976 Act) or exclusion orders (1978 Act) are available either to exclude one party from the matrimonial home, or to allow access to the other party who has been wrongfully excluded. Non-molestation injunctions and personal protection orders are available in cases of harassment or (in the Magistrates' Court) in cases of actual or threatened violence.

However, the domestic violence legislation only applies between married or cohabiting couples where there is (or very recently was) a "matrimonial home".[24] It cannot be used against other relatives or associates, for example an adult child, even living in the same household. Nevertheless the applicability of domestic violence remedies should not be overlooked in cases of abuse between spouses which are the product of long-standing violent relationships. Injunctions may of course be made ancillary to divorce or other matrimonial proceedings, when application for maintenance orders should also be made. Matrimonial remedies should not be discounted because of the age of the parties. Indeed, proper financial arrangements may be a prerequisite for one party being able to enter residential care.

Other remedies

When violence is perpetrated by family members outside the marital relationship or by strangers, recourse must be had to ordinary legal remedies, most usually an action for trespass or assault. However, as the case of *Patel v. Patel*[25] shows, an injunction is seen merely as a temporary device whilst the quantum of damages is assessed (in that case an action against a son-in-law claiming damages and an injunction in trespass). The Law Commission in its report on *Family Law, Domestic Violence and the Family Home*[26] has proposed that the protection of any new law in this field should extend to persons within a defined group of close relatives, to former as well as present spouses, and actual as well as past members of the same household. What they did not do was recommend the

---

[24] See *O'Neill v. Williams* (1983) 127 S.J. 595.
[25] [1988] 2 FLR 179.
[26] *Family Law, Domestic Violence and the Family Home* (Law Commission, 1993).

creation of a new tort of harassment or molestation, with remedies against those outside the immediate family or household.

FINANCIAL ABUSE

Little empirical research has been undertaken into the extent of the financial abuse of elderly people in the United Kingdom, but evidence from the United States of America in "When the Elderly are Abused: Characteristics and Intervention"[27] suggests that financial abuse may in fact be the most prevalent form of abuse. It may be insidious and difficult to detect, as in the case of the misuse of pension monies over a period of time, or it may involve a one-off transaction such as the "gift" of a large sum of money from a bank account. Elements of fraud or undue influence may appear in a number of cases. Though devices exist to regulate the management by others of the financial affairs of older people, for example enduring powers of attorney and receivership under the Court of Protection (see Chapter 12–Delegation of Financial Responsibility), these safeguards will cover only a minority of elderly people.

THE LAW OF CONTRACT

Generally the law favours the upholding of contracts which are, on the face of it, valid. Thus a contract made with a person suffering from mental disorder is valid except in two instances. First, if the other party knew of the patient's disability, the contract is voidable at the patient's option, and the burden of proof is on him to show that this disability prevented him from understanding the particular transaction in hand,[28] thus contracts made during lucid intervals are binding regardless of whether the other party knew of previous incapacities.[29] Secondly, where the patient's property is subject to the control of the Court of Protection, any contract concerning that property is not binding on the patient, but is binding on the other party.[30]

The question in many instances will be the validity of a contract for the sale of an asset at a much reduced price. There must be consideration for a contract to come into existence, and that consideration must be of some economic value, since "natural affection of itself is not a sufficient consideration".[31] The law will not, however, enquire into the adequacy of

---

[27] Powell and Berg, "When the Elderly are Abused: Characteristics and Intervention" in *Educational Gerontology*, Vol. 39(2), pp. 230–239.
[28] See *Re. K.* [1988] Ch. 310.
[29] See *Imperial Loan Co. v. Stone* [1892] 1 Q.B. 599.
[30] See *Baldwyn v. Smith* [1900] 1 Ch. 588.
[31] See *Bret v. J.S.* [1600] Cro. Eliz. 756; see also *Thomas v. Thomas* [1842] 2 Q.B. 851 and *White v. Bluett* (1853) 23 L.J.Exch. 36.

the consideration. Where there is a mistake as to value, the buyer is not precluded from taking advantage of the mistake that he knew the seller was making.[32] It is different if the seller is making a mistake, not merely of quality, but as to the terms of the contract, for example for the sale of an "Old Master" believed by the seller to be a painting by an unknown local artist.

Equity however does recognise a further class of "unconscionable bargains" whereby a purchase of property from a "poor and ignorant" vendor at considerable undervalue may be set aside where the vendor acts without legal advice: *Butlin-Sanders v. Butlin*.[33] Furthermore, if there is evidence of unfairness amounting to equitable fraud in the execution of a contract, that contract may be rescinded for the protection of a party suffering from mental incapacity, even if the lack of capacity is unknown to the other party: *Hart v. O'Connor*.[34] However, if there is no fraud or unconscionable conduct, the law applies and the contract is valid.

Duress and undue influence

Duress and undue influence make contracts voidable, rather than void. Duress may be of a physical nature but also of an economic nature, as in the threat to break a pre-existing contract: see *North Ocean Shipping Co. v. Hyundai Construction Co.*[35] The equitable doctrine of "undue influence" (see below), which has been exercised primarily in relation to gifts, is equally applicable to contracts.

Non est factum

Particular rules apply to written signed contracts: "When a document containing contractual terms is signed, then, in the absence of fraud, or [. . .] misrepresentation, the party signing it is bound, and it is wholly immaterial whether he has read the document or not" *per* Scrutton L.J. in *L'Estrange v. Graucob*.[36] If a third person acquires rights under the contract for value and in good faith, it cannot then be avoided (for fraud or misrepresentation). One would then have to argue that the document is void, using the doctrine of *non est factum*. Three factors must be proved: (1) that A's signature has been procured by the fraud of B, (2) that B's fraud was such as to lead A to believe that the document was fundamentally different in its effect from what was the case, and (3) that A was not guilty of negligence in so signing. In *Foster v. Mackinnon*,[37] an elderly man was induced to sign a bill of exchange by a fraudulent representation that it was a guarantee. He successfully pleaded *non est*

---

[32] See *Smith v. Hughes* (1871) L.R. 6 Q.B. 597.
[33] (1985) 15 Fam.Law 126.
[34] [1985] A.C. 1000.
[35] [1979] Q.B. 705.
[36] [1934] 2 K.B. 394 at 403.
[37] (1869) L.R. 4 C.P. 704.

factum. However, in *Gallie v. Lee*,[38] it was the effect, not the nature, of the document that was held to be the vital issue as to whether the transaction was void. There, an elderly widow, who could not read without her spectacles, which were broken, was induced to sign a document which she believed was a deed of gift of her house to her nephew, but which was in fact a deed of sale of the house to a third party. The document however was held not to be void, because it in fact it carried out her agreed objective, which was to allow her nephew to raise money on her house, and to divest herself of title to it.

NECESSARIES

The principles of the common law for the supply of necessaries were replaced by section 3(2) of the Sale of Goods Act 1979: "where necessaries are sold and delivered [. . .] to a person who by reason of mental incapacity [. . .] is competent to contract, he must pay a reasonable price for them." Notice that the price to be paid is not the agreed price, but a "reasonable price". Necessaries are defined as "goods suitable to the condition of life (of the person) [. . .] and to his actual requirements at the time of sale and delivery." "Necessaries" includes services as well as goods, for example the provision of medical treatment.

Where there is no concept of a "bargain", but the recipient is simply maintained at the expense of another person, there is a remedy at common law under the doctrine of agency of necessity: *Brockwell v. Bullock*.[39] Relatives, friends, etc., providing "necessaries" may thus recover payment under this head.

GIFTS

Many transactions which are sought to be impugned will not be contracts, but will be gifts. A gift from a mentally incapacitated donor may be set aside depending upon the circumstances of the case and the degree of incapacity proved. This varies from a low degree of understanding where the subject matter is trivial, to a high degree of understanding where the donor is disposing of his only asset of value. In *Re Beaney*[40] the defendant was suffering from an advanced state of senile dementia; her transfer of her house to her eldest daughter was held to be void even though she understood the absolute nature of the gift, as its value and the claims of other potential recipients were not appreciated by her.

---

[38] [1971] A.C. 1004.
[39] (1889) 22 Q.B.D. 567.
[40] [1978] 1 W.L.R. 770.

Undue Influence

Equitable remedies may be available to set aside gifts and other transactions if they have been procured by undue influence, but only if there has been some unconscionable conduct on the part of the defendant, together with evidence that the transaction is manifestly disadvantageous to the plaintiff.[41] It is immaterial that the advantage has been gained by a third party, and not by the person exercising undue influence.

What is required is a gift so large or a transaction so improvident "as not to be reasonably accounted for on the ground of friendship, relationship, charity or other ordinary motives on which ordinary men act" per Nourse L.J. in Goldsworthy v. Brickell.[42]

The existence of a "fiduciary relationship" between the parties raises a prima facie presumption of undue influence in circumstances where a degree of trust or confidence can be shown to exist. Such a relationship has been found to exist between mother and son[43]; elderly customer and bank manager[44]; employer and secretary/companion[45]; solicitor and client[46]; and husband and wife-to-be (both elderly).[47] All the circumstances of the case will be taken into account, as in Re Craig,[48] where an 84-year-old man had engaged a secretary/companion and had over a period of six years given her gifts worth nearly £28,000, equal to two-thirds of his estate. Though there was no actual evidence of undue influence, because of their value, none of the gifts could be accounted for on the grounds of "ordinary motives"; the relationship was one of confidence and there was a presumption of undue influence. Though the onus on the plaintiff (a disappointed beneficiary) was said to be a "heavy one", he was not required to prove that the relationship was one of domination, simply one of reliance.

The presumption could be rebutted by showing that "full, free and informed discussion" had taken place, resulting in the removal of the secretary's influence over her employer. The best way of doing this is by showing that independent advice was taken. In Re Coomber[49] it was sufficient to show that the mother's assignment of a business lease to her son, which was challenged by her other children after her death, had been drawn up by a solicitor who had ascertained that she understood the nature and consequences of her act. It was not necessary that she should have sought further legal advice or financial advice.

---

[41] See Bank of Credit and Commerce International v. Aboody [1990] Q.B. 923.
[42] [1987] Ch. 378 at 401.
[43] Re Coomber [1911] 1 Ch. 723.
[44] Lloyds Bank v. Bundy [1975] Q.B. 326.
[45] Re Craig [1971] Ch. 95.
[46] Re A Solicitor [1975] Q.B. 475.
[47] Zarnet v. Hyman [1961] 1 W.L.R. 1442.
[48] [1971] Ch. 95.
[49] [1911] 1 Ch. 723.

Simpson v. Simpson[50] was a case where proof of undue influence displaced the presumption of advancement between spouses. The residuary estate had been left to the plaintiffs (the children) by will. Subsequently the testator became ill and mentally incapacitated and between that time and his death, 70 per cent of the estate was transferred into a joint account with his wife. Though undue influence could not be presumed from the marital relationship alone, a combination of factors led to this conclusion: his declining mental capacity; his increasing dependence on his wife; the effect of the transfers on the dispositions made by will; and his failure to consult his solicitor who was an old family friend.

Normal equitable defences of laches, acquiescence and confirmation apply. The donor must commence proceedings within a reasonable period of time from the ending of the influence over him; in *Bullock v. Lloyds Bank*[51] this was four years. Personal representatives may take action on behalf of the deceased.

INSTITUTING PROCEEDINGS

Instituting proceedings on behalf of elderly people may raise some areas of difficulty.

A problem may arise in cases of common assault where the victim, and not the police, is required to institute proceedings: *Nicholson v. Booth and Naylor*.[52] There is an exception to this, however, in the case of *Pickering v. Willoughby*[53] where the victim is:

> "so feeble, old and infirm as to be incapable of instituting proceedings and is not a free agent but under the control of the person committing the assault, the information may be laid by a third person."

In that case a great nephew was permitted to lay the information where his elderly great aunt had been assaulted by the niece who had moved in to live with her.

Witnesses

Normally witnesses will be expected to attend and to give oral evidence on oath. This may cause difficulties where the witness is infirm or incapacitated. Section 23(1) and (2)(a) of the Criminal Justice Act 1988 however provided that a statement made by a person in a document shall be admissible in criminal proceedings, as evidence by him would be admissible if the person who made the statement is dead or, by reason of

---

[50] [1992] 1 FLR 601.
[51] [1955] Ch. 317.
[52] (1888) 57 L.J.M.C. 43.
[53] [1907] 2 K.B. 269 at 305.

his bodily or mental condition, unfit to attend as a witness. Thus both physical and mental infirmity are relevant to the question of fitness to attend court: *R. v. Setz-Dempsey; R. v. Richardson*.[54]

Section 23 is however subject to the general powers of the court to exclude evidence in section 28(1)(*b*) because it is not of probative value, for example, and to the discretion in section 25 to exclude documentary evidence in the interests of justice. A relevant factor is the reliability of the evidence given the degree of infirmity of the witness: *R. v. Neshet*.[55] See generally J. McEwan, "Documenting Hearsay Evidence—Refuge for the Vulnerable Witness".[56]

The witness must be able to understand the obligation involved in the oath as well as the duty to tell the truth: *R. v. Dunning*.[57] There is no provision analogous to that in the Children Act 1989, s.96, allowing children to give evidence without oath.

In civil cases, documentary hearsay evidence may be admissible under section 2 of the Civil Evidence Act 1968 if the witness is unable to attend because of physical or mental infirmity certified by a medical practitioner (s.8 and R.S.C., Ord. 38, r.25).

Corroboration

Many instances of abuse will go unwitnessed by others and some will be of such a sensitive nature that a corroboration warning may be required. In *R. v. Spencer*,[58] a case concerning special hospital patients, the House of Lords decided that although a full corroboration warning, such as that given in sexual offences, was not required, nevertheless juries had to be warned in clear terms of the dangers of convicting on the unsupported evidence of patients who might have a common grudge.

PROCEDURES

Many local authorities have devised administrative procedures to deal with allegations of abuse. Some of those are modelled on child protection procedures, involving case conferences and the keeping of "at risk" registers. Though there is no policy guidance akin to *Working Together*[59] in the field of abuse of the elderly, both the Association of Directors of Social Services (1991) and the Social Services Inspectorate (1993) have endorsed the idea of practice guidance, preferably on an inter-agency basis.

Lessons from the field of child protection, however, show that diligence needs to be exercised to see that fairness is observed in the

---

[54] *The Times*, July 20, 1993, C.A.
[55] *The Times*, March 14, 1990.
[56] [1989] Crim. L.R. 629.
[57] [1965] Crim L.R. 372.
[58] [1987] A.C. 128.
[59] *Working Together* (H.M.S.O., 1993).

operation of internal procedures; see for example *R. v. Norfolk County Council, ex p. M.*,[60] where there was no opportunity given for prior consultation before the name of the alleged abuser was placed on the child abuse register.

LAW REFORM

Reform of the substantive law so as to increase its effectiveness in cases of abuse or neglect has been proposed by the Law Commission in its Consultation Paper *Mentally Incapacitated and Other Vulnerable Adults: Public Law Protection*.[61] In dealing with the issues of abuse, the Law Commission sought to extend its brief beyond the protection of mentally incapacitated people to those who could be seen to be vulnerable, defined in paragraph 2.29 as those who by reason of old age, infirmity, or disability are unable to take care of themselves or protect themselves from others. However the Law Commission also proposed that such inclusion of vulnerability should not extend beyond the operation of emergency protection procedures to longer term intervention without consent. Powers to be given to the local authority might include a duty to investigate allegations of abuse or neglect; a right of entry to premises and access to the client; a power of assessment; and a power of removal. The model relies heavily upon the concept of "significant harm" introduced by the Children Act 1989, s.31, and that Act's repertoire of intervention orders. In any decision to be taken either by a local authority or by any future judicial forum, certain principles were held to apply. These were (para. 5.13):

> "that any decision taken or order made should be in the best interests of the person concerned and should respect his previous possession of capacity by taking into account:
>
> (a) his ascertainable past and present wishes and feelings
> (b) the need to encourage him to participate in any decision-making to the fullest extent of which he is capable, and
> (c) the general principle that the course least restrictive of the incapacitated person's freedom of decision and action is likely to be in his best interests."

The emergency provision of respite care, or in the longer term, guardianship may be possible responses to the finding of abuse, for the arrangement of which social services authorities will need to be involved (see Chapter 2—The Delivery of Social Services and Chapter 8—Compulsory Intervention).

---

[60] [1989] Q.B. 619.
[61] *Mentally Incapacitated and Other Vulnerable Adults: Public Law Protection* (Law Commission, 1993).

Chapter 10
Housing Matters

As people become older, their housing needs change; families have grown up and left, maintenance becomes more of a burden in both physical and financial terms, stairs and other features become less easy to live with. It is then that older people look to adapt or move out of the accommodation which has served them well for many years, into something smaller, easier to maintain and closer to facilities. The requirements for more suitable accommodation are common amongst older people, be they someone in a three-bedroomed council house or a home owner who has just completed paying off his mortgage. If people decide to stay in their own homes, they may wish to give consideration to repairs and improvements to make continued living there more comfortable. It may also be that the home is the major asset and they wish to try to unlock capital or provide an income.

There are situations when people may find themselves homeless, for example when one of a couple dies who has a right to reside under a family trust and the surviving partner has no rights, or because of other changes in family circumstances.

HOME IMPROVEMENT GRANTS

There are various grants available in respect of insulation, renovations or minor repairs, whether the claimant is an owner-occupier, private tenant, or housing association tenant, provided their income is low (generally someone in receipt of income support, housing benefit, family credit, council tax benefit or disability working allowance).

The more income or savings someone has, the less grant aid is available. Some grants are mandatory, for example renovation grants to make property suitable for human habitation, or discretionary, for example towards the cost of providing heating.

All landlords are responsible for repairs to the structure of their property and to the services supplying gas, water, electricity and for sewage installation.[1] Most councils and housing associations are generally responsible for major repairs although the tenant may be responsible for minor repairs and redecoration. So far as private tenants are concerned, in most cases landlords are responsible for repairs, but not generally responsible for improvements. It may be possible for the landlord to obtain an improvement grant, using slightly different rules and criteria, or it may be possible for the tenant to apply for an improvement grant himself, although he should obviously notify the landlord of his intentions.

Improvement grants are dealt with through the environmental health or housing departments of the local council, and on no account must work be commenced before the grant is approved, as this will lose all entitlement to grant assistance. If an owner-occupier sells the property within three years of receiving the grant, he may be required to pay some or all of it back. This rule does not apply if the owner-occupier dies or is an elderly person who has to sell in order to move into sheltered accommodation. Provisions relating to renovation grants are found in the Local Government and Housing Act 1989, Pt.VIII.

Renovation grants

These are available for larger repair and improvement works. In the case of serious disrepair, structurally unstable properties, dampness severe enough to damage health, inadequate lighting, heating or ventilation, lack of a wholesome water supply, insufficient facilities for preparing or cooking food or no suitably located fixed bath or shower and washhand basin with hot and cold water, a mandatory grant is available. Discretionary grants may be available to put a property into reasonable repair, convert a property to provide separate living accommodation, provide adequate thermal insulation, provide adequate facilities for space heating or provide "satisfactory internal arrangements", for example to deal with a staircase felt to be too steep. Renovation grants are means tested, with people over the income threshold possibly being eligible for part grant aid. Savings of £5,000 are ignored and, thereafter, £1 per £250 of savings is added to income to calculate eligibility. People aged between 60 to 74 years with a weekly income of less than £103.95 (£139.25 for a couple) should get full grant aid. Between 75 to 79 years the figures are £106.05 (£142.10 for a couple) and over 80, £110.40 (£147 for a couple). (These figures are up to date to January 1995.)

Insulation grants

These are available towards the cost of insulating lofts, lagging hot water tanks and pipes, lagging cold water tanks situated in lofts and having doors and windows draughtproofed.

The Energy Efficiency Office's Home Energy Efficiency Scheme (HEES) provides grants to people on low incomes for such basic

---

[1] Landlord and Tenant Act 1985, s.11.

insulations and from April 1, 1994, grants to all persons aged 60 without a means test. Grants are made up to a maximum of £128.50 for draught-proofing, £198.70 for loft insulation, and £305 for both jobs combined. (These figures are up to date to January 1995.) If the costs of the work are higher (which is unlikely unless the property is large), the extra cost has to be funded by the individual. In order to obtain a grant, approval for the works should first be obtained from the Energy Action Grants Agency (EAGA), PO Box 1NG, Newcastle-upon-Tyne, NE99 1NG. It can be contacted on Freephone 0800 181 667 for information and details of local contractors.

HEES is available to owner-occupiers, private tenants, local authorities and housing association tenants.

Disabled facilities grant

Under the Chronically Sick and Disabled Persons Act 1970, social services departments have a duty to assist in making arrangements for necessary adaptations to someone's home. This includes help with assessing what work is needed, including having plans prepared and liaising with other council departments, as well as providing grant assistance. An occupational therapist from the local social services may also help with advice and adaptations not covered by grant aid. A disabled facilities grant can be claimed by council tenants as well as by private tenants and owner-occupiers and in respect of modern properties which would not normally be eligible for grant aid.

The grant can be applied for if the householder is registered or registerable as disabled, or has such a person living with them. The Council has to be satisfied that the proposed works are necessary and appropriate to meet the needs of the disabled person (which will be done through the help of the advisor from social services), and that they are reasonable and practicable given the age and condition of the property. If satisfied, a mandatory grant is available. Works covered by such grant aid includes access into and around the property, improving heating, adapting heating or lighting controls to make them easier to use and providing suitable bathroom and kitchen facilities that can be used independently by the disabled person. Discretionary grants may be available for doing other works to make a property suitable for a disabled person.

A disabled facilities grant does not have to be repaid on sale of the property.

Minor works assistance

Minor works assistance may be available to help with minor repairs, improvements or adaptations but such aid is discretionary, and is only available to claimants on income support, council tax benefit, housing benefit, family credit or disability working allowance. The grant is to a maximum of £1,080 on any one claim with a maximum of £3,240 claimable within any three-year period. (These figures are up to date to January 1995.) It can be towards providing or improving thermal insulation, or "patch and mend" works in respect of properties in a clearance area to make such properties weatherproof until the occupier is moved out. In either of these cases, there is no age limit.

Minor works assistance is also available to applicants aged at least 60 who wish to "stay put" or where an applicant requires assistance with adaptation works for an elderly person to stay with them or move into their home, in which case the elderly person must be at least 60.

If a claim is for "staying put", the grant covers minor repairs, small improvements and adaptations, or basic safety and security measures. If major works are needed a renovation grant or disabled facilities grant may be more appropriate. If the grant is for adaptations for an elderly person to stay permanently with the applicant, it covers additional standard amenities, *e.g.* showers, toilets or handbasins, or additional cooking or heating facilities. Again, other grants may be more suitable.

COUNCIL TENANTS

The local council is responsible for repairs in respect of the structure and exterior of the property, electrical wiring, water and gas pipes, toilets, basins and sinks. Some small repairs and internal decoration are the responsibility of the tenant, but some councils have a programme of decorating one room every few years providing there is no younger relative living at home.

The Housing Department should be contacted about getting a repair done; if nothing happens an environmental health officer can be asked to inspect the property and advise the Housing Department as to what needs to be done. Some minor repairs, costing between £20 and £200, can be done by the tenant under the "right to repair" scheme and the cost claimed back, but the council may not meet the repair cost in full.

Succession

Under Housing Act 1985, s.87, a person is qualified to succeed the tenant under a secure tenancy (where the property is occupied by the tenant as his only or principal home) if he (the successor) occupies the dwelling house as his only or principal home at the time of the tenant's death and either:

(a) he is the tenant's spouse (there is no need to also show residence with the deceased); or

(b) he is another member of the tenant's family and has resided with the tenant throughout the period of 12 months ending with the tenant's death.

It does not matter that the tenant died in hospital, but a would-be successor who moved into the property after the tenant had gone into hospital where they subsequently died was held not to be residing with the tenant.[2]

A tenant under a periodic tenancy which has arisen where a secure tenancy for a certain term has come to an end by effluxion of time or by an order of the court, can be succeeded to (Housing Act 1985, s.89). In such cases, if more than one person is qualified to succeed, the tenant's spouse is preferred to other members of the family, and where two or more other members are eligible, the successor is the one as may be agreed between them and, in the absence of agreement, the one selected by the landlord.

Only one such succession is possible. There cannot be succession to a tenant who was himself a successor (Housing Act 1985, s.87). The definition in the Housing Act 1985, s.88, of a successor is wider than might be expected, including not only successor-tenants to previously secure tenants or periodic tenants, but also where a joint tenant has become the sole tenant.

Right to buy

Public sector tenants have the right to buy their home at a discounted price as provided for under Part V of the Housing Act 1985 as amended. Such rights are given to "secure" tenants; i.e. tenants of a local authority, a housing association or trust (but not charitable ones), an urban development corporation, the Development Board for Rural Wales or a housing action trust as created under the Housing Act 1988, who are individuals occupying the property as their only or principal home, or if joint tenants, that each is an individual and at least one of them occupies the dwellinghouse as his only or principal home (Housing Act 1985, ss.79–81). The secure tenant must have been one for a period or periods of at least two years, although not necessarily in the same property or with the same landlord. Some successor-tenants can count the time of a deceased tenant through whom they have acquired the successor tenancy (Housing Act 1985, s.87). The secure tenant must comply with the definition not only at the time he agrees to purchase but he must remain one until completion of the sale or else the right to buy is lost.[3]

If the tenant dies after agreeing terms to purchase the council property but before the conveyance is executed, there is no equitable interest in the right to purchase which can be vested in the tenant's estate, thereby giving the estate the right to purchase the property, despite delay on the part of the council in getting the paperwork prepared. In *Bradford Metropolitan City Council v. McMahon*,[4] Staughton L.J., at p 244, noted:

> "that Mrs Eggett might have obtained an injunction, immediately before she died, requiring the council to convey the house to her. It also follows that

[2] See *Foreman v. Beagley* [1969] 1 W.L.R. 1387, C.A.
[3] See *Sutton London Borough Council v. Swan* (1985) 18 H.L.R. 140, C.A.
[4] [1993] 4 All E.R. 237.

other secure tenants in the future may seek an injunction, if their health is precarious and their landlord dilatory."

The right to buy is not exercisable where there is a possession order, bankruptcy petition or receiving order against the tenant (Housing Act 1985, s.121) and completion cannot be compelled if there are four weeks' arrears of rent (Housing Act 1985, s.138(2)).

The purchase price is calculated by reference to the value of the property less a discount (Housing Act 1985, s.126). The valuation is taken at the date of the tenant's notice of claim to the council of his desire to purchase (Housing Act 1985, s.122) and is taken to be the price which at the time the property would realise if sold on the open market by a willing vendor, disregarding any improvements made by the tenant, or any failure by the tenant to keep the property in good internal repair, and also disregarding the fact that it is the tenant in residence (or a member of his family) who is the potential purchaser. If there is a conveyance it is based on the assumption that the vendor is selling for an estate in fee simple with vacant possession; if leasehold, the vendor is selling a lease of 125 years at a ground rent of not more than £10 per annum (Housing Act 1985, s.127).

The discount is calculated by reference to a basic discount of 32 per cent on the value of the house if the purchaser has less than three years' time as a secure tenant or in armed forces accommodation, or an aggregate of such times and, thereafter, a further 1 per cent for each complete year, the maximum discount being 60 per cent or £50,000, whichever is the lesser. If a flat, the discounts are 44 per cent and 2 per cent with a maximum of 70 per cent or £50,000 (Housing Act 1985, s.129).

The purchase must be in the name of the secure tenant. If he then makes a disposal within three years of purchase, there is an obligation to repay all or part of the discount, the repayment figure being reduced by one-third for each complete year after purchase (Housing Act 1985, s.155). A disposal for these purposes is a further conveyance of the freehold or an assignment of the lease, or the grant of a lease for a term of more than 21 years, otherwise than at a rack rent. There are certain "exempt" disposals, the most relevant for older people being if the property is vested in a beneficiary under a will or intestacy, in settlement of an order under the Inheritance (Provision for Family and Dependants) Act 1975 or if there are rearrangements within a family whereby joint purchasers redistribute amongst themselves or to members who would originally have qualified as a joint purchaser.

It has often been the case that older tenants have built up a substantial potential discount because of the length of their tenancy but either do not have sufficient capital to purchase the property outright at the discounted price, or their income is insufficient to fund a mortgage. Many purchasers have gone ahead with a younger relative having funded the purchase price, either by paying the price outright or by taking on the responsibility of the mortgage payments. At the time such an arrangement is entered into, the different parties should seek independent advice, almost certainly culminating in a trust deed, so that it is clear how the equitable interest is to be held, who is responsible for what outgoings, that the tenant/purchaser has the right to remain in residence for as long as they wish, and what happens to the proceeds of sale on death or earlier move into residential care. It may be possible for the tenant to require any member of his family who occupies the dwellinghouse as their only or principal home to share the right to buy with him under Housing Act 1985, s.123. Such a person may be his spouse or have been residing with him throughout the period of 12 months ending with the giving of notice, or the landlord must consent. Even if the property is purchased in joint names, a trust deed setting out the formalities of the arrangement while the relationship is still a good one is advisable in case it breaks down in the future.

Disadvantages

The disadvantages of buying under this legislation include:

(i) becoming responsible for the building's insurance (and possibly service charges if the property is a flat);
(ii) being responsible for all repairs;
(iii) housing benefit towards rent disappears and there may be no help for mortgage interest, the elderly person's income may not be sufficient for them to obtain the required mortgage, although they can consider a "maturity" interest only mortgage;
(iv) if financial help towards the purchase is provided by relatives, how is the elderly person protected if there is failure to pay on the mortgage; what happens if the relationship breaks down and the relatives want to realise their investment?;
(v) having become an owner-occupier, it may be harder to move into council-owned sheltered accommodation if the time comes.

Exemptions to the right to buy

Some housing which is deemed particularly suitable for occupation by the elderly is not eligible under the right to buy legislation as it is considered important for councils to maintain their stock of special housing.[5] This specifies dwellinghouses which are one of a group of dwellinghouses which are particularly suitable, having regard to their location, size, design, heating systems and other features, for occupation by elderly persons, and which it is the practice of the landlord to let for occupation by persons aged 60 years or more or by such persons and physically disabled persons, and special facilities (such as the services of a warden) are provided. The exception also extends to individual

---

[5] See the Housing Act 1985, Sched. 5, para. 11 as substituted by the Leasehold Reform, Housing and Urban Development Act 1993 and the Housing (Preservation of Right to Buy) Regulations 1993 (S.I. 1993 No. 2241).

properties if they are considered particularly suitable for occupation by elderly persons.

Private Tenants

The tenant of a private landlord may find one of several statutes relevant to his tenancy, depending on when the tenancy was first entered into, the length of the initial term, and the amount of rent payable.

If the lease was created after January 15, 1989, it is governed by the Housing Act 1988 and is either an assured tenancy (which can only be terminated by court order) or an assured shorthold tenancy (whereby the landlord can obtain possession at the end of the term or thereafter, if an automatic statutory periodic tenancy has come into existence, by giving two months' notice stating that he wants possession).

Succession under the Housing Act 1988

In a periodic tenancy, succession is restricted to the tenant's spouse (which includes a cohabitee) provided that the deceased was the sole tenant, the spouse was occupying the dwellinghouse immediately prior to death as his or her only or principal home, and the deceased tenant was not himself a successor (Housing Act 1988, s.17); for a fixed-term assured tenancy which has not yet expired, normal succession principles apply.

Rent Act 1977

For a tenancy prior to January 15, 1989, to be protected by Rent Act 1977 there must be "a tenancy under which a dwellinghouse (which may be a house or part of a house) is let as a separate dwelling" (Rent Act 1977, s.1). The tenancy must comply with rateable value and rental limits set out in section 4 and not be excluded by the provisions of sections 5 to 16 which include tenancies at a low rent, a dwellinghouse let with other land (in addition to the garden), where payments are made for board and lodging and where the landlord is resident in the same dwelling.

Once it has been established that the tenancy is a protected one under the Rent Act 1977, a set procedure must be followed in order to obtain possession, first by service of a notice to quit and then, if the tenant has not left voluntarily (which he is not obliged to do), by obtaining a court order which will only be made if the court is satisfied that suitable alternative accommodation is or will be available by the time the order takes effect or one of the cases in Schedule 15 has been made out. Some of the more likely cases for elderly people include case 3, deterioration of the dwellinghouse, where this is due to acts of waste, neglect or default of the tenant and the property has deteriorated; case 9, where premises are required by the landlord or his family; case 12, where it is required by the owner who let it before retirement but intended to occupy it on retirement and possession is now required.

Succession under the Rent Act 1977 (Schedule 1 as amended)

A statutory tenancy by succession can be claimed by a surviving spouse (which includes a cohabitee), if any, of the original tenant if residing in the dwellinghouse immediately before the death of the original tenant; if there is no surviving spouse, any person who was a member of the original tenant's family, residing with him at the time of his death and for a period of two years beforehand. Only one succession is allowed, but if there had already been one succession prior to January 15, 1989, a second succession is permitted.

LEASEHOLD REFORM ENFRANCHISEMENT

Leasehold Reform Act 1967

This enables tenants of privately owned houses held on long leases at low rents to acquire the freehold or an extended lease. The tenant must at the time he gives notice be occupying the house as his only or main residence, and have been so occupying under a long tenancy at a low rent for the preceding three years or for periods amounting to three years in the preceding 10 years. A successor to a deceased tenant may count the previous tenant's period of residence provided that the deceased tenant was also in occupation under the tenancy, the successor becomes entitled on death and he is a member of the deceased tenant's family.

A long lease is a tenancy granted for a term of years certain exceeding 21 years (Leasehold Reform Act 1967, s.3(1)).

The right to purchase the freehold relates to houses of any value (Leasehold Reform, Housing and Urban Development Act 1993, s.63) but various rateable value limits continue to apply if an extended term is all that is required.

A low rent is defined as one "at any time when rent is not payable under the tenancy [. . .] at a yearly rate equal to more than two-thirds of the rateable value of the property" (Leasehold Reform Act 1967, s.4(1)). The relevant rateable value is the latest of March 23, 1965, the property's first appearance on the valuation list, and the first day of the term. If the property does not come within this test, then there is a second low rent test, applying to the right to acquire the freehold only, inserted as section 4A of the Leasehold Reform Act 1967 by the Leasehold Reform, Housing and Urban Development Act 1993, s.65. This applies if either no rent was paid in the initial year of the tenancy, or the aggregate rent paid in the first year did not exceed two-thirds of the letting value of the property (where the tenancy was entered into before April 1, 1963), two-thirds of the rateable value where the tenancy was entered into between April 1,

1963 and April 1, 1990, or in other cases £1,000 if the property is in Greater London or £250 elsewhere. The term "rent" does not include payments to the landlord in respect of services, repairs, maintenance or insurance.

The Leasehold Reform, Housing and Urban Development Act 1993 provides for tenants of long-lease flats to collectively enfranchise themselves, or for individuals to extend their leases by way of a new 90-year term.

RAISING INCOME FROM THE HOME

Often the major asset is the home and the older person wishes to use it to raise an income or lump sum whilst continuing to live there. There are various schemes, some designed specifically for older people, to help do this.

If local authority grants are not available, some charitable organisations, such as some ex-service groups, will lend comparatively small sums of money against the security of the property.

If the older person has sufficient income, a normal repayment loan with a bank or building society may be possible, but the term of the loan is likely to be shorter than if the loan were being made to a younger person.

Some banks and building societies provide "maturity" interest-only loans, where only the interest is payable, the capital being repaid when the property is disposed of or on death. To be eligible for such a loan, the borrower has to be at least 60 years old.

Home income plans

Home income plans, also known as mortgage annuity schemes, involve the taking-up of a loan against a proportion of the property's value. The loan is used to purchase an annuity, part of the income of which is used to pay the interest on the loan and the net balance of which is paid to the annuitant as a supplement to their income. A proportion of the annuity, calculated by reference to the annuitant's age and other factors, will be liable to income tax, which will be deducted at source, and tax relief on the loan interest is also available (Income and Corporation Taxes Act 1988, s.365).

The proportion of the property's value which can be used for such a plan varies depending on the scheme, and can have an upper capital limit. The capital outstanding on the loan is repaid when the property is sold. It is possible for the original property to be sold and the loan transferred and charged against a replacement property, but the agreement of the annuity company to the transfer loan will be required. If the property is sold and the older person goes into care, the full amount of the annuity is received, less tax, no deductions being necessary to pay the mortgage interest, and is therefore available to meet residential care fees.

In some cases it may be possible to receive a small cash sum at the start of the loan, and, in addition to take out capital protection so that, if the annuitant dies within a few years of taking out the loan, some capital is returned to the estate. In such cases the amount of annuity income will be reduced.

If the older person is on income support or council tax benefit, a Home Income Plan may well not be beneficial. The extra income from the annuity will probably disentitle them to income support and reduce the council tax benefit, resulting in the older person being no better (or not much better) off in income terms and much worse off in capital terms. It may also disentitle them to help with dental treatment and glasses.

Most schemes have a minimum age before such a plan can be taken up, generally 70 years for a single person, 150 years for the combined ages of joint applicants, with a maximum loan of 70 to 75 per cent of the house value and a minimum loan of £15,001.

The costs of a surveyor's and legal fees have to be borne in mind, as well as future funding of adequate buildings insurance cover.

Once the older person (or survivor, if a couple) dies, the annuity ceases, but until it has been discharged or the property disposed of the interest on the loan remains to be paid. In recent years, with property prices having fallen and properties more difficult to sell, some beneficiaries have found themselves receiving little in terms of inheritance and possibly a worthless property once the loan, accrued interest, and disposal charges are taken into account.

Home reversion schemes

In order to realise a more substantial capital sum, it is possible to enter into a home reversion scheme, whereby the property, or a proportion of it, is sold to a reversions company, generally for a one-off lump sum, although a few will provide an annuity. The older person remans living in their property, responsible for maintenance and normal outgoings including insurance, possibly paying a nominal rent if the entire property has been sold, and, when the property is sold on the death of the older person (or the second death in the case of a couple), the entire value or relevant proportion sold passes to the reversions company. The lump sum received by the older person is worked out on an actuarial basis, and tends to be discounted quite heavily compared with its actual value.

There are minimum age requirements which vary depending on the scheme. Again, comparisons should be made of the administrative, legal and survey fees between the various schemes available on entering such an arrangement. With some schemes it is possible to transfer the arrangements to a replacement property, or to be paid an additional sum if the older person leaves the property early, e.g. to move in with relatives or into residential care.

Roll-up loan

There are now fewer of these plans available than in the 1980s. An annuity is paid, but nothing is deducted, or only a reduced amount is paid in respect of the interest due on the capital loan against the property which was used to buy the annuity. The interest rolls up and, in times of high interest, the total amount owed can double in five to six years. There is no tax relief on such loans, and the interest rate charged tends to be slightly higher. Some arrangements require interest to be paid once the rolled-up sum equals a preset percentage, often around 80 per cent, of the property's value. This may mean that the older person has to start paying interest on the loan at a time in their lives when they are least able to afford it or to understand what has happened.

CO-OWNERSHIP

The situation may often arise where younger relatives agree to be responsible for the care of their elderly relative, rather than the elderly person giving up their home and moving into residential care. Arrangements vary, sometimes the younger relatives give up their home to move in with their elderly relative, sometimes vice versa. Such arrangements often not only mean one party giving up their existing home, but also a certain amount of expenditure on the "common" home, be it to modernise, put in suitable additional facilities such as a downstairs toilet, or to add a "granny-annex".

It is preferable if, before taking any irrevocable steps, each party has taken independent advice and they have agreed between themselves as many aspects of the arrangement as possible. Separate representation is advisable to try and counter any charge of undue influence by a young, fit relative over someone elderly and possibly also infirm.

A trial period together to see how realistic the proposition might be, is a practical move. Each party needs to realise the day-to-day difficulties of different generations living together, differences in dietary preferences, in overall lifestyle, in noise levels and noise tolerance (be it children playing lively games, young people listening to heavy metal, or deaf elderly needing a high volume for the television). In addition, agreement needs to be reached about who is responsible for which household bills and what contributions are made by whom to the housekeeping.

If improvements are to be made to the "common" home, who is to apply for planning permission and/or building regulation approval? How will the improvements be paid for? Whilst one of the home improvement grants mentioned previously might be available for some works, there are no grants available for building on an extension (granny-annex) and it can take some time for the plans to be prepared and passed, and the building works to be completed, something which the elderly person may not be able to cope with particularly well if their health has already started to deteriorate.

What is to happen to the property itself? Should any contribution to improvements be reflected on the deeds? What happens to the property if the elderly person has to go into care, or after they die? Wherever possible, not only should things be clearly agreed and documented between the parties involved, but other relatives should be kept informed about developments so that there are no unseemly squabbles at the end of the day.

If the name of the elderly person is on the deeds there is at least some form of protection if things go wrong. If the deeds are expressed by way of joint tenancy, the property will pass automatically to the surviving co-owner or co-owners although the deceased's share in the property is still an asset for inheritance tax purposes (Inheritance Tax Act 1984, s.171). The joint tenancy can be severed by either party if the agreement does not work out, or, as a co-owner, each party can also look to force a sale and/or realise their share.

If contributions are unequal, then a tenancy in common, reflecting the proportions, should offer protection for each party. If the relationship breaks down subsequently, one of the owners goes bankrupt, or a mortgagee repossesses the property, at least the elderly person has a share in the property which can be identified, although he may not get back all of his investment, if property prices have fallen or the cost of the improvements, which he has paid for, have not increased the overall value of the property by an equivalent amount.

Should the deeds be in the names of the younger relatives only, there can be problems for the elderly person establishing what they are entitled to have back should the relationship fail and/or the property be sold.

Undue influence

Often the argument of undue influence will be relied upon to protect an elderly person when the family arrangements fail. In *Avon Finance Co. Ltd. v. Bridger and another,*[6] Mr and Mrs Bridger were let down by their son who raised his contribution towards his parents' retirement home by way of a finance company loan and then failed to meet the repayments. The son had told his parents the documentation which they signed related to the building society loan, which the parents knew about and the repayments of which they were making. The finance company failed in their action to obtain possession on the grounds that they had appointed the son as agent to deal with the paperwork and should have been aware that the relationship of child and elderly parent was such that undue influence was likely to be brought to bear. There was also a failure to see that the parents were given independent advice.

Where actual undue influence is exerted by one party on another, the party influenced can have the transaction set aside: *CIBC Mortgages plc v.*

---

[6] [1985] 2 All E.R. 281.

Pitt,[7] however, if undue influence is presumed (as opposed to actual) then the party influenced has to go on and prove that the transaction has been to their manifest disadvantage. In *Cheese v. Thomas*[8] a gentleman of 86 years contributed £43,000 towards the purchase of an £83,000 property bought in the name of his nephew, who borrowed his contribution to the purchase price, and soon defaulted on the mortgage. The property was sold for only £55,000 because of the collapse of the property market. The uncle brought proceedings that the transaction be set aside on the ground of undue influence, and that he get his £43,000 back. The judge at first instance found the transaction to be manifestly disadvantageous to the plaintiff, a finding confirmed by the Court of Appeal, as he had used all his money to purchase the right to live in a house for the remainder of his life and that right was insecure and tied him to a particular house. It was ordered that the proceeds of sale be split in the proportion 43 to 40 (which resulted in the uncle receiving only £28,700 of his original investment) as the objective of equity is to restore the parties as closely as possible to their original positions, so that the transaction would be set aside so as to achieve justice for both parties, rather than the defendant alone being left to shoulder the entire loss resulting from the drop in market value.

In *Baker v. Baker*[9] undue influence was not an issue. The elderly father did not succeed in getting all his capital back after the family relationship broke down and he moved out, the Court of Appeal finding that all he had lost was the right to live in the house rent-free, which amounted to a lesser sum than his original investment of £33,950, part of the money having been a gift to the defendants as their "inheritance".

THE PROVISION OF SPECIALISED ACCOMMODATION

Sheltered housing

This generally consists of grouped bungalows or a development of self-contained, one- or two-bedroomed, flats with a resident warden, some communal facilities and an alarm system in each unit for use in an emergency. Meals are not normally provided and the warden is there to keep a neighbourly eye on residents (possibly a daily call to check all is well), and to call for help in emergencies. The warden is not there to help with shopping, cooking, cleaning, personal care or nursing. There are often communal laundry facilities and a common room for group

---

[7] [1994] 1 A.C. 200.
[8] [1994] 1 All E.R. 35.
[9] (1993) 25 H.L.R. 408.

activities centred on the complex. The maintenance of the exterior and communal areas, the overall buildings insurance, gardening (except with some bungalows), and window cleaning are not the responsibility of the residents. If the housing consists of a purpose-built block of flats, there may be some form of security in terms of locked front doors and the need to remember passcodes in order to obtain access. Most such complexes are owned and run by local authorities or housing associations, but some are now privately owned and can be purchased.

Renting

There are often long waiting lists for such accommodation and many councils will not accept applications from owner-occupiers. Some housing associations also will not consider owner-occupiers or see them as a high priority. In any event most housing associations take 50 per cent of their tenants from local authority lists, so that getting into the rented sector of this type of housing, if you are an owner-occupier, can be rather difficult.

The tenant pays a rent which is based upon a realistic rent for the type of bedsitter, flat or bungalow provided and taking into account the additional costs of providing the warden and other communal services. Sometimes the rent includes a charge to cover mains services such as fuel and water, sometimes these have to be paid for separately to the relevant utility on a normal invoice.

Financial help towards the rent is available in the form of housing benefit, if the tenant does not have sufficient income and/or capital resources (less than £16,000) to fund the rent in his own right. Housing benefit is payable in respect of the rent and eligible service charges which include services such as the cleaning of communal areas, entry 'phones, caretakers, and emergency alarm systems in premises designed, adapted or particularly suitable for older people, but housing benefit is not available towards the water or fuel element of the sheltered accommodation charges (Housing Benefit (General) Regulations 1987[10]). The tenancy agreement is generally in the form of an assured tenancy in respect of tenants who have gone into occupation in recent years.[11]

Buying sheltered housing

The facilities offered in private complexes available for purchase on a long lease are similar to those provided in such accommodation run by local authorities or housing associations. Once the developer has

---

[10] S.I. 1987 No. 1971.
[11] See generally the Housing Act 1988.

completed the building works, it generally hands over the freehold to a separate management organisation which assumes responsibility for running the scheme. It is the management organisation which employs the warden and provides the other services. In addition to the lease-holder paying his own council tax, mains service bills and ground rent, there is a service charge to pay for those services provided by the management organisation. Provision is generally made in the service charge for part of the monies to go into a "sinking fund" for long-term major repairs and redecorations, although sometimes the contribution to the "sinking fund" is taken as a lump sum out of the proceeds of any sale of the accommodation. Serious consideration at the time of purchase needs to be given to the service charge; likely rises in the future, what it covers, and what happens about payment for major repairs.

There are likely to be restrictions with regard to any resale, the most common being that a purchaser must be over the age of 55, although some developers will allow children to buy such accommodation for their parents, the restriction being that the permanent occupier of the accommodation must be over 55 years.

There can also be problems as to whether the flat owner sells the property privately or by employing his own estate agent, or whether he is obliged to use the management organisation to negotiate the sale and, in either case, whether or not the management organisation levies an administration charge.

It is possible to enter into a variety of schemes whereby only part of the purchase price is paid. Some schemes mean only a percentage of the lease (say 70 per cent) is purchased, the balanced funded by a Housing Corporation subsidy, and on sale, only 70 per cent of the property's market value is paid over. Some builders will sell at a discounted price and again, the purchaser only receives back the same percentage of any resale price, unless the discounted price was a sales ploy to generate quick sales.

Shared membership schemes, often with housing associations, mean that rent is paid in respect of the percentage of the property unpurchased if that share of the property is more than 25 per cent. The full service charge still has to be paid. Most shared ownership schemes give the elderly person the same legal protection as is afforded to those buying leasehold property outright.

If the elderly person is purchasing the accommodation by way of mortgage, there may be help through income support in respect of interest payments for the mortgage. Income support may also be available to help towards the service charge.

Builders' sheltered housing schemes must comply with the National House Building Council's Sheltered Housing Code of Practice, which came into force on April 1, 1990, and which applies to all sheltered housing sold after that date, be it new or second-hand. Builders are instructed to ensure residents' rights are protected by a legally binding agreement between the builder and the management organisation and any builder in breach of the Code can be subject to disciplinary action.

HOMELESSNESS

The duties of local authorities towards homeless people are contained in
Part III of the Housing Act 1985. The local authority must provide
"suitable" accommodation (s.69) for persons who are:

(a) homeless (s.58);
(b) in priority need (s.59);
(c) not homeless intentionally (s.60); and
(d) who can satisfy the local connection test in sections 61 and 67(2).

The statutory provisions should be read in the light of the *Code of Guidance
for Local Authorities*.[12]

Homelessness defined

A person may be homeless even if he has accommodation which he is
entitled to occupy if it is "not reasonable for him to occupy the premises"
(s.58(2A)); an amendment introduced by section 14(2) of the Housing and
Planning Act 1986. Overcrowding, lack of facilities and medical needs
may thus be taken into account, as in *R. v. Wycombe Borough Council, ex p.
Homes*[13] where the accommodation was at the top of a hill and difficult to
get to; the applicant, who had difficulty walking, was "homeless". If the
local authority fails to take all relevant evidence, including medical
evidence, into account, any subsequent decision is challengeable by
judicial review: *R. v. Bath City Council, ex p. Sangermano*.[14]

Elderly people who only have a licence to occupy property because
they live, for example, with relatives, may be made homeless, or
threatened with homelessness (s.58(4)) because of domestic disputes. It
is worthwhile in such circumstances to make an application to the local
authority, particularly as any accommodation offered in consequence
must be "suitable" (s.69). This is likely to rule out bed and breakfast
accommodation for the majority of elderly people. A referral to the local
authority social services department for an assessment of need under
section 47 of the National Health Service and Community Care Act 1990
may trigger the process, as the social services authority may invite the
housing authority, when possible housing needs are identified, "to
assist, to such extent as is reasonable in the circumstances, in the making
of the assessment" (s.47(3)(b)).

---

[12] *Code of Guidance for Local Authorities* (3rd ed., 1993).
[13] *Legal Action*, December 1989, p. 15.
[14] (1984) 17 H.L.R. 94.

Priority need

"A person who is vulnerable as a result of old age, mental illness or handicap or physical disability or other special reason" has a priority need for accommodation (s.59(1)(*c*)).

The benefit of this also extends to people "with whom such a person resides or might reasonably be expected to reside." Vulnerability however must relate specifically to the ability to secure accommodation for oneself and in *R. v. Tower Hamlets London Borough Council, ex p. Begum*[15] it was held that an adult lacking mental capacity was not owed duties under Part III of the Housing Act. The applicant herself would not have been able to respond to the local authority's offer of accommodation which she was seeking on behalf of herself and her family. Her family could not qualify for housing because they were intentionally homeless. The relevant duty owed to a mentally incapacitated adult by the local authority was that contained in the National Assistance Act 1948, s.21.[16] The decision appears to run contrary to the trend of providing care in the community for disabled people and their carers.

Paragraph 6.9 of the Code of Practice, whilst encouraging local authorities to adopt a "flexible and pragmatic" approach to assessing the needs of the elderly, nevertheless militates against a finding of vulnerability on the basis of chronological age alone:

> "authorities should look not just at whether people are old, but at the extent to which their age has made it hard for them to fend for themselves."

Persons who do not have a priority need, but who are homeless, are owed a duty to provide advice and assistance in any attempts that they may make in securing accommodation (s.65(4)).

Intentional homelessness

Intentional homelessness may relate to a failure to keep up rent or mortgage payments, or to positive action such as the causing of a nuisance or another breach of a tenancy agreement. Paragraph 7.4 of the Code of Practice however makes clear that any act or omission must have been intentional, and should not be construed as such either where the applicant was in "real financial difficulties", or where he or she was incapable of managing their affairs. Persons who are intentionally homeless, but nevertheless in priority need, are owed a lesser duty by the local authority; to ensure that accommodation is made available for his occupation for such period as they consider will give him a reasonable opportunity of securing permanent accommodation (s.65(3)(*b*)).

---

[15] [1993] 2 All E.R. 65.
[16] See Chap. 2—The Delivery of Social Services, p. 17.

Local connection

The applicant does not have to prove a local connection with the authority to which he applies for housing. However, if he has a local connection elsewhere, that other authority can be expected to provide him with accommodation (s.67). People who have moved to live with relatives, prior to them having being made homeless, will however be protected from referral by section 67(1) if he or the person with whom the applicant can reasonably be expected to reside has a local connection with the authority to which the application is made. A local connection can exist through residence, employment, family associations or "special circumstances" (s.61(1)). Domestic violence, or the threat of such violence overrides the "local connection" provisions (s.67(2)(c)) to enable the victim to remain in the new area.

Challenging local authority decisions

Decisions may be challenged for the failure to take relevant considerations into account, for the application of a wrong legal test in any of the criteria that need to be proved, and for bias or inadequacy in the procedure used to establish homelessness.

A failure to make available suitable alternative accommodation in discharge of their duty towards the applicant is also challengeable by way of judicial review. The authority must consider representations made by the applicant as to why any particular accommodation is unsuitable (for example, medical evidence): R. v. Wycombe District Council, ex p. Hazeltine.[17]

Damages may also be available in an action for breach of statutory duty; as in R. v. Lambeth London Borough Council, ex p. Barnes (Olive),[18] where the applicant had spent over a year waiting for permanent accommodation. The Code of Practice suggests any temporary arrangements made should be as short as possible, when the authority has a duty to secure permanent accommodation, and it should not be used automatically or as a deterrent (para. 13.2).

An interim mandatory injunction[19] may be sought to require the housing authority to continue to provide accommodation whilst proceedings for judicial review are continuing. The applicant must however be able to show that he has a very strong case.[20] Such a tactic may be necessary as an adverse decision under section 64(1) on the duty to provide permanent accommodation would normally extinguish the duty under section 63(1) to provide temporary accommodation.

---

[17] (1993) 25 H.L.R. 313, C.A.
[18] (1993) 25 H.L.R. 140.
[19] See p. 104.
[20] R. v. Westminster City Council, ex p. Augustin [1993] 1 W.L.R. 730.

Chapter 11
Welfare Benefits and Finance

In any consideration of welfare benefits basic distinctions can be drawn between contributory and non-contributory benefits and means tested and non-means tested benefits. A general codification of the law took place in 1992 with what is now the Social Security (Contributions and Benefits) Act 1992 (S.S.C.B.A. 1992). The mixture of statute law and regulations is, however, exceedingly complex, and reference will need to be made to specialist texts when dealing with individual cases. Only those benefits of most direct relevance to people over the age of 60 or 65 are considered here.

RETIREMENT PENSIONS

Eligibility

Entitlement to a retirement pension depends upon the following factors:

(1) Having reached "pensionable age" which is 65 for a man, and 60 for a woman (S.S.C.B.A. 1992, s.122(1)). This rule discriminates on grounds of sex, but is not contrary to European law: *R. v. Secretary of State for Social Security, ex p. Equal Opportunities Commission.*[1] Article 7 of the European Community Directive on Social Security of December 19, 1978 on the progressive implementation of the principle of equal treatment for men and women in matters of social security allows member states for the time-being to set different ages for men and women to become entitled to retirement pensions. This "derogation" may, however, not be applicable to transitions from disability benefits at pensionable age (see below for discussion of this in relation to particular benefits).

(2) Making a claim for a pension to be paid. Only a maximum of 12 months will be paid in arrears (Social Security (Claims and Payments) Regulations 1987, reg. 19 and Sched. 4[2]). However, it is

---

[1] Case 9/91: [1992] 3 C.M.L.R. 233.
[2] S.I. 1987 No. 1968.

not necessary to give up work in order to claim a retirement pension and any earnings will not reduce the amount of pension received. A pension which is not claimed will be treated as deferred. However, women aged under 65 and receiving a widow's pension will be automatically granted a retirement pension and will not need to claim.

(3) The contribution conditions must be satisfied; this is an amalgam of the contributions record calculated over the working life. A category A retirement pension (S.S.C.B.A. 1992, ss.44 to 46) is payable on the claimant's own contribution record; a category B pension on the spouse's contribution record (S.S.C.B.A. 1992, ss.49 to 51) and a category D pension (S.S.C.B.A. 1992, s.78) is a non-contributory pension payable to those over 80 years.

All retirement pensions are taxable and taken fully into account for income support purposes.

Amounts payable

The pension paid may consist of a basic pension, plus an additional pension (based on earnings after April 5, 1979, under the state earnings related pension scheme, "SERPS", unless contracted out) (Social Security Pensions Act 1975, s.29) and a graduated pension (based on contributions between April 1961 and April 1975) (Social Security (Graduated Retirement Benefit) (No. 2) Regulations 1978.[3] An age addition of 25p a week is paid to those over 80 years. Persons in receipt of graduated retirement benefit who are over 80 are also entitled to an age addition: Social Security (Widows Benefit and Retirement Pensions) Amendment Regulations 1993.[4] A higher pension will be paid to those who defer entitlement to pension (see below).

Crediting contributions

The married woman's or widow's reduced rate contributions do not count towards pension entitlement. Home responsibilities protection was introduced from 1978 for those receiving child benefit for a child under 16, those in receipt of income support who do not have to sign on as unemployed because they are a carer, and those people who for 48 weeks in a relevant tax year spend 35 hours a week looking after someone receiving either the higher or middle rates of disability living allowance care component, attendance allowance, or constant attendance allowance (Social Security Pensions (Home Responsibilities & Miscellaneous Amendments) Regulations 1978, reg. 2).[5] Protection is automatic on the

---

[3] S.I. 1978 No. 393.
[4] S.I. 1993 No. 1242.
[5] S.I. 1978 No. 508.

first two heads, but has to be claimed if only the third condition is satisfied. However, a year in which a woman has elected reduced liability for contributions cannot be a year of home responsibility. Years of home responsibility are deducted from the number of years for which a person would otherwise have to satisfy the contribution conditions. Men aged 60 to 65 years who take early retirement from work will be credited with Class 1 credits if these are needed to fulfil their contribution conditions (Social Security (Credits) Regulations 1975, reg. 9A).[6]

Deferring the retirement pension

For the first five years after reaching pensionable age, it is possible to defer entitlement to either Category A or Category B pension or graduated retirement benefit and to accumulate thereby entitlement to a higher rate of pension. The amount thus gained is slightly less generous for those who reached pensionable age before April 6, 1979 (Social Security Act 1975, s.28(4)), but for those who retired after that date deferment for a whole five-year period will lead to an increase of 37 per cent on the basic retirement pension each week (S.S.C.B.A. 1992, Sched. 5, paras. 1 and 2). However, any day on which unemployment benefit, statutory sick pay or sickness benefit or invalidity benefit is paid cannot be counted towards the deferment of pension. A widow will become entitled to the increase that her husband would have gained provided that she does not remarry before the age of 60. A widower will be similarly entitled on his wife's deferment but only if he was over pensionable age when she died. There is a particular difficulty with women who are claiming graduated retirement benefit on their own limited contributions whilst their husbands defer their own pension. Prior to the decision in *Chief Adjudication Officer v. Pearse*[7] they were told by the Department of Social Security that by claiming their benefit in their own right, they were disentitled to any increase in their Category B pension awarded when their husband eventually received his deferred pension. According to the Court of Appeal in *Chief Adjudication Officer v. Pearse*[8] this was a misinterpretation of the law, and those affected are advised to ask leave to make a late appeal to the Social Security Appeal Tribunal against any decision to refuse an increment. New regulations in 1992, however, reinstated the receipt of graduated benefit as an obstacle to receiving an increment (Social Security (Widow's Benefit and Retirement Pensions) Amendment Regulations 1992).[9] In the majority of cases, therefore, married women whose husbands are deferring their pension

---

[6] S.I. 1975 No. 556.
[7] *The Times*, June 18, 1992.
[8] *ibid.*
[9] S.I. 1992 No. 1695.

will be best advised to defer the receipt of any small amount of graduated retirement benefit to which they may themselves be entitled.

The process of cancelling a decision to defer payment of pension is called de-retirement, and this can be done only once. A man whose wife is entitled to a Category B pension on his contributions cannot de-retire without his wife's consent (S.S.C.B.A. 1992, s.53(4)).

Proposals for change

The government has announced that the pensionable age for women will be increased from 60 to 65 between the years 2010 to 2020.[10] This will affect women born after April 5, 1950. The five-year maximum time-limit for deferment of pension is also to be abolished, and each year of deferment will produce an increment of 10 per cent as opposed to the current 7.5 per cent.

Retirement pension for widows and widowers

Widows who were under 60 when their husband died, and who have not remarried, can claim on their own or their husband's contribution record once they reach pensionable age (S.S.C.B.A. 1992, s.38). Widows who were over 60 years when their husband died and not receiving the full basic pension, will be able to claim a full pension based on his contribution record. Any additional pension is paid in full; but only one-half of any graduated pension based on his contributions. A retirement pension based on a late husband's contributions is not lost by remarrying over the age of 60, or by living with a man as his wife.

Men who were widowed on or after April 6, 1979, and who do not have enough contributions of their own, can rely on their late wife's contributions provided they do not remarry before they reach pensionable age.[11]

Pensions and people who are divorced

Those who are divorced after pensionable age, or who divorce before pensionable age and do not remarry, may be entitled to a retirement pension based on the contribution record of their former spouse. The spouse's contribution record throughout the years of marriage up to and including the year in which the decree was made absolute can be taken into account. If a person has been married more than once, only the most recent marriage counts for these purposes. These rules do not apply to

---

[10] See *Equality in State Pension Age*, Cm. 2420 (1994): see also D.H.S.S. leaflet EQPI.
[11] Social Security (Contributions and Benefits) Act 1992, s.48; see also Social Security (Widow's Benefit and Retirement Pensions) Regulations 1979 (S.I. 1979 No. 642).

those who were divorced before they reached pensionable age on April 5, 1979 (S.S.C.B.A. 1992, s.48(2)).

OCCUPATIONAL PENSIONS

Occupational pension schemes provided by employers give pension and life assurance benefits to employees which are separate from the benefits provided by the state. Section 53(2) of the Social Security (Pensions) Act 1975 first provided that approved pension schemes should be available to men and women on equal terms. This is backed up by section 2 of the Sex Discrimination Act 1986 which makes provisions relating to retirement, including the introduction of a maximum retirement age, unlawful if they involve discrimination against women. Payment of an occupational pension, however, will operate so as to reduce the amount of unemployment benefit payable, even though this is less favourable to men than to women, as at the age of 60 women will move on to retirement pension: see Social Security Decision No. R(U) 3/92.

Job mobility was enhanced as a result of section 10 of the Social Security Act 1986 which required that after two years' membership all occupational pension schemes must preserve a member's benefits rather than refund the contributions made. General and specific information relating to the operation of occupational pension schemes and entitlement under them must be given on request.[12]

The vast majority of occupational pension schemes are contracted out of the additional pension "earnings related" part of the state scheme (SERPS). The state scheme, however, will make up any shortfall of what the occupational scheme will pay compared to the additional pension which otherwise would have accrued. See Social Security leaflet NP 46 for details on calculations of this. Though a minimum level of return is thus assured, state funds cannot wholly compensate for bad investments made by occupational pension schemes.

Employees who do not wish to belong to their employer's occupational pension scheme, and those who are self-employed, may take out a personal pension, according to the provisions of section 18 of the Finance (No.2) Act 1987. Contracting out of the state scheme is available only to those paying Class 1 national insurance contributions. The position of widows and widowers is protected by the Occupational Pension Schemes (Protected Rights) Regulations 1987 and the Occupational and Personal Pension Schemes (Miscellaneous Amendments) Regulations 1992.[13]

---

[12] Occupational Pension Scheme (Disclosure of Information) Regulations 1986 (S.I. 1986 No. 1046). General regulation of both occupational and personal pensions is provided by the Pension Schemes Act 1993.
[13] S.I. 1987 No. 1117 and S.I. 1992 No. 1531 respectively.

Occupational pensions and the earnings rules

A person residing with a dependant and claiming an increase for them in invalidity benefit, severe disablement allowance or Category A retirement pension will not have an increase paid if their dependent earns more than £45.45 per week: Social Security Benefits (Dependency) Regulations 1977, regs. 8(2) and 12.[14]

In *Cottingham and Geary v. Secretary of State for Social Security*[15] the Court of Appeal decided that it was unlawful to take a wife's occupational pension into account as if it were earnings. The decision affects claims between March 11, 1988 and December 5, 1992. The Department of Social Security applies what are known as the "anti-test case" rules as a reason for not paying arrears prior to the date of the successful appeal: this policy may however be circumvented by seeking leave to make a late appeal to a Social Security Appeal Tribunal.

Occupational pensions and the equality of treatment

Equality of provision between men and women in occupational pension schemes has been considered by the European Court of Justice in two landmark judgments; *Barber v. Guardian Royal Exchange Assurance Group*[15a] and the *"Coloroll"* case.[15b] Both concerned the proper interpretation of Article 119 of the Treaty of Rome that men and women should receive equal pay for equal work. It was decided in *Barber* that a pension from an occupational pension scheme was to be considered as pay for the purposes of Article 119. *Coloroll* took this further by requiring equal access to pension schemes for part-time as well as full-time workers, and by equalising the age at which a full pension is payable. This means that part-timers will be entitled to make up missing contributions in order to qualify for a pension upon retirement, but it also means that the pensionable age for women in occupational schemes will be equalised with that of men. Normally this will mean that women will have to wait until the age of 65 for a full pension; and retiring at age 60 will in future be regarded as "early retirement" with lower entitlement. Non-service related benefits such as fixed lump-sum payments on death, must be paid at the same level for both sexes.

PERSONAL PENSIONS

Personal pensions are a new form of saving for retirement made possible by the provisions of section 54 of the Finance (No.2) Act 1987, and are now the only form of private pension provision available to the self-

---

[14] S.I. 1977 No. 343.
[15] [1993] Pensions Law Reports 79, C.A.
[15a] Case C–262/88: [1991] 1 Q.B. 344, European Ct.
[15b] Vroege (C–57/93) and Fischer (C–128/93), *Financial Times*, October 4, 1994, E.C.J.

employed. Persons in employment and paying full-rate national insurance contributions may choose a personal pension in preference to membership of an occupational pension scheme. Tax relief on enhanced contributions to personal pension schemes is increased incrementally for those aged 50 or over. Incentive payments by way of an additional rebate on national insurance contributions formerly applied to both personal and occupational pension schemes contracted out of SERPS. However, section 1 of the Social Security Act 1993 restricts such incentive payments to personal pension schemes, thus making personal pension schemes on this basis marginally more attractive than contracted out occupational pension schemes, but also limits the payment of the addition to those aged over 30 in the relevant tax year. Choosing a personal pension scheme requires proper professional advice, as does making the choice between a personal and an occupational pension, especially as the latter may include sickness and widows' benefits not available in a personal pension scheme. The state scheme (SERPS), based on the national insurance system, remains available to those who have neither an occupational nor a personal pension.

People who were improperly advised not to join or to leave occupational pension schemes in favour of taking out a personal pension may be able to claim compensation for losses thus incurred. This follows the publication in October 1994 of the Securities and Investment Board inquiry, entitled *Pension Transfers and Opt-Outs—Review of Past Business*. Reviews of relevant transactions during the periods 1988 to 1994 will be carried out over a two-year period. The scheme does not however cover those who opted out of SERPS during the same period.

WIDOWS' BENEFITS

Entitlement to widows' benefits depends entirely on the husband's contribution record, except where the husband died as the result of an industrial accident or disease, in which case the contributions condition is treated as satisfied automatically. Industrial death benefit is still paid to the widows of those who died from these causes before April 11, 1988.

Benefits comprise:

(i) the widow's payment, which is a lump sum payment of £1,000;
(ii) widowed mother's allowance; and
(iii) widow's pension.

Widow's payment is payable to women under 60 years when their husband died, or those over 60 years whose husbands were not entitled to a category A retirement pension (S.S.C.B.A. 1992, s.36). Entitlement is thus mainly limited to younger widows. Widowed mother's allowance is payable to women who are either pregnant by their husband or entitled to child benefit in respect of a qualifying child as defined by the

S.S.C.B.A. 1992, s.37(2). Widow's pension is payable to women up to the age of 65, though from 60 years onwards they can elect to draw retirement pension instead; this may be advantageous if any graduated pension is payable. The minimum qualifying age for widows' pension is 40 years if the husband died before April 11, 1988, or 45 years if he died after that date. However, women aged under 55 when they first qualified for their pension will receive a reduced amount.

Widowed mother's allowance and widow's pension are taxable but will not be affected by earnings. Remarriage brings entitlement to an end, but cohabitation only suspends entitlement.

INCOME SUPPORT

Income support is a non-contributory means tested benefit available to those whose assessed income is lower than the "applicable amount" needed to live on (S.S.C.B.A. 1992, s.124). People who have savings in excess of £8,000 or who work for 16 or more hours in a week are not eligible for income support. Income support is a "passport" benefit to other types of help such as housing and/or council tax benefit, renovating grants, free prescriptions, dental treatment, vouchers for glasses and fares to hospital. Generally, income support is paid in arrears at the end of a "benefit week"; however people over pensionable age or who are receiving a retirement pension or widow's pension are paid income support in advance. People who are over 60 years (men or women) do not have to "sign on" as unemployed in order to receive income support; as either one of a couple living together can claim, it is sensible for the one who does not have to sign on to do so.

Premiums

In calculating the "applicable amount", any one of nine different client group premiums may be added to the basic weekly rates to produce the sum of money actually payable. If more than one premium is payable generally only the larger will be paid. There are higher rates if you are claiming as a couple. The premiums are:

(i)   the disability premium;
(ii)   the pensioner premium (60 to 74);
(iii)   the enhanced pensioner premium (75 to 79);
(iv)   the higher pensioner premium (80-plus or disabled);
(v)   the lone parent premium;
(vi)   the family premium;
(vii)   the disabled child premium;
(viii) the carer premium;
(ix)   the severe disability premium.

The disability premium

The disability premium is payable only while the person who qualifies (and his/her partner) is aged under 60; over that age the higher pensioner premium will be paid (this is more generous). The severe disability premium, however, does continue after the age of 60, when it will be paid on top of the higher pension premium.

The severe disability premium

Severe disability premium will be paid to a single person who either receives the disability living allowance care component at the middle or higher rate, or the attendance allowance (or constant attendance allowance), and who is living alone and has no-one who receives invalid care allowance for looking after them. The qualifying conditions for each of a disabled couple are the same, but benefit will be halved if someone receives invalid care allowance for looking after one of the couple. It is quite possible to receive disability living allowance or attendance allowance for your own needs whilst looking after someone else[15c]; in this situation the carer premium is payable. The rules relating to "living alone" are complex but exclude those living with a "close relative", for example, a son, a daughter, parent, brother or sister: see *Chief Adjudication Officer v. Foster*[16] upholding the validity of the Income Support (General) Amendment (No.3) Regulations 1989.[17] Such a person is not regarded as living alone even if there is joint legal liability to pay rent or mortgage, or if the arrangement is a commercial one. However, if the accommodation is entirely separate, *e.g.* a granny flat, the person is treated as living alone and the severe disability premium can still be paid. Those people who are co-owners or joint tenants with a close relative and who were in receipt of income support with a severe disability premium before October 21, 1991, are protected by Income Support (General) Amendment (No. 6) Regulations 1991, reg. 4(9)[18] from the harsher rules which now apply.

The family premium

The family premium is payable if there is a child under the age of 19 in the household for which a claim is being made. Only one premium is paid, irrespective of the number of qualifying children. The lone parent premium is paid on top of the family premium, but not if the claimant is also entitled to disability premium or any of the pensioner premiums.

[15c] Determination of the rate of payment is based on the claimant's own personal needs, and not any additional needs she may have, *e.g.* for supervision, when getting up in the night to tend to a disabled husband: *Miller v. Secretary of State for Social Services, The Times,* May 4, 1994.
[16] [1993] 2 W.L.R. 292.
[17] S.I. 1989 No. 1678.
[18] S.I. 1991 No. 2334.

The carer premium

The carer premium can be awarded in addition to any other premium; it is paid to anyone who actually receives invalid care allowance or who has an underlying entitlement to invalid care allowance but cannot be paid it because of the overlapping benefit rules.

The pensioner premium and the enhanced pensioner premium

The pensioner premium is payable where the claimant, or their partner, or both, are between 60 and 74 years, and the enhanced pensioner premium is payable to those between 75 and 79 years (inclusive).

The higher pensioner premium

The higher pensioner premium is payable to all those over 80 years, or to those over 60 years who satisfy the requirements for the disability premium in that they or their partner are disabled or they themselves are incapacitated. "Disabled" in this context means either being registered blind or being in receipt of a qualifying benefit such as disability living allowance, attendance allowance, disability working allowance, invalidity benefit or severe disability allowance. "Incapacitated" means being incapable of work for 28 weeks prior to the claim, and continuing to be incapable of work at the time of making the claim. Normally, entitlement to a disability premium on the grounds of incapacity is limited to those aged under 60. However, under the "eight-week linking rule" those who were continuously in receipt of income support, including disability premium, within eight weeks of their 60th birthday, can progress to receive the higher premium as long as there is no subsequent break in entitlement to income support amounting to eight weeks or more. By a further application of the eight-week linking rule the claimant's entitlement to higher pensioner premium will continue even if the only reason they received higher pensioner premium was because their partner qualified under the disability condition. If their partner subsequently dies or separates from them, the higher pensioner premium will continue to be paid, provided there is no break of eight weeks or more in the claim for income support.

Working out the income support "applicable amount"

The "applicable amount" beyond which income support is paid is calculated according to a formula which includes:

(i) the personal allowance (the basic allowance for a single person, or a couple, and any dependent children);
(ii) any premium payable;
(iii) any income support housing costs;
(iv) any residential allowances.

Income support housing costs relate to mortgages and loans (housing benefit is available to tenants of the local authority, housing associations and private landlords). Claimants over the age of 60 are allowed more generous housing costs in that they are exempt from the rule that during the first 16 weeks of any claim to income support, only 50 per cent of any eligible interest payments on mortgages and loans can be included in the assessment. Interest on existing loans acquired for repairs or improvements to a home are counted as eligible housing costs for income support purposes: Income Support (General) Amendment Regulations 1993.[19] No deduction from housing costs for non-dependants over the age of 18 will be made in respect of any claimant who is, or whose partner is, registered blind, or who receives the care component of disability living allowance, attendance allowance or constant attendance allowance.

Those who are resident in a nursing home or residential care home will be eligible for a "residential allowance" of (from April 1995) £48 per week (£53 in London). For further details, see Chapter 5—Residential Care.

Calculating resources

Part V of and Schedules 8, 9, and 10 to the Income Support (General) Regulations 1987[20] cover the assessment of resources. Actual income, in some cases "notional" income for unpaid work, maintenance payments and any benefits payable under the national insurance scheme are all regarded as income. Attendance allowance and disability living allowance are disregarded except for those in residential or nursing care. An additional "tariff" income is also assumed, whether or not it is actually paid, from any capital between £3,000.01 and £8,000; this is calculated at the rate of £1 per week for every £250 (or part of £250) over £3,000. In particular the following types of capital are disregarded:

(i) the value of your home;
(ii) any arrears of benefit payable;
(iii) the value of any personal possessions;
(iv) the surrender value of a life insurance policy; and
(v) any payment from the independent living fund.

However, there are special rules relating to deprivation of capital (reg. 51(1)) "for the purpose of securing entitlement to income support or increasing the amount of that benefit", which allow the value of that capital (actual, not notional, capital) to be taken into account in calculating entitlement to income support. Giving capital to friends or relatives would come within the provision, or purchasing luxury items

---

[19] S.I. 1993 No. 30. The Income Support (General) Amendment Regulations 1994 (S.I. 1994 No. 1004) designate most loans taken out *whilst on income support* to buy or acquire an interest in the home as non-eligible. One exception is loans taken out or increased to make adaptations to meet the needs of a disabled person.
[20] S.I. 1987 No. 1967.

for one's own use, provided the relevant intention could be proved. The full value of the capital thus divested will not, however, be taken into account for all time; the diminishing capital rule in regulation 51A will reduce its notional value over time.

THE SOCIAL FUND

The social fund, which replaces the system of single discretionary payments administered by the Department of Social Security under the old supplementary benefits system, is in fact two distinct systems, one concerned with the making of regulated payments to which there is access as of right, and the second dealing with discretionary payments and loans, the availability of which are limited by budgetary constraints (S.S.C.B.A. 1992, s.138).

(1) Regulated payments

Decisions in respect of regulated payments are made by adjudication officers and are subject to the right of appeal to a Social Security Appeal Tribunal. Regulated payments comprise maternity payments, payments for funeral expenses and cold weather payments.

Funeral payments
Payments for funeral expenses extend to those in receipt of income support, family credit, disability working allowance, housing benefit or council tax benefit. The relevant regulations are the Social Fund Maternity and Funeral Expenses (General) Regulations 1987.[21] A claim may be made from the date of the death up to three months after the funeral, or up to 12 months after the funeral if there is a "good cause" for the delay. Claims may be made by a "close relative" who has taken responsibility for the funeral or cremation, which must have taken place in the United Kingdom. The reasonable cost of all essential expenses for a "simple" funeral will be made, including the cost of one return journey to arrange or to attend the funeral. The following are deducted from the funeral payment:

(i) any savings that the claimant may have above £500 (£1,000 if aged over 60);
(ii) any of the deceased's assets which are available without probate of letters of administration being granted; arrears of attendance allowance come within this category[22];

---

[21] S.I. 1987 No. 481. See also the Social Fund Maternity and Funeral Expenses (General) Amendment Regulations 1994 (S.I. 1994 No. 506).
[22] Social Security Decision No. R(IS) 12/93.

(iii) any sum due to the claimant because of death, for example from an insurance company or occupational pension scheme, but not a widow's payment[23];

(iv) any contribution from a charity or relative, except where this is for non-essential items.

Additional expenses, for example, other travelling expenses, *may* be met from the discretionary part of the social fund.

Cold weather payments
Cold weather payments of £7 (£8.50 from November 1, 1995) a week will be made on those rare occasions when the Metrological Office declares a "period of cold weather" defined as any seven-day period during which the average of the actual or forecasted mean daily temperature is at or below freezing. Payment will be made to those who qualify on the following grounds:

(i)   they receive a disabled child premium;
(ii) they are responsible for a child under 5 years;
(iii) they receive a disability or severe disability premium or any of the pensioner premiums.

The Social Fund Cold Weather Payments (General) Amendment Regulations 1993[24] disentitle people in receipt of a residential allowance (that is those in residential care) from cold weather payments.

(2) Discretionary payments

Decisions on discretionary payments from the social fund are made by social fund officers, and are reviewed by social fund inspectors; there is no right of appeal to a tribunal (Social Fund (Application for Review) Regulations 1988[25]).

Three types of help are available:

(1) crisis loans;
(2) budgeting loans;
(3) community care grants.

Crisis loans
Crisis loans can be given to meet short-term needs in an emergency, or after a disaster such as a fire or flood. Even people not on income support may qualify, provided they have no savings, and no access to any funds to meet their needs. The maximum loan is £1,000. The loan must be the only means of preventing serious risk to the health or safety of any member of the applicant's family.

---

[23] reg. 8.
[24] S.I. 1993 No. 2450.
[25] S.I. 1988 No. 34.

Budgeting loans
Budgeting loans are available only to people who have been in receipt of income support for 26 weeks. Savings above £1,000 will disqualify them (£500 if aged under 60). The highest amount of money that can be outstanding at any one time is £1,000. Their purpose is to spread large one-off expenses over a long period. Repayment is usually through deductions from weekly benefit; no loan will be given to a person assessed as unable to repay it. The normal maximum repayment period is 78 weeks. Budgeting loans (Secretary of State's Directions, para. 12) are not available for domestic assistance and respite care, housing costs including residential charges, or medical, surgical, optical, aural or dental items or services.

Community care grants
Community care grants come out of a different budget from that for loans. The same savings restrictions apply. They are payments to help people move out of institutions into the community, or to avoid going into institutional care. If a local authority has a statutory duty to meet a particular need, for example, under section 2 of the Chronically Sick and Disabled Persons Act 1970, a community care grant cannot be made available to meet that need.

Priority groups include elderly people, people with all types of disability, including those who are chronically sick, families under stress, and people without "a settled way of life" who are undergoing resettlement. Examples (not exhaustive) of community care grants are:

(i)   setting-up home or start-up grants;
(ii) removal expenses;
(iii) connection and reconnection fees for fuel and domestic appliances (but not telephone installation);
(iv) furniture and domestic appliances;
(v)   bedding;
(vi) travelling expenses to visit a patient in hospital, or residential care.

As the capacity to make such grants depends upon other demands on the budget, availability is likely to differ from place to place and from time to time.

The community care element of the grant has a number of different elements:

(1) Enabling people to stay out of care, by the provision of a number of aids to daily living such as high seat chairs or orthopaedic mattresses, or extra bedding in cases of incontinence.
(2) Enabling people to move to more suitable accommodation by paying removal costs and the costs of refurnishing. A crisis loan (see above) may be available for the payment of rent in advance.
(3) Enabling people to move house to care for elderly friends or relatives, as well as enabling the elderly person themselves to move nearer to sources of support.

(4) Enabling people to re-establish themselves in the community following a stay in institutional or residential care. In *R. v. Secretary of State for
Social Services, ex p. Stitt; R. v. Social Security Fund Inspector, ex p.
Sherwin; R. v. Same, ex p. Roberts,*[26] it was held that undue importance
should not be attached to administrative guidance which took into
account only stays of more than three months. The place where
care has been provided must however be an institution specifically
set up to provide care for those unable to live independently.

Housing Benefit

Housing benefit is a means tested benefit which can assist with the
payment of rent (but not mortgage payments) (S.S.C.B.A. 1992, s.130).
Those who are on income support need to make a separate claim for
housing benefit. Housing benefit is calculated according to a formula laid
down in the Housing Benefit (General) Regulations 1987.[27] Benefit can
only be claimed for "eligible housing costs"; these exclude water and
sewerage charges, charges for meals and/or fuel, and certain service
charges. The provision of a warden service, communal rooms and an
emergency alarm system in specifically adapted accommodation is
eligible to be included in the calculation of housing benefit, as is a charge
made in respect of counselling and support by a landlord: *R. v. North
Cornwall District Council, ex p. Singer; same v. same, ex p. Barett; same v. same,
ex p. Bateman.*[28]

The local authority may refuse to take the full cost of rent into account
if the accommodation is deemed to be unreasonably high, but for those
aged over 60 the local authority must also be satisfied that suitable
cheaper accommodation is actually available (reg. 11). Deductions are
made for non-dependants living in the same household. People who
have savings in excess of £16,000 cannot claim housing benefit. Housing
benefit is not payable towards fees in a nursing home or residential care
home, except for those already receiving such benefits on October 29,
1990. People who are temporarily away from home (including those in
respite care or in hospital) can continue to claim housing benefit in
respect of their main residence for up to one year.

Living with relatives

People living with a close relative are not eligible for housing benefit
unless the arrangement is a commercial one (reg. 7(*a*)): a close relative is a
parent, son, daughter, step-parent, step-son, step-daughter, parent-in-

---

[26] [1991] C. O. D. 68.
[27] S.I. 1987 No. 1971.
[28] *The Times*, January 12, 1994. The Housing Benefit and Council Tax Benefit (Amendment)
Regulations (S.I. 1994 No. 470) however restrict entitlement to where a landlord spends the
majority of his time engaged not in counselling but in other eligible activities, thus
jeopardising many sheltered lodgings schemes.

law, son-in-law, daughter-in-law, brother or sister. A proper commercial arrangement however should not be regarded as one designed to take advantage of the housing benefit scheme even if the accommodation is provided by a relative: *R. v. Solihull Metropolitan Borough Council Housing Benefits Review Board, ex p. Simpson.*[29] Self-contained accommodation, for example a "granny-annex", will attract housing benefit. If living accommodation is shared, however, deductions will be made in respect of "non-dependants", a term which would include adult children and elderly relatives. However, payments received from non-dependants do not count as "income". No non-dependant deductions are made where the housing benefit claimant is registered blind or in receipt of attendance allowance or the care component of disability living allowance (reg. 63(6)).

COUNCIL TAX BENEFIT

Council tax, which is payable to the local authority, comprises both a property element (equivalent to 50 per cent of the charge), and a personal element (2 × 25 per cent of the charge). Details of the scheme are contained in the Local Government Finance Act 1992 and the Council Tax Benefit (General) Regulations 1992.[30] There are indefinite exemptions from council tax for certain dwellings which are unoccupied; these include premises vacated by someone who is in hospital, a residential care home or a nursing home, or living elsewhere in order to give or receive personal care. Other dwellings are exempt for a six-month period, these include premises which form part of the estate of a deceased person from the time when probate or letters of administration are granted.

There is only one council tax bill for each domestic dwelling, but there exists joint and several liability to pay that bill between persons having the same legal interest in the property whether as freeholder, leaseholder or licensee.

There are four ways of reducing liability (applied in this order):

(1) the disability reduction scheme;
(2) a status discount;
(3) the council tax reduction scheme; and
(4) council tax benefit.

The disability reduction scheme

The disability reduction scheme operates by reducing by one band the valuation of property for the purposes of the council tax. It applies to dwellings which are the sole or main residence of a disabled person

---

[29] *The Times*, January 5, 1994.
[30] S.I. 1992 No. 1814.

(Local Government Finance Act 1992, s.80(6)(a)), though that person does not necessarily have to be the person liable to pay the council tax. Eligibility is governed by the Council Tax (Reductions for Disabilities) Regulations 1992.[31] A "qualifying individual" must be "substantially and permanently disabled" (reg. 1(2)), though there is no need to show that he is in receipt of other benefits as a result of that disability. The dwelling must have a second bathroom or kitchen, or some other room which is predominantly required for meeting the needs of the qualifying individual by reason of the nature and extent of his disability. Alternatively, sufficient floor space may be needed to use a wheelchair within the living accommodation in the dwelling concerned.

Status discount

A status discount is automatically available when there is only one person living in the dwelling since the personal element in the council tax is calculated on a two-person household. A sole householder will therefore automatically be eligible for a 25 per cent reduction in the charge. The presence of the householder himself, or other persons in the household, may be disregarded in calculating the chargeable amount by virtue of the Council Tax (Discount Disregards) Order 1992[32] and the Council Tax (Additional Provisions for Discount Disregards) Order 1992.[33] Most relevant here are disregards relating to persons permanently resident in residential or nursing care, persons who are severely mentally impaired, and certain carers. A person is regarded as severely mentally impaired if he has a severe impairment of intelligence and social functioning (however caused) which appears to be permanent and who is entitled either to a disability benefit for income maintenance, or to an attendance allowance or to the higher or middle care component of disability living allowance. Medical evidence will be required. Subject to this, some elderly people may be eligible. Live-in carers who are not the spouse or partner of the person that they care for 35 hours a week or more are also entitled to a status discount, but only if the other person actually receives attendance allowance (but only at the higher rate), or the higher care component of disability living allowance. The 50 per cent property element in the council tax is not affected by these status discounts; eligibility for council tax benefit in respect of the property element will be calculated in the usual way, according to the value of income and capital.

The council tax reduction scheme

The council tax reduction scheme is a transitional scheme covering the two years from April 1993 to April 1995. The local authority will award a

---

[31] S.I. 1992 No. 1335.
[32] S.I. 1992 No. 548.
[33] S.I. 1992 No. 552.

reduction automatically to those who would otherwise have been worse off as a result of the changeover from the poll tax in April 1993.

Council tax benefit

Council tax benefit (Local Government Finance Act 1992, s.103) is the major scheme whereby liability can be reduced. There are in fact two types of council tax benefit known as "main council tax benefit" and "second adult rebate". The former is income-related and restricted to those with capital of less than £16,000. The second adult rebate, however, is available regardless of income or savings when there is a second adult with a low income living in the same household. The maximum benefit payable is 25 per cent. This is a new benefit that was not available under the old rate rebate or poll tax system. It could benefit a householder who has an elderly relative on a low income living with them, provided that other person is not jointly liable to pay council tax on the home.

Invalidity Benefit

Invalidity benefit is the general term used to describe invalidity pension and invalidity allowance (S.S.C.B.A. 1992, ss.33–34). It is payable to those incapable of work who have previously been entitled to statutory sick pay or sickness benefit for a period of 168 days. Certain widows and widowers under pensionable age may be entitled to claim invalidity pension following bereavement even though they were not first entitled to sickness benefit (S.S.C.B.A. 1992, s.40). The basic invalidity pension may be increased by an earnings related addition from the State Earnings Related Pension Scheme (SERPS).

Invalidity allowance

Invalidity allowance is paid in addition to invalidity benefit for those men incapacitated for work before the age of 60, and women incapacitated before the age of 55. However, invalidity allowance will not be paid to those receiving an additional invalidity pension under SERPS. Invalidity allowance, once payable, continues to be paid in addition to any future retirement pension.

Income support may be paid on top of invalidity benefit if total income is less than the "applicable amount".[34] Invalidity benefit is also a qualifying benefit for disability premium or higher pensioner premium. "Therapeutic work", for which a person can earn up to £42 a week, may be undertaken, with prior agreement, during the time that invalidity benefit is paid (Social Security (Unemployment, Sickness and Invalidity Benefit) Regulations 1983, reg. 3(3)).[35] National insurance contributions

---

[34] p. 188.
[35] S.I. 1983 No. 1598.

will also be credited during any time spent on invalidity benefit, but if retirement pension is deferred in order to remain on invalidity benefit no entitlement to an increased pension is thereby accrued.

Invalidity benefit and retirement pension

Invalidity benefit is not taxable, unlike retirement pension. It may be advantageous therefore to defer entitlement to pension for up to five years and to remain on invalidity benefit during that time, though the amount of benefit will be reduced if there is an inadequate contribution record unless the incapacity is due to an industrial accident or disease.[36] Men whose wives are still working may also find it advantageous to remain on invalidity benefit until aged 70 as they may still be entitled to an increase for their spouse under the tapered earnings rule: Social Security Benefit Dependency Regulations 1977, reg. 8(6).[37] This applies to those who have been continuously entitled to an increase in the same benefit since September 14, 1985, which may make changing benefit disadvantageous.

The unequal position of women

The unequal position that men and women are placed in because of the differences in pensionable age was declared unlawful under European Community Law by E.C. Council Directive 79/7 (the *Graham* case).[37a] Women with incomplete contribution records have their invalidity benefit reduced to the level at which retirement pension would be payable at age 60; men do not have such a reduction made until the age of 65. Women who become incapable of work between the ages of 54 and 59 are also not entitled to invalidity allowance which would be payable if they were male. The Department of Social Security has appealed the *Graham* case to the Court of Appeal which has in turn referred the issue to the European Court. In the meantime women affected by the decision should appeal or ask for a review of their case. If they have already been persuaded to claim retirement pension at age 60 they may consider whether they should de-retire.

The Social Security (Incapacity for Work) Act 1994

The Social Security (Incapacity for Work) Act 1994 introduces a new incapacity benefit to replace both sickness benefit and invalidity benefit with effect from April 1995. Section 1 of the Act introduces new sections 30A and 30B into the Social Security Contributions and Benefits Act 1992, which detail the circumstances in which incapacity benefit will be paid.

---

[36] Social Security (Unemployment, Sickness and Invalidity Benefit) Regulations 1983 (S.I. 1983 No. 1598). reg. 18.
[37] S.I. 1977 No. 343.
[37a] *Secretary of State for Social Security and Chief Adjudication Officer v. Graham (Rose)*, January 18, 1994, C.A.

Further details of the scheme are contained in certain regulations.[37b] Only an outline of those changes to people of pensionable age are discussed here.

Incapacity benefit will comprise (i) short-term incapacity benefit, payable at a lower or higher rate, and (ii) long-term incapacity benefit. The lower rate of short-term incapacity benefit is paid for the first 196 days of incapacity and the higher rate is paid for the remainder of the first year of incapacity. Only after the first year will long-term incapacity benefit be paid. This may be contrasted with the transition from sickness benefit to invalidity benefit after six months of "sickness". Incapacity is a narrower concept than sickness. Different tests of incapacity apply according to whether a person has previously been in employment. If so, an "own occupation" test (Social Security Contributions and Benefits Act 1992, s.171B) applies for the first 197 days of incapacity; in all other cases, an "all work" test applies (s.171C). Certain people are eligible for payment of incapacity benefit at the long-term rate after only 196 days (s.30B(4)). These are people who are terminally ill, or who are entitled to the highest rate of disability living allowance.

People of pensionable age are not eligible for payment of incapacity benefit at the long-term rate (s.30A(5)). Their entitlement is limited to payment of short-term incapacity benefit, but only if their period of incapacity for work began before they reached pensionable age (s.30A(2)). Section 30B(3) further provides that in the case of a person of pensionable age, the rate of incapacity benefit will not exceed the rate at which the relevant retirement pension would be payable. Section 30A(2) also specifies that persons who seek to defer their pension in order to remain on incapacity benefit can only do so if they were entitled to a Category A pension, or a Category B pension in respect of a deceased spouse. Incapacity benefit, unlike invalidity benefit, will be taxed.

Particular rules apply to widows and widowers (ss.40 and 41 respectively of the Social Security Contributions and Benefits Act 1992, inserted by para. 8 of Sched. 1 to the Social Security (Incapacity for Work) Act 1994). A widow is not entitled to incapacity benefit if over pensionable age, but if incapacitated before that age she shall be entitled to a Category A retirement pension.

Transitional provisions have yet to appear in regulations. The intention however seems clear to be to move people of pensionable age away from disability benefits and on to retirement pension, whilst introducing more stringent medical tests of incapacity for work.

SEVERE DISABLEMENT ALLOWANCE

Severe disablement allowance (SDA) is payable where a person's national insurance contributions are insufficient to enable him or her to qualify for invalidity benefit (S.S.C.B.A. 1992, s.68). Claimants must be at

---

[37b] Social Security (Incapacity Benefit) Regulations (S.I. 1994 No. 2946), Social Security (Incapacity Benefit) (Increases for Dependants) Regulations (S.I. 1994 No. 2945).

least 80 per cent disabled, and must have been incapable of work for at least 196 days. SDA is available to people aged 16 and over but below pensionable age. Remaining on SDA beyond pensionable age may be advantageous as it is tax free; it is also a way of qualifying for the higher pensioner premium paid with income support.[38] A recent decision has extended eligibility for SDA to those who were entitled to SDA or its predecessor, non-contributory invalidity pension, before September 10, 1984, when section 165A of the Social Security Act came into force replacing "eligibility" with the need to claim.[39] This includes married women who were wrongly excluded from benefit because of the discriminatory rules then in force. Claims for arrears may be possible even as far back as 1984. Entitlement depends upon continuation of the same period of interruption of employment. A decision of the European court is awaited: *Johnson v. Chief Adjudication Officer (No.2)*.[40]

Discrimination against women

A recent decision of the European court, *Thomas v. Chief Adjudication Officer*,[41] decided that it was unlawful to discriminate against women by disallowing claims to SDA (and to invalid care allowance (see below)) by women above the pensionable age of 60 when men could claim up to age 65. Such discrimination was not "necessary to guarantee the consistency and the financial equilibrium of the system" because both benefits were non-contributory. Claims by women aged 60 to 64 should therefore now be accepted.

INDUSTRIAL INJURIES BENEFITS

Benefits under the industrial injuries scheme are paid to people who are disabled as a result of an accident at work or a prescribed industrial disease as defined by the Social Security (Industrial Injuries) (Prescribed Diseases) Regulations 1985.[42] The main benefit is disablement benefit, supplemented by constant attendance allowance and exceptionally severe disablement allowance. The extent of disablement is assessed on a percentage basis. Reduced earnings allowance is also payable for those whose injury is pre-dated October 1, 1990[43]; this will be lost if the claimant gives up regular employment. Deferring entitlement to a

---

[38] See p. 190.
[39] Social Security Decision No. R(S) 2/91.
[40] Social Security Decision No. R(IS) 10/92.
[41] [1993] Q.B. 747, E.C.J.
[42] S.I. 1985 No. 967.
[43] See the Social Security (Industrial Injuries) (Regular Employment) Regulations 1990 (S.I. 1990 No. 256).

retirement pension beyond the age of 60 or 65 may therefore be advisable in some cases.

WAR DISABLEMENT PENSION

The war pensions scheme provides pensions for people disabled as a result of service in H.M. forces, which are tax-free. Disablement is assessed on a percentage basis, with those less than 20 per cent disabled being given a lump sum gratuity and not a pension. Entitlement to non-means tested benefits is unaffected, and £10 of a war disablement pension is ignored as income for the purposes of means tested benefits. Supplementary allowances are payable, including a mobility supplement and a constant attendance allowance. There is no upper age limit for claiming mobility supplement (unlike the upper age limit of 66 for claiming the mobility component of disability living allowance). An age allowance is paid automatically from the age of 65 for those assessed as at least 40 per cent disabled. Local authorities have a discretion, known as a "local scheme", to disregard war disablement pensions and war widows' pensions in the calculation of housing benefit: sections 134(8) and 139(6) of the S.S.C.B.A. 1992.

Full information is available from the War Pensions Helpline on 01253 858858, and claims can be made by writing to the Director of War Pensions, War Pensions Directorate, North Fylde Central Office, Norcross, Blackpool FY5 3TA. There is no time-limit for making a claim for a war disablement pension, or seeking a review. Appeals for disablement arising from Second World War and later can be made to the Pensions Appeal Tribunal.

DISABILITY LIVING ALLOWANCE AND ATTENDANCE ALLOWANCE

Disability living allowance has replaced attendance allowance and mobility allowance for disabled people under the age of 65 (S.S.C.B.A. 1992, s.71); claims for this benefit can however be made up until that person's 66th birthday. For people over the age of 65 who are in need of care and supervision because of their mental or physical condition, the relevant benefit is still attendance allowance (S.S.C.B.A. 1992, s.64). Both disability living allowance and attendance allowance are non-contributory, non-means tested and non-taxable benefits. There is a qualifying period of three months for disability living allowance and six months for attendance allowance. A medical examination is not normally necessary as the majority of claims are decided upon information provided by claimants themselves. The basis of the entitlement is the need for assistance or care; it does not matter that there is no-one at present providing that care. There is no monitoring either of how the allowances are spent.

Disability living allowance—mobility component

Disability living allowance is divided into two components payable at different rates; the care component and the mobility component. The mobility component is payable at a higher rate for those unable or virtually unable to walk and approximates to the old mobility allowance, though it now explicitly includes those who are both deaf and blind and those people who are severely mentally impaired with severe behavioural problems. The lower rate is now payable to those people who, though they are able to walk, cannot do so without guidance or supervision from another person. Early claims are advisable since no one can claim once they have reached their 66th birthday, but once entitlement is granted, the mobility component can then be paid for life: Social Security (Disability Living Allowance) Regulations 1991.[44] No particular distance of walking is specified in the regulations. However, the walking referred to is "out of doors" which may serve to include people who are especially vulnerable in cold or damp conditions. "Circumstances peculiar to the claimant" are not to be taken into account; for example the fact that the claimant is able to walk some distance but not to the nearest bus-stop, or that he is unable to use public transport. People with dementia who are in need of supervision outdoors are likely to qualify for the lower rate of mobility component. The motability scheme which assists with the leasing or purchase of cars by people with disabilities is limited to those who receive the higher rate mobility component.

Disability living allowance—care component and attendance allowance

The care component of disability living allowance is paid at three weekly rates, the lowest of which includes people who are unable, by virtue of either physical or mental disability, to prepare a cooked meal for themselves if they have the ingredients, known as "the cooking test", or who require attention from another person for a significant portion of the day, known as the "limited attention" condition. There is no equivalent lowest rate in the payment of attendance allowance. Eligibility for attendance allowance and for the middle or higher rate of the care component of disability living allowance depend upon the same criteria. The claimant will need to show (S.S.C.B.A. 1992, s.72(1)) that he is so severely disabled, physically or mentally, that he requires, in connection with his bodily functions, either frequent attention throughout the day, or prolonged or repeated attention during the night. The attention needed must be in connection with bodily functions, for example eating,

---

[44] S.I. 1991 No. 2890.

dressing, walking, going to the toilet,[44a] but frequency may be achieved by the aggregation of a number of different care needs. "Prolonged" attention is normally that which exceeds 20 minutes, and repeated attention is twice nightly or more. It is not necessary for the attention to be required every night. As an alternative to the "attention" conditions, the claimant may seek to rely on the fact that he needs either continual supervision from another person throughout the day in order to avoid substantial danger to himself or others, or that he needs another person to be awake for a prolonged period or at frequent intervals during the night to avoid substantial danger to himself or others. Supervision may be precautionary and essentially passive in nature; it does not necessarily require direct intervention on the part of the supervisor. The amount of attention required involves weighing the remoteness of the risk, for example the house being set alight, against the seriousness of the consequences should this occur. The test is what is "reasonably required", not what is medically essential. Advice from the Department's own medical advisor that the house door should be shut so as to minimise risks from wandering was held to be unreasonable in Social Security Decision No. R(A) 3/90: in this case, official guidance on assessing the risks of epilepsy was not to be regarded as a presumption against entitlement. Where benefit is withdrawn, there must be positive evidence to support the reinterpretation of the claimant's position.

Day or night?

Since different rates are paid for day time and night time attention or supervision, it may be necessary to define "night". In *R. v. National Insurance Commissioners, ex p. Secretary of State for Social Services*[45] "night" was defined as "the dark hours, beginning when the household, as it were closes down for the night". Thus preparation for bed is a day-time and not a night-time activity.

Terminal illness

Special rules apply to persons who are terminally ill. They are deemed to satisfy the conditions for the higher rate care component of disability living allowance or for the higher rate of attendance allowance, and to have done so throughout the necessary qualifying period for that benefit (S.S.C.B.A. 1992, s.66(1)). A person is regarded as terminally ill if he is suffering from a progressive disease and can reasonably be expected to die within six months as a result of that disease (S.S.C.B.A. 1992, s.66(2)). An application for review or an appeal on an existing claim can be made on the basis that that person is now terminally ill. A claim may be made

---

[44a] In *Mallinson v. Secretary of State for Social Security* [1994] 1 W.L.R. 630, H.L., it was accepted that guidance provided to a blind person constituted "attention in connection with his bodily functions".
[45] [1974] 1 W.L.R. 1290.

by another person on behalf of the person who is terminally ill without their knowledge or authority (S.S.C.B.A. 1992, s.66(2)(*b*)); in this way, the person who is terminally ill need not be told about their prognosis. The benefits agency is usually able to deal with claims based on terminal illness within 10 days.

Factors affecting benefit

Attendance allowance and the care component of disability living allowance overlap with constant attendance allowance under the industrial injuries and war pensions schemes, and the mobility component of disability living allowance also overlaps with the war pensioners' mobility supplement. Income support, housing benefit and council benefit will however be paid at a higher rate when the claimant or their partner is eligible for disability living allowance or attendance allowance. Carers may also be entitled to invalid care allowance.

The mobility component of disability living allowance is unaffected by stays in hospital or scheduled accommodation; the care component and attendance allowance are affected, and cannot be paid when the stay is longer than 28 days.[46] Two or more periods separated by 28 days or less will be added together towards the 28-day limit.[47] Respite care therefore needs to be carefully planned so as not to fall foul of these rules.

The care component of disability living allowance and attendance allowance as well cannot be paid after the first 28 days of residence in local authority accommodation provided under Part III of the National Assistance Act 1948. Also excluded is any accommodation where the cost is or may be borne wholly or partly out of public funds, though persons living in these forms of accommodation prior to April 1, 1993, when the community care changes were introduced have "preserved rights"[48] to existing benefits. Otherwise, the only people who can continue to claim or to receive these benefits after moving into residential care homes or nursing homes are those who are wholly privately funded.

Claims, reviews and appeals

Claims are dealt with initially by adjudication officers at regional disability benefit centres. There is a power to refer claimants or classes of claimants to doctors appointed by the Department of Social Security for medical examination (Social Security Administration Act 1992, s.54(2)). Refusal to attend for medical examination "without good cause" will defeat the claim (s.54(6)). The Disability Living Allowance Advisory

---

[46] See the Social Security (Disability Living Allowance) Regulations 1991 (S.I. 1991 No. 2890), regs. 8 and 9; see also the Social Security (Attendance Allowance) Regulations 1991 (S.I. 1991 No. 2740), regs. 6 and 7.
[47] See the Social Security (Disability Living Allowance) Regulations 1991 (S.I. 1991 No. 2890), reg. 10; see also the Social Security (Attendance Allowance) Regulations 1991 (S.I. No. 2740), reg. 8.
[48] See Chap. 5—Residential Care, p. 58.

Board acts as a consultative body on medical matters. Limited period awards are common on first claims, but an award can be made for life. The decision made on the claim can be challenged by asking for a review "on any ground" (Social Security Administration Act 1992, s.30(1)); this is in effect a fresh hearing of the case. An appeal against the decision of an adjudication officer on review lies to a disability appeal tribunal, if the dispute relates to a disability question; otherwise, it is to a social security appeal tribunal.

THE INDEPENDENT LIVING FUND

The Independent Living Fund was originally devised as a fund-awarding body to replace the weekly cash help that used to be available to some people with disabilities under the old supplementary benefit scheme. The original Independent Living Fund closed its doors to new applicants from November 25, 1992. Two new funds were set up to take the Independent Living Fund's place from April 1, 1993; these are the Independent Living (1993) Fund and the Independent Living (Extension) Fund. The extension fund will continue to make payments to severely disabled people in the community to help meet the actual costs of domestic help and personal care, but only if those people were already receiving payments from the old Independent Living Fund. This includes people over the age of 65, who were eligible under the old scheme. Protection will however be lost if the person ceases to receive payment from the Fund for more than 26 weeks, for example if he is in hospital.

The Independent Living (1993) Fund is open only to new applicants between the ages of 16 and 65; priority will be given to younger people in work. Help will not normally be given to people who are terminally ill. A contribution of 50 per cent of the disability living allowance paid will be required. Access to the scheme is via the local authority; in effect the Independent Living (1993) Fund will operate to "top up" services that the local authority can provide between the minimum threshold level of £200, and the £500 upper limit. The maximum award is therefore £300 per week. Applicants must be entitled to disability living allowance care component at the highest rate, and either be in receipt of income support, or have less than £8,000 capital and an income below income support levels once the cost of care needs is deducted.

The new arrangements reflect the status of the local authority as the leading authority in assessing need under section 47 of the National Health Service and Community Care Act 1990 (see Chapter 3—Community Care). Responsibility for meeting care needs above the £500 limit reverts to the local authority. The Independent Living (1993) Fund circumvents the restriction imposed on local authorities by section 45(4)(a) of the Health Services and Public Health Act 1968, that they can provide services but not financial assistance, and in effect enables disabled people themselves to a limited extent to act as their own care manager. The Independent Living Extension Fund and the Independent Living (1993) Fund can both be contacted at P.O. Box 183, Nottingham NR8 3RD.

INVALID CARE ALLOWANCE

Invalid care allowance is an allowance paid to carers in their own right subject to certain stringent limitations (S.S.C.B.A. 1992, s.70). These limitations are as follows:

(1) The person for whom care is provided must be receiving either the higher or middle rate of the care component of disability living allowance, or attendance allowance, or constant attendance allowance.
(2) The care given must be "regular and substantial" for 35 hours per week or more. The 35 hours must be given to one individual in need of care and cannot be aggregated: Social Security (Invalid Care Allowance) Amendment (No. 2) Regulations 1993.[49]
(3) The carer must not be gainfully employed (earning a maximum of £50 per week) or in full time education.
(4) The carer is not under the age of 16.

Invalid care allowance is not means tested but is taxable, except for any increase in respect of dependent children. Class 1 National Insurance contributions are credited during any period for which invalid care allowance is claimed. A maximum 12 months arrears of benefit can be paid. A person receiving invalid care allowance is not required to be available for work as a condition of entitlement to income support. A break of 12 weeks in any period of six months does not affect entitlement to invalid care allowance; holidays and periods in hospital are aggregated for this purpose. Only four of those weeks however can be time spent in hospital because after that entitlement to the care component of disability living allowance or attendance allowance ceases.

Overlapping benefits

Rules relating to overlapping benefits mean that invalid care allowance cannot be paid at the same time as unemployment benefit, maternity allowance, invalidity benefit, sickness benefit, retirement pension, widow's benefit or severe disablement allowance. However, those who claim invalid care allowance shortly before reaching pensionable age can thereafter have their retirement benefit topped up to the £33.70 invalid

---

[49] S.I. 1993 No. 1851.

care allowance rate. This is an advantage to people who would otherwise not have enough contributions for a full-rate retirement pension. A claim for income support or employment benefit may be treated as one for invalid care allowance (Social Security (Claims and Payments) Regulations 1987, Sched. 1[50]); it may be advantageous to argue that a claim should have been so treated if eligibility for unemployment benefit or income support fails on other grounds.

A major disadvantage in claiming invalid care allowance is that the person being cared for thereby loses their entitlement to severe disability premium, which is worth £35.05. However, if the carer cannot be paid invalid care allowance (perhaps because of the overlapping benefit rules) it may be worth making a formal claim anyway in order to become eligible for the £12.65 per week carers' premium included in the calculation of income support, housing benefit and council tax benefit.

A particular difficulty arises with those who would be entitled to severe disablement allowance and invalid care allowance. Under regulation 4(5)(b)(i) of the Social Security (Overlapping Benefits) Regulations 1979,[51] the claim for invalid care allowance always takes precedence, unless application is made to reverse the priorities and to have the whole of the invalid care allowance payable as severe disablement allowance. There is an important advantage in doing this in that the person being cared for will not lose their severe disability premium if the carer is paid severe disability allowance, but will do so if he/she is paid invalid care allowance. Entitlement to the carers' premium with income support is unaffected by the election to be paid severe disablement allowance.

Invalid care allowance over pensionable age

Under the legislation, no one is entitled to invalid care allowance once they are over pensionable age (65 years for men, 60 years for women) unless they were entitled to it immediately before they reached that age, or would have been but for overlapping benefit rules (S.S.C.B.A. 1992, s.70(5); Social Security (Invalid Care Allowance) Regulations 1976, reg.10).[52] These rules however discriminate against women and for that reason were held to be contrary to European Law. The European Court (*Thomas v. Chief Adjudication Officer*[53]) confirmed that women aged 60 to 65 ought to be entitled to claim invalid care allowance (and severe disablement allowance) even after reaching pensionable age. An anti-discriminatory interpretation would mean also that it is unlawful to discriminate against men; and that Social Security (Invalid Care Allow-

---

[50] S.I. 1987 No. 1968.
[51] S.I. 1979 No. 597.
[52] S.I. 1976 No. 409.
[53] Case 328/91, [1993] Q.B. 747, European Ct.J. A common upper age limit of 65 years was belatedly introduced by the Social Security (Severe Disablement Allowance and Invalid Care Allowance) Amendment Regulations 1994 (S.I. 1994 No. 2556).
[54] S.I. 1976 No. 409.

ance) Regulations 1976, reg.11,[54] which limits continuing entitlement to invalid care allowance for men to those who were eligible immediately before the age of 70, is also contrary to European law. This would mean that both men and women who were receiving invalid care allowance immediately before the age of 65 should continue to be entitled to receive it even if they have ceased caring for someone.

Going into Hospital

Sickness and invalidity benefit, severe disablement allowance, widows' benefits and retirement pensions are paid in full for the first six weeks of any hospital stay. After six weeks benefit is reduced; the amount of reduction depends upon whether that person has or has not got dependants. Further reductions take place after 52 weeks in hospital, so that the patient receives only a basic personal allowance per week. In some cases benefit may cease altogether if the patient is incapable of acting for himself and the doctor in charge of treatment certifies that no sum of money, or only a part of what otherwise would be received, can be used for the patient's personal comfort or enjoyment (Social Security (Hospital In-Patients) Regulations 1975, reg.16[55]).

Attendance allowance and the care component of disability living allowance cease after four weeks in hospital; the mobility component of disability living allowance is however unaffected. Sickness or invalidity benefit is payable instead of unemployment benefit, immediately upon admission to hospital.

In all cases, periods in hospital separated by less than 28 days are counted as one period. Planning for periods of respite care therefore needs to be done with this in mind.

If there are any dependants, and a return home from hospital is not contemplated, it may be financially beneficial to seek a separate assessment for the person who remains at home from the benefits agency. Regulation 16(1) to (3) and para. 4(8) of Schedule 3 to the Income Support (General) Regulations 1987[56] allow applications as for a single claimant if the partner is permanently in Part III accommodation, in a residential care home or nursing home, or where he/she has been in hospital for 52 weeks.

Absence from Great Britain

Retirement pensions and widows' benefits are payable during an absence abroad, but subject to the exceptions discussed below will not

---

[55] S.I. 1975 No. 555.
[56] S.I. 1987 No. 1967.

be uprated for those who are not "ordinarily" resident in Great Britain.[57] Attendance allowance and invalid care allowance are also payable during temporary absence abroad. Entitlement is governed by the S.S.C.B.A. 1992, s.113(1) and the Social Security Benefit (Persons Abroad) Regulations 1975.[58]

Special rules relate to countries where there are reciprocal agreements and to the European Community. European Community social security law provides for the co-ordination of different national schemes[59] so that periods of residence or contributions paid in one European Community country count towards entitlement to benefit in others. This means that those who change their place of ordinary residence within the European Community have their entitlement to benefits (including uprating of benefits) protected. These arrangements relate to the payment of invalidity benefit, severe disablement allowance, widows' benefit, retirement pension, industrial injuries and guardian's allowance: attendance allowance, invalid care allowance and disability living allowance were, however, excluded form the scheme from June 1, 1992.[60] Further information is available from the overseas branch of the benefits agency.

Income support is normally only paid to those actually living in Great Britain. There are exceptions contained in regulation 4(2)(c) and (3) of the Income Support (General) Regulations 1987[61] where the claimant is not required to sign on (this applies to all people over the age of 60), and where the claimant's partner qualifies for a pensioner, disability or severe disability premium.

DISPOSING OF PROPERTY

Elderly people often express a wish to give away assets to members of a younger generation during their lifetime rather than everyone waiting to inherit under the will. There are so many reasons as there are people, but the main ones are a feeling of living too long and wishing to see the younger generation "get on" and enjoy the monies, to save inheritance tax, and an attempted avoidance of future care home fees.

The client's clear instructions need to be taken, and, if necessary, different members of the family should take independent advice. Any suggestion of undue influence needs to be considered and the elderly

---

[57] Social Security Benefit (Persons Abroad) (Amendment) (No. 2) Regulations 1994 (S.I. 1994 No. 1832).
[58] S.I. 1975 No. 563.
[59] ibid.
[60] Social Security Benefit (Persons Abroad) Amendment Regulations 1992 (S.I. 1992 No. 1700).
[61] S.I. 1987 No. 1967.

person needs to realise that once a gift is made, the asset is gone and cannot be recovered.

Often the major asset is the principal residence. Any gift needs to be thought through and the elderly person protected by a lease back, right to reside or some other protection to try and guard against the consequences of the children selling over their head, dying before their parent, divorcing or going bankrupt. Such a gift is not effective for inheritance tax purposes if the donor remains in residence, being a gift with a reservation (see Chapter 14—Formalities of Death).

So far as the avoidance of care home fees is concerned, see Chapter 5—Residential Care in connection with the notional capital rules. For income support purposes there is no time-limit as to how long ago a gift was made, the overriding principle being the reason for the gift—if to help a benefit claim then the fact of the gift, whenever made, is ignored and the asset treated as "notional" capital within the claimant's hands, to disqualify the claimant from eligibility for income support.

Under community care, the relevant provision is the Health and Social Services and Social Security Adjudications Act 1983, s.21.[62] Under this section the local authority can pursue assets transferred not more than six months prior to a person beginning to reside in Part III (now including private) accommodation if such assets are transferred not for full consideration and "knowingly and with the intention of avoiding charges for the accommodation." The local authority pursues the asset into the hands of the transferee up to the extent of the benefit accruing to the transferee (s.25(5)). If the transfer was made more than six months prior to the move into care it is suggested that the full charge will still be levied on the resident, and, once fees are unpaid, he is sued for the unpaid debt and the bankruptcy legislation invoked.

Income tax allowances

Most income is taxable, but certain items are tax free including disability living allowance, attendance allowance, invalidity benefit, income support (if 60 years or over or receiving this without needing to be available for work), council tax and housing benefit, war disablement and war widow's pension, the first £70 of interest from a National Savings Bank ordinary account, and the proceeds on encashment of National Savings Certificates.

The state pension is therefore liable to income tax, but is generally covered by personal allowances, and so elderly people in receipt of this alone tend not to be bothered by the inland revenue.

The basic allowances increase, dependent on age, for example:

---

[62] See Chap. 5—Residential Care, p. 63.

Personal Allowance	(for 1994/95)
under 65	£3,525
aged 65–74	£4,630
aged 75 and over	£4,800

Married Couple's Allowance	(for 1994/1995)
both under 65	£1,720
one or both aged 65–74	£2,995
one or both aged 75 or over	£3,035

In addition there might be eligibility on behalf of a widow for a widow's bereavement allowance of £1,720 in the year of death and the following year (such allowance is not available to a widower) and a blind person's allowance of £1,200.

The higher age allowances are reduced to the basic personal allowance or married couples allowance if the gross income is more than £14,600, the reduction working on the formula that for £2 of income over the £14,600 limit, £1 of the allowance is lost until the age allowance is reduced back to the basic allowance applicable to individuals under 65 years.

If, in addition to pensions, the gross income from investments in banks and building societies and other income would take the individual over the relevant personal allowance and into the tax bracket, an individual is not allowed to try and juggle things so as to have some accounts paying interest gross to use up the balance of unused personal allowance with other accounts paying net, unless the investment is one which naturally pays gross interest, such as national savings products. All accounts should pay net and, at the end of the year, certificates should be obtained from the bank or building society under the Income and Corporation Taxes Act 1988, s.352, and tax repayment claims should be submitted in order to reclaim the tax overdeducted up to the unused personal allowance limit.

Husbands and wives are now taxed independently so that consideration may be given to transferring savings from husband to wife (as it is generally the wife who has less pensionable income) in order to use up the balance of personal allowances. Before assets are transferred, consideration needs to be given as to whether or not, in a wider context, this is advisable. From an inheritance tax point of view, the assets are not taxable at the time of transfer from husband to wife, but the consequence of the gifted assets, along with other assets in the wife's hands, needs to be considered because of the eventual inheritance tax position on her death. Also, what if the partner to whom assets have been transferred has to go into residential care? If all the savings are in one partner's hands and it is that partner who goes into care, then they will be assessed on those assets when calculating liability as to payment for fees.

Retirement lump sums

Upon retirement or when collecting a "private" pension, the recipient is often entitled to a lump sum in addition to the weekly or monthly pension payments. This is a convenient time to overhaul finances as a whole and seek best advice as required under the Financial Services Act 1986 with a review of all assets and income, and consideration as to what future plans and needs are likely to be. The solutions will be individual, being dependent on the amount of capital received, other assets and future income requirements.

Chapter 12

Delegation of Financial Responsibility

As people become older, the situation frequently arises when they either do not want to continue with the responsibility of handling their finances and business affairs, or ill-health affects them to such an extent that dealing with their money becomes something which they are unable to do in a meaningful way. There are methods whereby a third party can be appointed to deal with some or all aspects of an individual's finances and business affairs, but which method is relevant depends on the individual's wishes, the types of financial matters to be handled, and his mental capacity.

This chapter looks at the benefits agency methods of payment of state benefits, other than the claimant signing his weekly order book, agency and appointeeship, and the use of powers of attorney or Court of Protection receivership for dealing with all of an individual's business affairs from bank accounts to investments, to dealing in land.

Agency and Appointeeship

There are occasions when a recipient of state benefits is unable to physically call at the Post Office to sign his order book and obtain his pension, etc. It is possible for benefits such as retirement pension, attendance allowance, and even income support to be paid directly into the claimant's bank or building society account every four or 13 weeks in arrears, or weekly in the case of income support, requiring the claimant's signature once on the initial authorisation form.

Physical disabilities

If direct bank arrangements are not what is required, then it is possible for the claimant to nominate a third party, as agent, to collect the benefits instead, if the claimant has a physical incapacity. This is done by the claimant striking out the words "I acknowledge receipt of the above sum" on the front of the relevant weekly slip of their pension book, signing the front as normal, and then completing the back of the slip with details of the nominated agent adding a further signature, as authorisation. The nominated agent then completes a further statement confirming who they are, that the claimant is alive at the time of encashment, acknowledging receipt of the payment, and that the amount received will be paid over immediately.

If the claimant wishes the agency arrangement to continue for some time, the above procedure has to be followed each time. Alternatively, form AP1 can be completed and submitted to the benefits agency and they will issue an agency card which states that the named agent is authorised to collect the claimant's benefits. The claimant still has to sign the front of each order, and the agent produces the card to the post office by way of identification.

It is up to the claimant to inform the benefits agency of any changes in circumstances, for example admission to hospital or a change in means affecting eligibility for income support. The claimant must have the mental capacity to understand what he is doing, otherwise no valid appointment of an agent can be made. If the claimant is a resident in local authority Part III accommodation it is possible to nominate an official of the local authority (by office, not by name) to act as agent. The "signing agent" as he is known, is able to obtain payment by signing the order book as if he were the claimant, unlike a normal agent.

For residents in private care, the normal agency rules, or appointeeship mentioned below, are possibilities, but they are not recommended. Many registration authorities do not approve of home owners handling residents' personal finances, and require strict accounting procedures to be followed. Where the resident has no relatives or other representative, there is often no alternative to someone from the home encashing the benefits.

Mental incapacity

If the claimant lacks mental capacity, the Secretary of State for Social Security has the power to make a third party appointee for the claimant (Social Security (Claims and Payments) Regulations 1987, reg. 33[1]). The benefits agency should ascertain that the claimant is unable, for the time being, to act and that no receiver has been appointed by the Court of Protection. On receipt of a written application, the appointment is made, as a result of which the appointee has the right to act as if he were the claimant. He can claim and receive benefits (his signature alone will do) but he also has a duty to report relevant changes which affect entitlement. The monies received always belong to the claimant and must be used for his needs. Generally, the benefits agency appoints a close relative or friend, and will satisfy itself both as to the incapacity of the claimant and the suitability of the proposed appointee by considering medical evidence and/or visiting the persons concerned.

---

[1] S.I. 1987 No. 1968.

The appointment can be revoked at any time by the Secretary of State (reg. 33(2)(A)), by the appointee resigning after one month's written notice, or on notification of the appointment of a receiver.

Arrangements similar to appointeeship can be made for collecting pensions, salaries, etc., for people who are mentally incapable when the payer is a government department, the armed forces or some local authorities. Again, medical evidence will be required and it may be conditional on the Court of Protection being informed at some future date.

THIRD PARTY MANDATE

It is possible for someone with a physical disability to make arrangements for a third party to operate a particular bank or building society account or carry out a particular transaction. Each bank or building society has its own requirements, which may vary from an initial letter of authority and evidence of the signatures of all involved, to a new form being completed for each separate transaction.

POWERS OF ATTORNEY

For business and financial affairs as a whole to be placed on a more formal footing, a power of attorney might be considered. Nowadays there is a choice between a general power, as prescribed by the Powers of Attorney Act 1971, or an enduring power, in accordance with the provisions of the Enduring Powers of Attorney Act 1985. It comes down to why the power of attorney is needed, as to which type is chosen. In either case, the basic principles remain the same:

(i) the power of attorney must be granted by deed (Powers of Attorney Act 1971, s.1, as amended by Law of Property (Miscellaneous Provisions) Act 1989, s.1) and in the case of an enduring power in the prescribed form (Enduring Powers of Attorney Act 1985, s.2(1)(a));

(ii) the donor must have mental capacity at the time of executing the deed;

(iii) the donor has the choice as to who shall operate his affairs;

(iv) does the donor trust his attorney?;

(v) more than one attorney can be appointed but do they act jointly or jointly and severally (Powers of Attorney Act 1971, s.10(1); Enduring Powers of Attorney Act 1985, s.11(1));

(vi) is it to give general power or to be limited in its use?;

(vii) an attorney cannot make a will for a donor;

(viii) the maxim *delegatus non potest delegare* applies—the attorney cannot delegate his authority, although having reached a decision he can employ agents to carry that decision out;

(ix) the attorney is entitled to recover expenses properly incurred in the performance of his duties and may be entitled to remuneration;

(x) the attorney is under a duty to discharge his responsibilities with reasonable skill and care;

(xi) the attorney must not make secret profits and, in any transaction between himself and the donor, ensure that all material facts are disclosed and that he has acted completely fairly and free from the taint of self-interest; and

(xii) the donor is liable for the attorney's acts in so far as they are with the ostensible authority of the attorney.

The major differences are:

(i) a general power ceases on the supervening mental incapacity of the donor unless it is an irrevocable power (*Drew v. Nunn*[2]), whilst an enduring power carries on into the donor's mental incapacity although registration of the power in the Court of Protection must be undertaken (Enduring Powers of Attorney Act 1985, s.1(1));

(ii) an attorney cannot make gifts for the donor (*Re Bowles' mortgage*[3]) under a general power unless specifically authorised but there is a limited power of gifting under an enduring power (Enduring Powers of Attorney Act 1985, s.3(5));

(iii) an attorney cannot take on trustee powers under a general power unless specifically authorised whereas the Enduring Powers of Attorney Act 1985, s.3(3), authorises an attorney under a general or limited enduring power to execute or exercise powers or discretions vested in the donor as trustee;

(iv) an attorney's duties under an enduring power vary depending on whether or not he is acting pre-registration, during an application for registration (where his authority is limited to maintenance of the donor or others or to prevent loss to the donor's estate (Enduring Powers of Attorney Act 1985, s.1(2) and (4)) or after the power has been registered;

(v) the bankruptcy of a donee of a general power may not necessarily revoke the power but the bankruptcy of a donee of an enduring power will revoke the power whatever the circumstances of the bankruptcy (Enduring Powers of Attorney Act 1985, s.2(10)). In the case of a joint appointment, the bankruptcy revokes the power (Enduring Powers of Attorney Act 1985, Sched. 3, Pt. 1). In the case of a joint and several appointment the

---

[2] [1879] 4 Q.B.D. 661.
[3] (1874) 31 L.T. 365.

remaining attornies carry on and it is just the appointment of the bankrupt which ceases (Enduring Powers of Attorney Act 1985, Sched. 3, Pt. 11).

General power of attorney

The statutory basis for general powers of attorney is the Powers of Attorney Act 1971, but much reference also has to be made to common law. The attorney's consent to being appointed is not required, and he can always refuse to act should he so wish.

The donor must have mental capacity at the time he signs the general power so that he understands the implications of the authority which he is giving to the attorney. Once the donor no longer understands, the legal validity of the general power ceases with the loss of mental capacity. It is for this reason that it is suggested general powers are only used for "one-off" transactions or if it is felt, with certainty, that the donor's mental capacity will not fail.

The general power of attorney can be limited both in the scope of what the attorney is empowered to do and as to the period for which the attorney's authority can last.

Revocation of the power is an unilateral act of the donor's, unless the power granted was irrevocable. It can be express, by deed, or implied, by an act on the part of the donor incompatible with the continued operation of the power. It is generally wise for the donor to go on to inform those who had knowledge of the grant of the power of its revocation, for example his bankers. There is protection of both the donee and third parties where acts are performed in ignorance of the revocation (Powers of Attorney Act 1971, s.5).

Enduring power of attorney

Mental capacity
For a power of attorney to be an enduring power it must be made whilst the donor is still mentally capable. It can be made any time after March 10, 1986, but must comply with the formalities of the relevant set of regulations made under the Enduring Powers of Attorney Act 1985 in force at the time of execution of the power by the donor, currently the Enduring Powers of Attorney (Prescribed Form) Regulations 1990.[4]

The donor's capacity at the time of execution of the power does not have to be particularly sophisticated. Hoffman J. in *Re K.*[5] accepted that a donor might be mentally incapable of managing his affairs on his own behalf within the terms of the Mental Health Act 1983, s.94(2), but still capable of understanding the implications of appointing someone else to act under an enduring power. It would mean that registration of the enduring power of attorney would follow virtually immediately.

---

[4] S.I. 1990 No. 1376.
[5] [1988] 2 FLR 15.

Hoffman J. set out the matters which the donor needs to understand at the time of execution for the enduring power of attorney to be valid:

> "First (if such be the terms of the power), that the attorney will be able to assume complete authority over the donor's affairs. Secondly (if such be the terms of the power), that the attorney will in general be able to do anything with the donor's property which he himself could have done. Thirdly, that the authority will continue if the donor should be or become mentally incapable. Fourthly, that if he should be or become mentally incapable, the power will be irrevocable without confirmation by the court."[6]

Form of the enduring power of attorney
The form is made up of three parts: A, B, and C, and although adaptable to individual circumstances, must contain certain basic items. Part A, headed "About using this form" is mandatory and is an explanation to the donor of the implications of his entering into an enduring power.

Part B identifies the enduring power of attorney as belonging to the particular donor, and so recites details such as his full name, address and date of birth. It then goes on to name the attorney(s), whether or not two or more attorneys act jointly or jointly and severally, and to specify if general or limited authority is being given in relation to all property and affairs or only specified items and whether or not there are any restrictions or conditions under which the attorney must act. There must be a statement that the donor intends the power to continue even if he becomes mentally incapable, and a further statement as to whether or not the donor has read, or had read to him, the notes forming Part A. If a preprinted form is used, the alternatives not required must be deleted. It is possible to use a shortened form merely detailing the relevant information and authority being given, but the relevant marginal notes relating to the facts given in the shortened Part B must be retained as these notes are part of the prescribed form.

Part B is signed by the donor and then witnessed, not by the attorney, and neither it is suggested by the wife or husband of the donor. If the donor is unable to form a signature, but can make a mark, then this is acceptable, but the attestation should be amended suitably. It is possible for a third party to sign the power on the donor's behalf and at his direction, but execution in this form requires two witnesses.

Part C is signed by the attorney, and there is a separate Part C for each attorney should there be more than one. Until an attorney has executed Part C the power is not a valid enduring power (although it can be used as an ordinary power) and, once completed, is only valid so far as that attorney is concerned. If there is a joint appointment, all attorneys must sign for the enduring power of attorney to be valid. In signing, the attorney is confirming that he realises he has a duty to register the power in the Court of Protection if the donor is becoming or has become

---

[6] *per* Hoffman J. at p. 20.

mentally incapable, acknowledging that he has a limited power to make gifts (unless this has been specifically restricted) and that he is an adult. It is possible for a minor to be named as attorney and the appointment will be valid so long as it is shown he was an adult at the time he executed the enduring power of attorney and, at that stage, the donor still had capacity. The witnessing requirements are similar to Part B.

It is possible for individuals or a trust corporation to be appointed attorneys but not a partnership. It has been suggested that an appointment such as "the senior partner for the time being" in a firm of solicitors is a valid appointment, but the clause would need to be carefully drafted so that the attorney could be clearly identified.[7] The attorney must not be bankrupt at the time of execution of the enduring power of attorney (Enduring Powers of Attorney Act 1985, s.2(7)(*a*)) and, if an attorney becomes bankrupt subsequently, his authority is terminated "whatever the circumstances of the bankruptcy" (Enduring Powers of Attorney Act 1985, s.2(10)).

The document cannot be an enduring power of attorney if it gives the attorney a right to appoint a substitute or successor (Enduring Powers of Attorney Act 1985, s.2(9)). It is possible for alternative appointments to be made, *i.e.* "X but if X dies Y" as the court's view is that the appointment is of only one person at a time.

According to the Court of Protection, in 1991 the majority of enduring powers of attorney registered (98.4 per cent) were unrestricted in their authority, although it is possible for the donor to specify what property can or cannot be dealt with by the attorney, whether he is to have general authority over the donor's property and affairs to the same extent as the donor himself, or whether he is limited to paying bills, unable to sell the property or must only follow certain courses of action having consulted members of the family. A restriction can be placed in the power that the attorney can only act under it if satisfied that the donor is or is becoming mentally incapable. Each time an enduring power of attorney is prepared, consideration should be given as to whether or not the individual's circumstances necessitate the power containing qualifications as opposed to a blanket authority.

If a professional attorney is appointed the addition of a charging clause might be considered. Most powers of attorney do not contain one and the attorney relies on an implied term as to payment. The explanatory information in Part A does state "If your attorney(s) are professional people, for example solicitors or accountants, they may be able to charge for their professional services", so the court appears to have considered it likely. If all else fails it has been suggested that the Enduring Powers of Attorney Act 1985, s.8(2)(*b*)(iii) can be used to resolve any difficulties.

---

[7] See Lewis, "Enduring Powers of Attorney Act 1985" (1986) L.S. Gaz. 3566.

Registration

Once the attorney has reason to believe that the donor is or is becoming mentally incapable the attorney has a duty to register the enduring power of attorney in the Court of Protection (Enduring Powers of Attorney Act 1985, s.4). There is no requirement as to the need for medical evidence to back up this belief, but a prudent attorney is well advised to consult the donor's medical advisors for confirmation of the onset of mental incapacity as a medical report obtained at this stage can help circumvent future difficulties.

Once an application to register the enduring power of attorney has been made, the attorney's powers under it are limited until the application has been determined (Enduring Powers of Attorney Act 1985, s.1(1)). Strictly, the attorney should not do anything under the authority of the power until the registration process is completed except to take action to maintain the donor or to prevent loss to his estate (Enduring Powers of Attorney Act 1985, s.1(2)(*a*)) or to take action to maintain himself or other persons in so far as permitted under the Enduring Powers of Attorney Act 1985, s.3(4).

Where it considers it necessary, the court has power under the Enduring Powers of Attorney Act 1985, s.5, to give directions where it has reason to believe the donor may be or may be becoming mentally incapable and whether or not the attorney has commenced a registration application. The court's powers are on the same basis and in the same circumstances as under the Enduring Powers of Attorney Act 1985, s.8(2), once a power has been registered.

As part of the registration process the attorney has to give notice of his intention to apply for registration to both the donor and a minimum of three relatives using Form EP1 as prescribed by the Court of Protection (Enduring Powers of Attorney) Rules 1994.[8] The relatives to be notified are selected according to a list detailed in Schedule 1, para. 2 to the Enduring Powers of Attorney Act 1985, as follows:

(*a*)   the donor's husband or wife;
(*b*)   the donor's children;
(*c*)   the donor's parents;
(*d*)   the donor's brothers or sisters, whether of the whole or half blood;
(*e*)   the widow or widower of a child of the donor;
(*f*)   the donor's grandchildren;
(*g*)   the children of the donor's brothers and sisters of the whole blood;
(*h*)   the children of the donor's brothers and sisters of the half blood;
(*i*)   the donor's uncles and aunts of the whole blood;
(*j*)   the children of the donor's uncles and aunts of the whole blood.

Once a class of relatives has been identified, then all members of that class are to be notified however many people that entails. If the attorney

---

[8]   S.I. 1994 No. 3047.

happens to be a relative within one of the relevant classes, he does not have to serve notice upon himself (Enduring Powers of Attorney Act 1985, Sched. 1, para. 3(1)) but can count himself as one of the three people requiring to be served. All notices must be served within 14 days of each other.

Notification to the relatives is effected by sending the prescribed notice to them by first class post (Court of Protection (Enduring Powers of Attorney) Rules 1994, r.16(2)[9]). By contrast, notification to the donor must be served personally (r.16(1)). If a co-attorney is not also applying for registration then he must also be notified of the application, by post, using the prescribed form EP1.

It is possible for the attorney to apply to the Court of Protection to be dispensed from the requirement to give notice to either the donor or a particular relative (Sched. 1, paras. 4(2) and 3(2)) and the court will grant such application if satisfied:

(*a*) that it would be undesirable or impracticable for the attorney to give him notice; or
(*b*) that no useful purpose is likely to be served by giving him notice.

An application to dispense with service on the donor on the ground that he is unlikely to understand what is happening is unlikely to succeed. If the grounds are such that the donor did not wish a particular relative to be informed or the donor's health would suffer by the fact of service on him, then these contentions must be backed evidentially.

If the whereabouts of a person entitled to be served are unknown to the attorney and cannot be reasonably ascertained by him, or such person is a minor or themselves mentally incapable, then Schedule 1, para. 2(2) provides that such a person is not entitled to receive notice. A dispensation does not, therefore, have to be specifically applied for, but it may mean notice having to be given to other relatives in order for the requisite minimum number to be served.

The application to the court is made on Form EP2 which sets out the fact that the attorney has reason to believe the donor is or is becoming mentally incapable, details of all the persons who have been served and when and contains a certificate that the provisions of the Enduring Powers of Attorney Act 1985 and Rules have been complied with. The application must be lodged with the court not later than 10 days after whichever is the later of:

(1) notice having been given to the donor and every relative entitled to receive notice and every co-attorney; or
(2) leave has been given to dispense with notice (the Court of Protection (Enduring Powers of Attorney) Rules 1994, r.8).[10]

---

[9] *ibid.*
[10] *ibid.*

If the notice period is missed application has to be made to have the time extended, each case being decided on its own merits.

A registration fee is payable and this is currently £50.

Objection to registration
The grounds upon which an objection to registration can be made are set out clearly on the EP1 and are as follows:

(i)   that the power purported to have been created by the instrument is not valid as an enduring power of attorney;
(ii) that the power created by the instrument no longer subsists;
(iii) that the application is premature because the donor is not yet becoming mentally incapable;
(iv) that fraud or undue pressure was used to induce the donor to make the power;
(v)   that the attorney is unsuitable to be the donor's attorney (having regard to all the circumstances and in particular the attorney's relationship to or connection with the donor).

Any objection does not have to follow a particular form, except that it be in writing, but must set out the name and address of the objector, the name and address of the donor (if not also the objector), any relationship of objector to donor, the name and address of the attorney and the grounds for objecting to the registration (the Court of Protection (Enduring Powers of Attorney) Rules 1994, r. 10[11]).

If a valid notice of objection is received by the Court before the expiry of the period of five weeks beginning with the latest date on which the attorney gave notice to any person under Schedule 1; or it appears from the application that there was no relative to whom notice has been given; or the court has reason to believe that if appropriate enquiries were made evidence might be brought to light which would satisfy one of the grounds of objection, then the court neither registers the enduring power of attorney nor refuses the application until it has made or caused to be made such inquiries (if any) as it thinks appropriate in the circumstances (Enduring Powers of Attorney Act 1985, s.6(4)).

Where objections are lodged in court a preliminary hearing date is fixed for the giving of directions. If the matter does not resolve itself easily in the light of whatever information might be revealed as a result of these directions being complied with, then the court fixes a hearing at which attendance may well be required and the matter resolved. It is possible to appeal any decisions made by a nominated officer of the court to the Master, and from the Master to a judge.

At the end of the day, the court can register, possibly giving directions enabling it to supervise how the attorney exercises his powers. If the court refuses to register the power it may appoint a receiver using its

---

[11] *ibid.*

powers under Part VII of the Mental Health Act 1983. Where the refusal to register is on the grounds of fraud or undue pressure being used or that the donor is unsuitable, the court must revoke the power (Enduring Powers of Attorney Act 1985, s.6(7)). If the refusal is on any ground other than that the application is premature, then the power must be delivered up to be cancelled unless the court directs otherwise (Enduring Powers of Attorney Act 1985, s.6(8)).

Post registration

If having considered the objections, or having been satisfied with the result of any enquiries, the court orders the registration to proceed or no valid objection to the registration is received within the five-week period in which such objections can be made, the enduring power of attorney is returned by the court to the attorney. The original enduring power of attorney will have been sealed and stamped by the court with the date of registration. If an objection to registration on apparently valid grounds is received after registration, it can be considered and is treated as an application to cancel the registration (Enduring Powers of Attorney Act 1985, s.8(2)).

The attorney can carry on managing the donor's affairs within the authority given him by the enduring power of attorney but he no longer need consult the donor. The attorney must act reasonably and within legal constraints. It is prudent to keep accounts, but the court will not wish to see them unless it has particularly directed so. The court does not supervise the attorney's actions, but does have power to intervene if matters are brought to its notice which it feels deserve investigation. It is also possible for the attorney to approach the court for guidance if he is uncertain how to proceed in particular circumstances (Enduring Powers of Attorney Act 1985, s.8). Even so:

> "the court's powers are primarily directed to the proper supervision of the attorney, and to giving consents or authorisations which are necessary to supplement the powers but which are not inconsistent with restrictions imposed by the donor of the power."[12]

Revocation

An enduring power of attorney may be revoked in one of three ways, automatically, by the donor, or by the court.

Section 2(10) of the Enduring Powers of Attorney Act 1985 provides for automatic revocation on the bankruptcy of the attorney, whether or not the enduring power of attorney has been registered. If the attorney is a

---

[12] *per* Vinelott J. in *Re R. (Enduring Power of Attorney)* [1990] 1 Ch. 647 at 652.

sole or joint appointment then the registration will be cancelled, if joint and several, the registration will be amended to allow the non-bankrupt attorney to continue acting.

The donor can revoke an enduring power of attorney at any time before registration as if it were an ordinary power, so this can be express or implied, oral, in writing or by deed. Under the Enduring Powers of Attorney Act 1985, s.8(3), the court must confirm any revocation if satisfied that the donor has done whatever was necessary at law to effect an express revocation and was mentally capable of revoking the enduring power of attorney when he did so (whether or not he is so when the court considers the application).

Once an enduring power of attorney has been registered, any attempted revocation by the donor must be confirmed by the court (Enduring Powers of Attorney Act 1985, s.7(1)). The donor must apply to the court which applies the section 8(3) test above.

The court may revoke an enduring power of attorney if it finds an objection founded in the use of fraud or undue pressure to induce the donor to create the enduring power of attorney or the attorney's unsuitability as attorney has been made out (Enduring Powers of Attorney Act 1985, s.6). It may also revoke an enduring power of attorney when exercising any of its powers under Part VII of the Mental Health Act 1983 (for example appointing a receiver).

If the attorney wishes to disclaim an enduring power of attorney, no such disclaimer, whether by deed or otherwise, is valid unless and until the attorney gives notice of it to the donor (Enduring Powers of Attorney Act 1985, s.2(12)). If at the time of disclaimer the attorney has reason to believe the donor is or is becoming mentally incapable, then the attorney must give notice of the disclaimer to the court, and the disclaimer is not valid unless and until the attorney has done so (Enduring Powers of Attorney Act 1985, s.4(6)).

Once an enduring power of attorney is registered, again no disclaimer is valid unless and until the attorney has given notice to the court (Enduring Powers of Attorney Act 1985, s.7(1)(b)). In the latter circumstances the court can then decide whether or not a receivership is necessary for proper management of the donor's affairs in the future.

Registration is cancelled if the court is satisfied that the donor is and is likely to remain mentally capable, or on being satisfied of the death or bankruptcy of the donor or the attorney (Enduring Powers of Attorney Act 1985, s.8(4)).

There is a limited power to make gifts under the Enduring Powers of Attorney Act 1985, s.3(5), which applies if the enduring power of attorney does not contain any conditions or restrictions preventing such gift-giving. The power is not as wide as is generally imagined, but may only be used "to make gifts of a seasonal nature or at a time, or on an anniversary, of a birth or marriage, to persons (including himself) who are related to or connected with the donor" (s.3(5)(a)). There is also the ability to gift to charities to whom the donor made or might be expected to make gifts (s.3(5)(b)).

An attorney under a registered power has no power to make a will, but must look to the court's jurisdiction under the Mental Health Act 1983 so far as statutory wills are concerned.

It is advisable to suggest to clients, possibly when making wills, that they should also consider the making of an enduring power of attorney and keeping it in reserve in case the need should arise when they may require a third party to manage their finances. The advantages of an enduring power of attorney include the ability to select for oneself who will deal with one's finances, rather than relying on a court appointment, and the comparative ease and lack of expense when using an enduring power, as opposed to the more restrictive regime and cost to one's estate when a receivership is involved.

COURT OF PROTECTION

Mental incapacity

The Court of Protection's jurisdiction is derived from Part VII of the Mental Health Act 1983, and its practice is regulated by the Court of Protection Rules 1994.[13]

In order for the court to exercise its powers over a person's affairs, it must first be satisfied that such person is "incapable, by reason of mental disorder, of managing and administering his property and affairs" (Mental Health Act 1983, s.94(2)). It is therefore advisable to ascertain that the patient (as he is known) is not suffering from a drink or drug problem (where the court has no jurisdiction), or some acute health problem which will respond to treatment and so obviate the need for proceedings.

The court has its own medical certificate, Form C.P.3, which is best completed by a medical practitioner with knowledge of the patient, generally his general practitioner, but it can be a specialist. The court produces guidance notes with the form to help the doctor complete it and it is worth sending these notes to the doctor along with an explanation of what is required as many general practitioners are unfamiliar with the court's requirements and do not always provide adequate information. The doctor's fee is payable out of the patient's estate.

If there is uncertainty about the patient's capacity or needs, a request can be made for the patient to be visited by one of the Lord Chancellor's Visitors. These are Medical, Legal and General Visitors who are not officers of the court but work in close co-operation with it. At the court's direction they can visit the patient to assess a particular problem and

[13] S.I. 1994 No. 3046.

provide a report, which may be restricted in to whom it can be revealed and the contents of which may be examined in relevant proceedings (Mental Health Act 1983, ss.102 and 103).

Procedure

Proceedings are commenced by means of a first application, which is completed in duplicate on Form C.P.1 and submitted to the court along with the medical certificate and relevant evidence to back up the application. A commencement fee is payable, now £100 (r. 79).

If a short form rule 9 certificate is required, a letter may be sufficient, if full proceedings are contemplated then the court requires much greater detail and Form C.P.5, certificate of family and property, needs to be completed.

The C.P.5 requires details of the applicant and full details of the patient. The questions to be completed are fairly comprehensive, starting with the name, address and relationship of the applicant and moving on to the same details in respect of the patient. Full details of immediate kin are also required as is confirmation that these relatives are informed of the fact of the application. The court also needs to know whether or not there is a guardianship order in effect or a power of attorney in existence. It also encourages sight of any will. In order that a complete picture of the patient can be built up there is space for a life history of the patient, including details of interests or hobbies so that, if the money will stretch, charitable contributions can be maintained and provision made for holidays or other items which the patient can benefit from or enjoy. There are questions as to current and future income and expenditure, details of assets and whether it is proposed that these be maintained or liquidated, and whether or not there are current or potential liabilities.

The more detail available to the court the quicker and more comprehensive the initial orders will be, but, if producing exact details of investment balances or next-of-kin is difficult, there should be no delay in making the application if it is obvious that one is necessary. It is better to have the matter underway with interim orders dealing with immediate problems or supplemental orders sorting out the difficult ones rather than delaying things so that nursing homes become restless because of unpaid bills or properties deteriorate because they have not been marketed.

Once the application has been made, the court fixes a hearing date (at which attendance is not usually required) and returns one copy of the Form C.P.1 endorsed with the hearing details. The patient has to be served with notice of the hearing, the court producing Form C.P.6 which has to be given to the patient personally. The person serving the patient then completes Form C.P.7 detailing the fact of service and this is returned to the court. There is provision for service on the patient to be dispensed with (rule 26(1), but the court prefers notification to take place as the patient may be able to provide information which could be relevant or may express dislike or distrust of the proposed receiver. It is generally only if there is medical evidence of service being prejudicial to the patient's health that dispensation will be granted. Service must take place at least 10 clear days before the hearing date.

The court may produce interim orders or certificates under rule 44 prior to the formal hearing date if it considers this advisable. For example, monies may be ordered to be released from a bank account in order to meet residential home fees or the giving up of a tenancy may be authorised. It may be that all that is required to handle the patient's affairs is some form of authority under rule 9, and thereafter using the benefits agency's device of appointeeship to collect pensions, etc., will be more than adequate. The rough guideline is whether or not the patient's assets are worth less than £5,000.

If a full receivership is the solution, after the hearing the court produces a draft of its proposed first general order, in duplicate, for consideration. The order can be fully comprehensive, dealing with a variety of matters as set out in the Mental Health Act 1983, ss.95 and 96.

The usual format is first to appoint a receiver. This is normally one named individual. The court inclines against a joint appointment as this can prove more costly for the patient as well as involving practical difficulties; nor does a joint appointment solve political difficulties between various family factions. Generally, the order goes on to authorise the receiver to collect, on the patient's behalf, all income to which he is entitled, from state benefits to investment income. If particular investments are to be realised the order will go on to authorise the relevant bank or building society to pay over to the receiver (if he is to handle the money for payment of debts, etc.), or lodge the funds in court. If land is to be sold, it may be ordered at this stage. There may also be clauses as to the retention in safe keeping of wills, deeds, documents of title or valuable chattels, a requirement as to the production of annual accounts and provision as to the payment of costs.

The court may request additional information at the time the order is being approved, for example, sight of investments or certificates of balance in respect of bank accounts. It may also require the proposed receiver to be fidelity bonded, the amount of security being linked to the income likely to pass through the receiver's hands. Until the security is taken up and the court informed that it is in place, the sealed copy of the order will not be released. The cost of the annual premium is borne by the patient's estate. If the receiver is a practising solicitor then bonding is not required.

It may be that the court will require Form C.P.12, receipt and undertaking to be completed by the solicitor or bank ordered to have deposited with them any will, deeds or other articles for safekeeping during the patient's lifetime or until further order. If the sale of a property is ordered the court will require the solicitor dealing with the transaction to undertake to place the proceeds of sale on deposit pending the court's directions as to investment. It may be that the court will accept the completed Form C.P.12 and any undertaking soon after the sealed order has been issued.

The approved or amended draft is returned to the court along with any outstanding information and a request for an adequate number of copies of the sealed order. The final order is then engrossed and sealed by the court and copies sent out. The receiver receives his own personally marked copy along with a booklet from the court explaining his duties.

Receivership

Once the order has been made it is produced to the relevant authorities, pension payers, etc., so that its terms can be carried through. The receiver should open a bank account immediately in the name of "AB Receiver for CD" and operate this account in such a way as to pass all the patient's monies through this account and see that all liabilities are discharged through the account as well. This makes not only the handling of the patient's affairs easier, but also the production of the annual accounts. If required by the court these coincide with the anniversary date of the order. The court provides the forms upon which the accounts are prepared and examines them against receipts and bank statements. It may be that if the patient's affairs are relatively straightforward the normal accounting procedures will be dispensed with and a more simple form substituted. This is also a convenient time for the patient's affairs to be reviewed, for consideration to be given about changes in investment, the investment of surplus income or the need for capital to be released to meet future expenditure.

In addition to the commencement fee the court charges an annual administration fee, due on the anniversary of the receiver's appointment and based on the disposable income available for the patient in each accounting year. It is possible for the payment of the whole or part of this fee to be postponed or waived where hardship might otherwise be caused or circumstances are otherwise exceptional (r.86).

If, as a result of the court's directions, an asset has to be disposed of which has been specifically devised or bequeathed in the patient's will, then the potential beneficiary's interest is preserved in the net proceeds of sale (Mental Health Act 1983, s.101). The fund representing them is specifically "earmarked" in some way. Even so, the patient's needs come first so that resort is made to these funds for the patient's benefit if necessary if there are insufficient funds available elsewhere.

The court has wide powers so far as the patient's affairs are concerned, but has no power to insist where a patient should live or to consent to medical treatment. Over and above the general management of finances and consideration of annual accounts it can deal with the patient's interest in a partnership or family company, the sale or purchase of a residence, his rights under a will or intestacy and any tax planning which this might involve, and the making or amending of a will (see Chapter 13—Wills, Intestacy and Family Provision).

If the patient is a trustee, the court will require an application to appoint a new trustee in place of the patient pursuant to the Mental Health Act 1983, s.96(1)(*k*) or the Trustee Act 1925, ss.36(9) or 54. The relevant section will depend on whether or not the patient is merely a trustee, has a power of appointment but is not a trustee, or is entitled to a beneficial interest. As well as the need for medical evidence (which may be covered by receivership proceedings) there will need to be an application, consent to act by the proposed new trustee, a certificate as to the fitness to act of the proposed new trustee, undertakings with regard to the patient's interest and possibly a draft deed of appointment. Increasingly this will become relevant as more cases arise where one of a couple who own the matrimonial home jointly becomes unable to manage their affairs and they move into a smaller property, sheltered accommodation, or residential care.

If the patient's mental health recovers on what would appear to be a permanent basis then an application can be made for the receivership to be discharged (Mental Health Act 1983, s.99(3)).

If a receiver wishes, or the court considers it expedient, he may retire and a new receiver be appointed (s.99). Often receivers wish to be relieved of their responsibilities because of age or ill health. When considering whom to appoint initially it may often be more practical to appoint someone of the next generation rather than the patient's spouse or sibling. If the receiver dies, the court may well include directions as to the completion of accounts for the period from the last accounts to death and dealing with the balance on the account.

On the patient's death the court's jurisdiction ends and the receiver's duties are to obtain directions for the winding up of the receivership. The court will require sight of the death certificate and any grant of representation or, if none, a statement of the assets and the consent of the executors or all the principal beneficiaries on an intestacy as to the payment out of funds in court. Final directions will consist of dealing with funds in court, passing or dispensing with the receiver's final account, discharging the fidelity bond, settling the court's administration fees and arranging for solicitor's fees to be agreed or taxed. The receiver should hand the balance on the receivership account to the personal representative and should not operate the account after the patient's death except to possibly pay the funeral account.

A solicitor's costs in respect of all matters in the Court of Protection can be taxed. The court has agreed a scale of fixed costs with the Law Society for many of the usual transactions from applying for the appointment of a receiver to annual management fees and fees for preparing the receiver's annual account. It is worth considering the current scale particularly for conveyancing matters and preparation of routine accounts. The costs, unless otherwise ordered, are payable out of the patient's estate.[14]

---

[14] *Re E.G.* [1914] 1 Ch. 927.

Chapter 13
Wills, Intestacy and Family Provision

Wills, the operation of the intestacy rules, and the inadequacy of family provision for dependants are particularly relevant to older people and it is easier and cheaper for all concerned if the client can be persuaded to review his financial and family affairs and update his will to take into account prevailing circumstances.

WILLS

At the time a will is executed the testator must have testamentary capacity. In addition, for a will to be valid in England and Wales, it must comply with the formalities of the Wills Act 1837 as amended by the Administration of Justice Act 1982, unless it is a privileged will (basically that of a soldier, member of the Royal Air Force or Navy on actual military service or mariner or seaman at sea[1]).

Capacity

So far as testamentary capacity is concerned, the testator must not only be able to understand what he is disposing of and to whom, but must also have the capacity to realise the extent of his assets and those towards whom he has responsibility. He is not expected to provide for all possible relatives or dependants, but at least be aware of those for whom he may have decided to make no provision.[2]

The testator must have testamentary capacity at the time any will or codicil is executed, even if his understanding has faded from the time he gave instructions to such an extent that he understands that he is executing a will which complies with the instructions given but he is unable to understand the detailed provisions.[3]

---

[1] See the Wills Act 1837, s.11; see also Wills (Soldiers and Sailors) Act 1918.
[2] *Banks v. Goodfellow* [1870] 5 Q.B. 549.
[3] *Perera v. Perera* [1901] A.C. 354.

The presumption is that the testator has capacity at the time a will or codicil is executed. If there is uncertainty or the likelihood of the will or codicil being contested in the future, then there is merit in obtaining a medical opinion of the testator's capacity at the time of execution, and, preferably, have the medical advisor act as one of the witnesses, making a record of his examination and medical findings for future reference.[4] This is particularly advisable if the testator is frail, close to death, particularly elderly, favouring the person initially approaching the solicitor with purported instructions or doing something vastly different from previously expressed intentions. If the will or codicil is contested, it is for the person propounding it to prove the testator's testamentary capacity at the time.[5]

Formal requirements

The formalities required by the Wills Act, s.9, as amended by the Administration of Justice Act 1982, s.17, are :

> "It is in writing;
> Signed by the testator or by some person in his presence and by his direction;
> It appears that the testator intended by his signature to give effect to the will;
> The signature is made or acknowledged by the testator in the presence of two or more witnesses present at the same time;
> Each witness either signs and attests the will, or acknowledges his signature, in the presence of the testator;"

The testator's signature no longer has to be "at the foot or end" of the will so long as it is apparent that he intended to give effect to his will by that signature.

If the testator is unable to form a clear signature, possibly through illiteracy, but more often with the older client because of blindness, stroke or extreme feebleness, then the attestation clause should be extended to show that the will was either read over to or by the testator and that he understood and approved the contents. If such an extended attestation is not used, than an affidavit of due execution will need to be filed when applying for probate, setting out the circumstances of why the signature (or lack of it) is as it is. See the Non-Contentious Probate Rules 1987, r.12.[6] If the will was signed by someone else on the testator's behalf then the attestation clause should be extended to explain this, or, again an affidavit explaining the facts will be necessary (r.13).

Alterations and obliterations

There is a presumption that unattested alterations, interlineations and erasures were made after execution with the result that probate is

---

[4] *Re Simpson dec'd* (1977) 121 S.J. 224.
[5] *Re Flynn dec'd* [1982] 1 W.L.R. 310.
[6] S.I. 1987 No. 2024.

granted in respect of the original wording, the alterations, etc., being ignored. If the alteration means the original words are not apparent then probate is granted in blank in respect of that part of the will that is no longer ascertainable.

The burden of proving that an alteration was made prior to execution rests on the person seeking to rely on it.

If the alteration was made after execution, then, to be valid, it has to be executed in like manner to the original will (Wills Act 1837, s.21). In order to establish whether the alteration was present at the time the will was executed and so as to give directions to the form in which the will is to be proved, the registrar shall require evidence (r.14).

If the will is not in an unmarked state when it is found, the registrar requires evidence as to its condition when found and an explanation as to whether or not any other documentation is missing or needs to be incorporated in order to ascertain exactly what should be proved (r.14).

Mistake

It is possible for a will to be rectified if the court is satisfied that the will fails to carry out the testator's intention as a consequence of clerical error or a failure to understand the testator's instructions (see the Administration of Justice Act 1982, s.20). Generally an application for rectification must be made within six months of a grant of representation being taken out (s.20(2)).

Revocation

A will is revoked by the subsequent marriage of the testator (Wills Act 1837, s.18) unless the will is specifically made in expectation of marriage by the testator to a particular person and he intends that the will should not be revoked on marriage (Administration of Justice Act 1982, s.18). Marriage, however, may not revoke a disposition in a will in exercise of a power of appointment, notwithstanding the testator's subsequent marriage unless the property so appointed would in default of appointment, pass to the testator's personal representatives (Administration of Justice Act 1982, s.18(2)).

Voluntary revocation is a question of intention on the part of the testator. It must be a present intention as opposed to a future one, and may be evidenced by the testator's declaration or by inference of the nature of the act done. The same standard of testamentary capacity is required to destroy a will as is necessary to make one.[7]

The revocation can be effected by a later will or codicil duly executed, by some writing declaring an intention to revoke the will and duly executed as a will, or by burning, tearing or otherwise destroying the will by the testator or someone in his presence and by his direction with the intention of revoking it (Wills Act 1837, s.20).

---

[7] *Re Sabatini* (1969) 114 S.J. 35.

The will must be injured, with the intention it be revoked, to such an extent that it destroys the entirety of the will, although the materials of which the will is composed do not have to be destroyed. Merely striking through the will with a pen or writing "cancelled" across is insufficient to be valid revocation. There must be physical destruction.

It is possible for revocation to extend to either the whole will or only some part of it (Wills Act 1837, s.20).

A revocation is prima facie absolute unless it is shown to be conditional, in which case the burden of proof lies on the person seeking to show the revocation to be conditional. In cases of physical destruction, the question of whether the revocation is conditional is one of fact; where there is a subsequent will or codicil it is a question of construction (*Re Finnemore dec'd*[8]).

It may be that a revocation is intended to be dependent upon another disposition which has already been or is intended to be made. If this is established the revocation may fail if the operative dependent disposition fails to take effect. It is a question of fact in each particular case.

COURT OF PROTECTION AND STATUTORY WILLS

If an individual is a patient of the Court of Protection or there are doubts about his ability to manage his affairs and possibly also to make a will, the guidance of the Court of Protection can be sought and the possibility of a statutory will considered. If the Court's directions are not sought, there may be future difficulties, not only surrounding the validity of the will because of the patient's potential lack of capacity, but also with regard to the payment of costs in respect of the work done in connection with the will.

Execution of will by patient

Where an individual's personal affairs are subject to an Order of the Court of Protection and it appears that he wishes to make a will, the Court will require evidence of the patient's testamentary capacity. Can he understand the nature of the document to be executed, the extent of property to be disposed of, and the claims of those to whom he might be expected to have a responsibility? (*Banks v. Goodfellow.*[9])

A medical report is obtained, possibly by way of the Court requesting one of the Lord Chancellor's Medical Visitors to visit the patient and report, or alternatively by consulting the patient's own medical advisors, where it is preferred that the report is provided by the medical attendant with the most senior status.

---

[8] [1991] 1 W.L.R. 793.
[9] (1871) L.R. 11 Eq. 472.

If the medical report indicates that the patient has testamentary capacity, instructions for the will can be taken. The solicitor must still be satisfied, both at the time of instruction and the time of execution, that the patient has testamentary capacity. It is advisable that the doctor who provided the medical report (if not the Lord Chancellor's Medical Visitor) be one of the witnesses to the will.

Once executed, the Court requires that a copy of the will be forwarded so that directions for safe custody can be made. Any previous will made should not be destroyed but retained and its envelope marked with the details of the newly executed will.

Statutory will

If the Court has evidence that the patient does not have testamentary capacity, the Court has power to make a will on the patient's behalf (Mental Health Act 1983, s.96(1)(e)). The objects of any such will must fall within the general functions of the judge with respect to the property and affairs of the patient as set out in the Mental Health Act 1983, s.95, *i.e.*:

(a) for the maintenance or other benefit of the patient;
(b) for the maintenance or other benefit of members of the patient's family;
(c) for making provision for persons or purposes for whom or which the patient might be expected to provide if he were not mentally disordered; or
(d) otherwise for administering the patient's affairs.

Principles taken into account

The approach to be taken by the Court when making a statutory will was considered in *Re D.(J)*.[10] This was decided on the provisions of the Mental Health Act 1959, but the principles when applying the Mental Health Act 1983 remain the same. The principles or factors to be taken into account on making a statutory will are:

(1) It is to be assumed that the patient is having a brief lucid interval at the time the will is made.
(2) During the lucid interval it is assumed that the patient has full knowledge of the past as well as full realisation that as soon as the will is executed he will relapse into the actual medical state that previously existed, with the prognosis as it actually is.
(3) It is the actual patient who should be considered, not a hypothetical one, taking account of his antipathies or affections, although not to give effect to those "beyond reason".
(4) The patient is to be regarded as advised by a competent solicitor.

---

[10] [1982] Ch. 237.

(5) The patient is to be envisaged as taking a broad brush approach rather than an accountant's pen.

The principles detailed above can be applied when the patient once had capacity. It has recently been decided that the Court also has jurisdiction to make a will for a patient who is born with a severe mental disability and so has never had testamentary capacity: see *Re C. (a Patient).*[11] The assumption is made that the patient would have been a normal decent person who would have acted in accordance with contemporary standards of morality. In that particular case the patient had inherited family monies so as to have an estate of £1,600,000. She had cousins, some of whom had not been aware of her existence prior to the Court proceedings, and had lived in one National Health Service hospital for 65 years from the age of 10. After minor legacies (including one of £15,000 to the grandchild of a cousin who suffered from Down's Syndrome, where the Court felt that the patient would wish to recognise her "community of misfortune" with the child[12]) the rest of the estate was split equally between charity and the family. Some of the patient's estate was distributed immediately by lifetime gift, and some by the will.

Form of application

The Court issues a Practice Note, P.N.9, which lays down its requirements when applying for a statutory will on behalf of the patient. A transaction fee of £100 is payable to the Court on the application.

The persons who can apply are the receiver, any person who has made an application for the appointment of a receiver, any person who might be entitled under any known will or on intestacy, any person for whom it might be considered the patient should provide if he were capable, an attorney under a registered enduring power of attorney, or any person whom the Court may authorise (Court of Protection Rules 1994, r.20[13]).

The hearing is before the Master in Chambers (unless the Master considers there are points which require reference to the judge) and the solicitor having conduct of the proceedings is expected to attend. The Court has power to direct that the patient is represented by the Official Solicitor (Court of Protection Rules 1994, r.15[14]) and generally does so.

Evidence

Evidence is by way of affidavit or affirmation with exhibits. The affidavit must comply with the Practice Direction (Mental Health: Affidavits).[15] For ease of filing the exhibits should not be stitched into the affidavit but should be exhibited separately.

---

[11] [1991] 3 All E.R. 866.
[12] *ibid. per* Hoffman J. at 872.
[13] S.I. 1994 No. 3046.
[14] *ibid.*
[15] [1984] 1 W.L.R. 1171.

In order for the Court to have a complete picture of the patient, in such circumstances the affidavit should contain the following information:

Details of the patient's family and a family tree.
Details of the patient's assets with current valuations.
Estimate of the patient's income and expenditure.
Details of the patient's likely future needs, and any changes which might cause the estate to increase or decrease.
Details of the patient's general health, domicile, his address and type of accommodation.
Financial details of the proposed beneficiaries and the likely inheritance tax and capital gains tax effects of the proposed will and of any lifetime gifts.
An explanation of the likely effect of the proposals on the patient's assets, more relevant if lifetime gifts are proposed, and whether immoveable property will be affected by the proposed will.
Current evidence of lack of testamentary capacity.
A copy of any existing will.
A draft of the proposed will.

Parties to be notified

On receipt of the application, the Court directs the parties to be notified. The Court has a general discretion which it can exercise in relation to the particular facts of each case.

In the ordinary case where there is no apparent urgency, all persons who might be materially or adversely affected should be notified of the application. This will normally include next of kin on an intestacy or beneficiaries named in previous wills (*Re B*[16]).

The fact that notification may cause upset within the patient's family is not sufficient reason for notification to be dispensed with.

In an emergency (*e.g.* the imminent death of the patient), the Court can dispense with the notification. In *Re Davey*[17] the Court had to balance the effects of the intestacy rules passing a substantial part of the estate to a much younger husband of not two months standing, who worked at the nursing home where the patient had become resident only six months previously, as opposed to the making of a statutory will in favour of blood relatives who had featured in a will made three months previously. The other relatives had no way of preserving their position if the patient died without a statutory will, whereas the husband had the opportunity of bringing proceedings under the Inheritance (Provision for Family and Dependants) Act 1975. The patient died seven days after the order to make the statutory will.

The practice in such cases is to give notice to the parties affected immediately after the hearing, and, if the patient survives, it is always

---

[16] [1987] 1 W.L.R. 552.
[17] [1981] 1 W.L.R. 164.

open for a further application to be made and a subsequent will ordered in the fullness of time.

Execution

Any statutory will should be expressed to be signed by the patient acting by the person authorised by the Court (Mental Health Act 1983, s.7) and must be:

(a) signed by the authorised person with the name of the patient, and with his own name, in the presence of two or more witnesses present at the same time; and

(b) attested and subscribed by those witnesses in the presence of the authorised person; and

(c) sealed with the official seal of the Court of Protection.

Safe custody of will

Once a will has been executed the Court will direct where it is to be deposited for safe custody. It is usually with the solicitors who prepared it or at the bank where the receivership bank account is maintained.

The will is kept subject to the Court's directions. A receipt and undertaking (Form C.P.12) is required to be filed confirming receipt of the will and undertaking not to part with it during the patient's lifetime except on the Court's direction.

Disclosure of contents

The contents of a will held subject to the Court's directions cannot be disclosed. However if the Court has the information it will disclose matters relating to specific funeral directions.

Disposal of assets

It may be that specific assets, including realty, are disposed of during the course of the receivership, although specifically devised or bequeathed in the will. The beneficiary's interest in that asset is preserved by the operation of the Mental Health Act 1983, s.101, insofar as property remains in the patient's estate which represents the property disposed of previously.

INTESTACY

There may be a total or a partial intestacy, dependent on whether or not the deceased left no will, total intestacy, or a will which does not dispose of his entire estate, so that a partial intestacy applies to those assets undisposed of by the will.

Surviving spouse and issue

The distribution on intestacy is governed by the Table of Distribution in the Administration of Estates Act 1925, s.46. The amount of the fixed statutory legacy is amended by statutory instrument.

As from December 1, 1993 the distribution of an estate where the deceased left a surviving spouse and issue is that the widow(er) takes the personal chattels as defined by the Administration of Estates Act 1925, s.55 (1)(x) and a statutory legacy of the first £125,000.[18] The residue is divided into two halves, one-half to the issue on statutory trusts absolutely and one-half giving a life interest to the widow(er) and then passing to the issue on statutory trusts in reversion.

Surviving spouse and no issue

Where there is a surviving spouse and no issue, the widow(er) takes the personal chattels and the first £200,000 and one-half of the remainder absolutely.[19] The other half passes to parents absolutely, where none, to brothers and sisters of the whole blood in equal shares, the issue of those who have predeceased the intestate taking *per stirpes* the share to which their parents would have been entitled. If there are no parents or brothers or sisters or their issue, the widow(er) is entitled to the entire estate whatever its value.

Spouse's rights

When paying a statutory legacy to the surviving spouse, interest is due from the date of death to the date of payment, the interest rate being at such rate as the Lord Chancellor may specify by order, currently 6 per cent.[20] A surviving spouse has the right to require the personal representative of the deceased to redeem the life interest to which he or she might be entitled on the intestacy (Administration of Estates Act 1925, s.47[21]). The life interest is capitalised, reckoned in accordance with special rules calculated by reference to the Intestate Succession (Interest and Capitalisation) Order 1977.[22] To take advantage of this entitlement the surviving spouse must inform the personal representatives in writing within 12 months from the date on which representation was first taken out. In exceptional cases this limitation period can be extended by the court.

---

[18] See the Family Provision (Intestate Succession) Order 1993 (S.I. 1993 No. 2906).
[19] *ibid.*
[20] See the Intestate Succession (Interest and Capitalisation) Order 1977 (S.I. 1977 No. 1491) and the Intestate Succession (Interest and Capitalisation) Order 1977 (Amendment) Order 1983 (S.I. 1983 No. 1374).
[21] Added by the Intestates' Estates Act 1952.
[22] S.I. 1977 No. 1491.

In addition, under the Intestates Estates Act 1952, s.5 and second Schedule a surviving spouse has the right to require that an interest in a dwelling house in which the intestate's surviving spouse was resident at the time of the intestate's death and which forms part of the intestate's estate, can be appropriated towards the surviving spouse's absolute interest in the estate. The Intestates Estates Act 1952, second Schedule sets out the steps to be followed in order for this to be done.

The surviving spouse's right to appropriate the former matrimonial home is exercisable even where the value of the home is more than the value of the surviving spouse's interest: see *Phelps, Wells v. Phelps*.[23]

No surviving spouse

If there is no surviving spouse, the estate is distributed on statutory trusts amongst all the members of the first class of relatives, when a member of that class is identified, the order of priority being as follows:

> Issue who obtain full age or marry under that age, children or predeceasing children taking their parents' share *per stirpes*.
> Parents or the surviving parent.
> Brothers and sisters of the whole blood and issue of such as died in the intestate's lifetime.
> Brothers and sisters of the half blood and issue of such as died in the intestate's lifetime.
> Grandparents.
> Uncles and aunts of the whole blood and issue of such as died in the intestate's lifetime.
> Uncles and aunts of the half blood and issue of such as died in the intestate's lifetime.
> If no blood relative in accordance with the above classes, then the Crown, Duchy of Lancaster or Duchy of Cornwall.

The statutory trusts of issue are set out in the Administration of Estates Act 1925, s.57, and apply so that an entitlement is held on trust and does not vest until the beneficiary attains the age of 18. The statutory powers of advancement and maintenance (Trustee Act 1925, ss.31 and 32) apply; lifetime gifts may be taken into account and infants may be permitted the use and enjoyment of personal chattels (Administration of Estates Act 1925, s.47(1)).

The statutory trusts for relatives other than issue are on the same terms but the bringing of lifetime gifts into account does not apply.

Illegitimacy is not to be taken into consideration in determining the rights of succession of an illegitimate person, or determining the rights of succession to the estate of an illegitimate person, or the rights of

---

[23] [1980] Ch. 275.

succession through an illegitimate person in respect of deaths on or after April 4, 1988 (Family Law Reform Act 1987, s.18).

POWERS AND DUTIES OF PERSONAL REPRESENTATIVES

Vesting of powers

The executor's powers arise at the time of the deceased's death as they are derived from the will. In practice, not much can be done without production of the grant of probate, which confirms the executor's powers, as those with control of the assets, banks, etc., will refuse to deal with the executor until they see proof of the executor's title.

If there is no will, none of the relatives have authority to deal with the estate until a grant of letters of administration is obtained, as it is from the grant that the administrator derives his authority. Until letters of administration are granted, the deceased's assets vest in the President of the Family Division (Administration of Estates Act 1925, s.9). Once letters of administration are granted then the deceased's assets vest in the administrator and such vesting also dates back to the deceased's death insofar as this will validate acts done for the benefit of the estate prior to the grant, which acts are viewed objectively.

Dealing with assets without a grant

Assets in joint names, such as share holdings or bank accounts, will pass automatically to the co-owner on production of the death certificate, as will land held as beneficial joint tenants.

If assets have been nominated (some Post Office or trustee bank accounts have been dealt with in this way, although it is no longer possible to nominate an account), then production of the death certificate is sufficient for them to pass to the nominee.

Life policies written up in trust can be paid out to the trustees of the policy and then on to the beneficiaries on production of the policy and death certificate. Some pension funds may also pay out by way of discretionary trusts, where the deceased had nominated to the pension fund trustees whom he wishes the trustees to consider when distributing the funds, although such nominations are for the guidance of the trustees only and occasionally the pension fund trustees may distribute funds to relatives or dependants not nominated by the deceased.

If the remaining assets are worth less than £5,000 in total, the need for a grant can be dispensed with and banks, etc., will generally act on sight of the original will, death certificate, claim forms signed by the executor (probably including an indemnity), and possibly a statutory declaration. If the case is one of intestacy, the consent of all the other beneficiaries may be required confirming the bank may deal with one family member on everyone's behalf (Administration of Estates (Small Payments) Act 1965).

Actions prior to grant

The personal representatives need to obtain details of assets and liabilities as well as ascertaining the whereabouts of documents of title. They are then in a position to complete an Inland Revenue account if applicable and submit the oath to lead probate.

If the estate is liable to inheritance tax funds needs to be raised to pay that proportion of the tax due on delivery of the account. Most building societies will allow cheques to be drawn on the deceased's account in favour of "Inland Revenue" if the position is explained. Banks are less obliging, but will agree the opening of an executor's loan account for a limited period. Interest paid on the loan for inheritance tax purposes can subsequently be set off against the personal representative's liability to income tax during the administration period (Income and Corporation Taxes Act 1988, s.364(1)).

Actions post-grant

Once the grant of representation has been obtained, together with sufficient additional office copies, it should be registered with all the relevant authorities where assets are held, such as banks, building societies, company registrars in respect of shareholdings, etc., and the Inland Revenue in order to clear pre-death income tax and capital gains tax liabilities.

Accompanying the grant should be the investment representing the asset and, if possible, a signed authority to encash or transfer it. If assets specifically bequeathed are not needed to discharge liabilities, they should be transferred to the relevant beneficiaries sooner rather than later. As a specific gift includes the right to all income, etc., earned by the asset concerned from the date of death, it makes it easier to transfer the assets so that the income passes direct into the beneficiary's hands as soon as possible, rather than having to account, subsequently, for income received by the personal representative prior to the transfer.

Sufficient assets should be realised as soon as possible in order to clear any loan raised to pay inheritance tax, to discharge the funeral account and any debts left by the deceased, and to pay pecuniary legacies. The balance of any monies raised should be placed on deposit pending completion of the administration.

The personal representative should be satisfied as to the identity of the beneficiaries as he is under a duty to distribute the deceased's estate to the persons entitled under the will or intestacy (Administration of Estates Act 1925, s.25).

If uncertain of the extent of the deceased's liabilities or of having identified all the beneficiaries such as "the children of A", protection is afforded under Trustee Act 1925, s.27, by the placing of advertisements giving notice of the personal representative's intention to distribute the assets in accordance with the claims which have been notified to him.

The residuary beneficiaries should be consulted as to how they would like to receive their inheritance, *i.e.* by way of the assets being transferred *in specie* or whether everything is to be encashed and the balance paid over. The personal representative may have a power of appropriation under the will, if not, the Administration of Estates Act 1925, s.41, gives the personal representative a statutory power to appropriate which can be exercised as long as it does not affect prejudicially any specific devise or bequest and consent is obtained from the beneficiary to whom the asset is to be appropriated. At common law, a residuary beneficiary may insist on an appropriation of his share of an easily divisible asset rather than the proceeds which the sale of it may realise (*Re Marshall*[24]). As long as by doing this the beneficiary does not obtain an unfair advantage *vis à vis* the other beneficiaries (*Lloyds Bank plc v. Duker*[25]).

The assets are transferred from personal representative to beneficiary by the method of transfer applicable to the particular asset as between individuals, *e.g.* stock transfer forms for shares, withdrawal and transfer slips for building societies. Land can be transferred by way of conveyance by deed, but it is more usual to do so by way of written assent under the Administration of Estates Act 1925, s.36, with a memorandum being endorsed on the grant of representation.

Once liabilities and pecuniary legacies have been discharged, specific bequests transferred, the pre-death tax position cleared, and the remaining assets realised or appropriated to the residuary beneficiary, the personal representative is in a position to prepare estate accounts. These accounts should be clear and concise and record the transactions in the estate to show the beneficiaries how the amount of their final entitlement has been reached. The beneficiary should acknowledge receipt of the cash or other assets and be handed tax certificate form R185E in respect of the administration income which is evidence of the tax paid by the personal representative and which enables the beneficiary to then deal with his personal tax position in respect of this income.

If a trust arises, because of a life interest under the will or intestacy, a contingency needing to be attained, or a discretionary or other form of trust or settlement being created in the will, then the personal representative should be able to identify a time when the administration of the estate ceases and the formal running of the trust begins. If the trustees are different from the personal representatives, the transfer of assets makes that fact easy to identify. If personal representatives and trustees are the same, it can be less easy to see when the change in role may have taken place.

---

[24] [1914] 1 Ch. 192, C.A.
[25] [1987] 1 W.L.R. 1324.

It is advisable for there to be a recognisable transfer from one capacity to the other as the duties and responsibilities of personal representative and trustee are different, for example:

> Personal representatives have a duty to the estate as a whole, trustees just to their individual beneficiary.
>
> An action against a personal representative is statute barred after 12 years for beneficiaries, and action against a trustee for breach of trust is statute barred after six years (Limitation Act 1980, ss.21, 22).
>
> Personal representatives have joint and several authority in relation to pure personalty, trustees must always act jointly.
>
> A sole personal representative may give a valid receipt for the proceeds of the sale of land, a sole trustee has no such power and a co-trustee must be appointed.
>
> If a sole or last surviving personal representative dies, unless there is a chain of representation under the Administration of Estates Act 1925, s.7, a fresh grant, letters of administration *de bonis non*, must be obtained and a new personal representative completes the administration. If the last surviving trustee dies, his personal representatives have power to appoint a new trustee (Trustee Act 1925, s.36).

The generally accepted ways of evidencing the change in capacity are, in addition to accounts being drawn to establish the exact trust assets transferred, for land to be assented to the personal representatives on trust for sale, for stocks and shares to be registered in their names (possibly with a designation "A's A/C") and for bank and building society accounts to be transferred to them as trustees.

Once the above has been done, accounts approved and assets distributed, the administration of the estate is complete.

Family Provision

Whilst a will may comply with the statutory formalities as to validity or the intestacy rules provide to whom an estate should pass, there may be individuals who consider that they have not been provided for when they should have been, or that the provision made is not adequate. The Inheritance (Provision for Family and Dependants) Act 1975 was enacted to enable such people to claim against an estate.

Classes of applicant

In order to being an action under the Inheritance (Provision for Family and Dependants) Act 1975, s.2, the applicant must bring himself within one of the classes of person set out in section 1(1):

(*a*) the wife or husband of the deceased;

(*b*) a former wife or former husband of the deceased who has not remarried;

(*c*) a child of the deceased;

(d) any person (not being a child of the deceased) who, in the case of any marriage to which the deceased was at any time a party, was treated by the deceased as a child of the family in relation to that marriage.

(e) any person, (not being a person included in the foregoing paragraphs of this sub-section) who immediately before the death of the deceased was being maintained, either wholly or partly, by the deceased.

Section 1(3) of the act goes on to provide that for the purposes of (1)(e) above, a person should be treated as being maintained by the deceased, either wholly or partly, as the case may be, if the deceased, otherwise than for full valuable consideration, was making a substantial contribution in money or money's worth towards the reasonable needs of that person.

Basis of application

There is only one ground on which a claim can be based, which is the disposition of the deceased's estate effected by his will or the law relating to intestacy, or a combination of his will and that law, is not such as to make reasonable financial provision for the applicant (Inheritance (Provision for Family and Dependants) Act 1975, s.1(1)).

The act goes on to provide two meanings for "reasonable financial provision" depending on whether the applicant is a surviving spouse or one of the other classes of claimant.

If the applicant is a surviving spouse, except where the couple were judicially separated at the date of death and a decree was in force and the separation continuing, "reasonable financial provision" means such financial provision as it would be reasonable in all the circumstances of the case for a husband or wife to receive, whether or not that provision is required for his or her maintenance (Inheritance (Provision for Family and Dependants) Act 1975, s.1(2)(a)).

The test is wider than mere dependency and the courts may consider a divorce analogy test based on what provision the applicant might reasonably be expected to receive had the marriage been terminated by divorce rather than death (Inheritance (Provision for Family and Dependants) Act 1975, s.3(2) (*Moody v. Stevenson*[26]). The approach should be seen as establishing a minimum entitlement, as Oliver L.J. has stated in *Re Besterman dec'd*[27] that "the overriding consideration is what is reasonable".

For other applicants, "reasonable financial provision" means such financial provision as it would be reasonable in all the circumstances of

---

[26] [1992] Ch. 486.
[27] [1984] 1 Ch. 458 at 469.

the case for the applicant to receive for his maintenance (Inheritance (Provision for Family and Dependants) Act 1975, s.1(2)(b)).

When looking at maintenance, claims by adult able-bodied children are discouraged: *Re Coventry*.[28]

There can be difficulties when the claimant is a co-habitee, if the parties have contributed equally to the outgoings of their mutual home. It then becomes difficult for the surviving cohabitee to establish that he was being maintained by the deceased, with the deceased making a substantial contribution in money or money's worth towards the reasonable needs of that person as required by section 1(3).

When to apply

An application under the Inheritance (Provision for Family and Dependants) Act 1975, s.2, must be brought within six months from the date on which representation in respect of the estate of the deceased is first taken out (Inheritance (Provision for Family and Dependants) Act 1975, s.4). Providing the originating summons is issued within the time-limit, it does not matter that it has not been served.

The court has a discretion to permit an application to be made out of time. The Act does not set down any guidelines as to how the court should exercise its discretion. All the circumstances should be considered with the onus being on the applicant to establish sufficient grounds for the court to extend the general rule. A substantial case needs to be established, therefore, that it would be just to extend the time; the courts will consider the circumstances surrounding the application and how promptly the applicant has acted, whether or not negotiations have been undertaken to settle the claim, whether or not the estate has been distributed and whether or not the applicant has an arguable case.

An application cannot be made prior to a grant of representation being obtained (*Re McBroom dec'd*[29]). This can cause practical problems if it would appear that no-one is likely to apply for a grant, and it is suggested that a grant is applied for by a nominee of the applicant under the Supreme Court Act 1981, s.116, so that proceedings can then be issued.

Powers of the court

The court's powers with regard to the types of order it can make if satisfied that reasonable financial provision has not been made for the claimant are set out under the Inheritance (Provision for Family and Dependants) Act 1975, s.2(1), as follows:

(a) an order for the making to the applicant out of the net estate of the deceased of such periodical payments and for such term as may be specified in the order;

[28] [1980] Ch. 461, C.A.
[29] [1992] 2 FLR 49.

(b) an order for the payment to the applicant out of that estate of a lump sum of such amount as may be so specified;

(c) an order for the transfer to the applicant of such property comprised in that estate as may be so specified;

(d) an order for the settlement for the benefit of the applicant of such property comprised in that estate as may be so specified;

(e) an order for the acquisition out of property comprised in that estate of such property as may be so specified, and for the transfer of the property so acquired to the applicant or for the settlement thereof for his benefit;

(f) an order varying any ante-nuptial or post-nuptial settlement (including such a settlement raised by the will) made on the parties to a marriage to which the deceased was one of the parties, the variation being for the benefit of the surviving party to that marriage or any child of that marriage or any person who was treated by the deceased as a child of the family in relation to that marriage.

If the order is for periodical payments, it can specify the amounts to be paid, express such amount as equivalent to the whole of the income of the net estate, or so specify a proportion of the income of the net estate, or direct that part of the net estate be set aside for meeting the periodical payments from the income of such part of the net estate as is set aside.

Matters to which the court is to have regard

The Inheritance (Provision for Family and Dependants) Act 1975, s.3, sets out the matters to which the court is to have regard when determining in what manner to exercise its powers under the Inheritance (Provision for Family and Dependants) Act 1975, s.2, that is to say:

(a) the financial resources and financial needs which the applicant has or is likely to have in the foreseeable future;

(b) the financial resources and financial needs which any other applicant for an order under section 2 of the act has or is likely to have in the foreseeable future;

(c) the financial resources and financial needs which any beneficiary of the estate of the deceased has or is likely to have in the foreseeable future;

(d) any obligations and responsibilities which the deceased had towards any applicant for an order under section 2 or towards a beneficiary of the estate of the deceased;

(e) the size and nature of the net estate of the deceased;

(f) any physical or mental disability of any applicant for an order under section 2 or any beneficiary of the estate of the deceased;

(g) any other matter, including the conduct of the applicant or any other person, which in the circumstances of the case the court may consider relevant.

In addition, when considering a claim from a surviving or former spouse, the court may have regard to the age of the applicant, the duration of the marriage and the contribution made by the applicant to the welfare of the family of the deceased, including any contribution made through looking after the home or caring for the family.

Joint property

In considering making an order under the Inheritance (Provision for Family and Dependants) Act 1975, s.2, the court has power under the Inheritance (Provision for Family and Dependants) Act 1975, s.9(1), to treat as part of the net estate of the deceased his severable share of property where immediately before his death he was beneficially entitled to a joint tenancy. For the deceased's share of a beneficial joint tenancy to be considered, the application must be made within six months of the date of the grant; there is no provision for the court to be able to extend this time-limit.

In *Jessup v. Jessup*[30] the court awarded a widow a lump sum of £10,000 from the deceased's severable share (worth £21,000) of a property which he had owned jointly with his mistress, and which had passed to her by survivorship. The mistress had also received the deceased's death in service benefit of £40,000. The widow had inherited the deceased's estate of approximately £2,500.

When valuing the deceased's share of the property the court will take into account the deceased's share in the value of a life policy which paid out on death and so greatly enhanced the value of the jointly held property by redeeming the mortgage: *Powell v. Osbourne*.[31]

Dispositions intended to defeat financial provision

The court has powers to look at *inter vivos* dispositions made by the deceased if it appears these may have been made in order to defeat an application for financial provision under the Inheritance (Provision for Family and Dependants) Act 1975, s.2.

The donee of such a disposition can be ordered to provide for the applicant such money or other property as may be specified. The court must be satisfied that:

(1) less than six years before his death the deceased with the intention of defeating an application for financial provision under the Act, made a disposition;

(2) full valuable consideration for the disposition was not given by the person to whom or for the benefit of whom the disposition was made or by any other person; and

---

[30] [1992] 1 FLR 591.
[31] *The Times*, December 3, 1992.

(3) the exercise of the powers conferred by Inheritance (Provision for Family and Dependants) Act 1975, s.10, would facilitate the making of financial provision for the applicant under the Act

before it can make an order.

If the donee of an *inter vivos* disposition is dead, the court can proceed against the personal representatives of the donee, but cannot make an order in respect of property already distributed by those personal representatives.

In considering matters when making an order exercising its powers under the Inheritance (Provision for Family and Dependants) Act 1975, s.10, the court must have regard to:

(*a*) the circumstances in which the disposition was made;
(*b*) any valuable consideration which was given;
(*c*) the relationship, if any, of the donee to the deceased;
(*d*) the conduct and financial resources of the donee;
(*e*) the circumstances of the case; and
(*f*) matrimonial proceedings and disentitlement orders.

It is possible in matrimonial proceedings for the parties to exclude the right of each other in the future to apply for an order under the Inheritance (Provision for Family and Dependants) Act 1975, s.2. When making such a provision, the court should be satisfied that it is just to make such an order and must have evidence to show the likely size of the estate and the beneficiaries in the future: *Whiting v. Whiting*.[32]

---

[32] [1988] 2 FLR 189.

Chapter 14

Formalities of Death

REGISTERING THE DEATH

A death should be registered within five days and must be registered in the registration sub-district in which it took place or in which the body was found (Births and Deaths Registration Act 1953). The five-day period can be extended by a further nine days as long as the Registrar of Births and Deaths has received written communication that the doctor has signed a medical certificate as to the cause of death.

The "informant", the person with responsibility for registering the death, is usually the closest relative, if none, then any person present at the death, the occupier of the premises where the death occurred (it can therefore be an administrator of a hospital or the proprietor of a residential home), anyone living in the house who knew about the death or the person making the funeral arrangements.

To register the death, the informant has to produce the medical certificate of the cause of death issued by the doctor looking after the deceased in his last illness, unless this certificate has already reached the registrar direct, which it will have if the death was reported to the coroner and there was a post-mortem examination without inquest.

It is helpful to have the deceased's birth and marriage certificates available as they will help answer most of the registrar's questions. If the National Health Service medical card is available, that should be taken and will be retained by the registrar.

Having entered the death in the register, which is signed by both the informant and the registrar, the registrar issues a green Disposal Certificate authorising either burial or cremation, which is handed to the funeral director, and a white Registration of Death Certificate which is free but only for use in obtaining National Insurance benefits. For other purposes a certified copy of the certificate of the entry of the death in the register needs to be purchased at the price of £2.50 per copy. If not purchased from the registrar within a couple of months of registration, the records are all passed to the superintendent registrar of the district and the cost of obtaining copies of the certificates will have been increased to £5.50.

DISPOSAL OF THE BODY

Assuming the coroner is not involved, possession of the corpse passes to the executors if the deceased died testate and to the next-of-kin if intestate. It is normally the executors or next-of-kin who will arrange the funeral.

If the deceased left funeral directions, these are merely wishes and are not legally binding (*Williams v. Williams*[1]), but will usually be followed by those making the arrangements.

Checks need to be made in case a grave space has already been purchased, in which case a certificate containing the relevant details will have been issued at the time of purchase. This is particularly likely if the deceased's spouse pre-deceased; a double grave space may have been purchased at that time.

Increasingly, pre-paid funeral plans are being entered into so that a check of the deceased's papers needs to be done to ensure that the correct funeral directors have been instructed as different firms are tied in with different plans. Depending on the plan purchased, it may be that the funeral is already paid for in total, or that the only expenses are extras ordered by the family, such as an additional car for the mourners.

If there are unlikely to be sufficient assets in the estate to pay the funeral account, a grant from the social fund may be available (Social Fund Maternity and Funeral Expenses (General) Regulations 1987[2]). The applicant for such a payment must be the person responsible for arranging the funeral and needs to be in receipt of income support, family credit, disability working allowance, housing benefit, or council tax benefit, or the "partner" of someone in receipt of such benefits. Help from the Social Fund will only be granted if the claimant or their "partner" have less than £500 in savings (or £1,000 if aged 60 or over). There is a time limit of three months in making a claim against the Social Fund. From April 1994 help will not be available unless there is a link between the deceased and the claimant and it is clear that that person should be responsible for the costs but cannot afford them. Payments will continue to be made to the partner of the deceased, a close relative where there is no other close relative who should take responsibility for the costs, or any other person who has good reason for taking responsibility for the costs.

Donated bodies and therapeutic use

If the deceased wished his body to be used for medical education or, research, or for therapeutic purposes (corneal grafting or organ transplantation), as well as expressing those wishes in his will, it is sensible for them to be communicated to the executors or next of kin, and his doctor

---

[1] (1882) 20 Ch. D. 659.
[2] S.I. 1987 No. 481. See also the Social Fund Maternity and Funeral Expenses (General) Amendment Regulations 1994 (S.I. 1994 No. 506).

and for a donor card to be carried as such instructions need to be acted on promptly after the death. Corneas can be removed within a few hours of death but other organs need to be removed whilst the heart is beating, although the body may be brain-stem dead.

A body may be used for therapeutic purposes under the provisions of the Human Tissue Act 1961 and for medical education or research under the Anatomy Act 1984. The tests as to whether a donated body can be used for either therapeutic purposes or medical education or research are broadly similar. The person lawfully in possession can give consent for such use if:

(a) the deceased, either in writing or orally in the presence of two or more witnesses during his last illness, requested that use; and
(b) the person lawfully in possession has no reason to believe that the request was subsequently withdrawn.

Alternatively, the person in lawful possession, having made such reasonable enquiries as may be practical can give consent for such use if he has no reason to believe:

(a) that the deceased had expressed an objection to such use and had not withdrawn it;
(b) that the surviving spouse or any surviving relative of the deceased objects to such use.

Both Acts treat the person who controls or manages a hospital, nursing home or other institution as being in lawful possession of any body lying there. If it is believed that an inquest might be necessary, no consent can be given.

It may well be that if donated parts are removed for therapeutic purposes the rest of the body will not be acceptable for medical education or research. A donated body may not be accepted for research purposes if it is not offered to the medical school quickly enough, the medical school has sufficient corpses at the time, or the body offered is not undamaged. Bodies which have been subject to a post-mortem examination or which have parts missing are generally not accepted.

The Coroner

Coroners are appointed for each coroner's district in a metropolitan county or Greater London by the council of that district or borough and/ or non-metropolitan counties by the council of that county (Coroners Act 1988, s.1). The county may be divided into coroner's districts, in which case a coroner is assigned to a particular district.

A coroner's jurisdiction is normally limited to the area for which he is appointed coroner. Usually a coroner holds an inquest in the area where the body lies, but it is possible for the inquest to be held elsewhere if the death occurred elsewhere (Coroners Act 1988, s.14), for example victims involved in an accident where there are multiple deaths may be taken to different hospitals in different coroner's districts, but one coroner is likely to hold the inquest into all deaths, possibly the coroner for the district where the accident occurred.

A coroner's duties include enquiring into the death, including the cause of death, of certain persons by holding an inquest or by having a post-mortem examination made.

Once a coroner is informed of the death within his jurisdiction and there is reasonable cause to suspect that the person died a violent or unnatural death, or has died a sudden death of which the cause is unknown, or in such a place or such circumstances as to require an inquest, he must hold an inquest touching the death. Where a medical cause of death is accompanied by concurrent events which might be considered unnatural, a coroner is under a duty to hold an inquest (*R. v. Poplar Coroner, ex p. Thomas*[3]).

There is a duty on every person to give information which may lead to the coroner having notice of circumstances requiring the holding of an inquest; and , at common law, it is an offence to dispose of a body in order to prevent an inquest being held. A Registrar of Births and Deaths must report the death to the coroner where there was no medical practitioner present at the last illness; no duly completed certificate of cause of death has been supplied; the deceased was not seen by a medical practitioner after death or within 14 days prior; the cause of death is unknown, or the registrar has reason to believe that death was unnatural or caused by violence or neglect, or attended by suspicious circumstances; or a death which appears to have occurred during an operation and before recovery from the effect of anaesthetic; or one which appears from the contents of any medical certificate to have been due to an industrial disease or industrial poisoning (Registration of Births and Deaths Regulations 1987[4]).

A coroner has a duty at common law to take possession of anyone killed violently or dying suddenly and to retain custody of the body until the inquest is concluded, although he has a discretion to order an early release.

A coroner or his officer is justified in searching not only the body but the effects of the deceased and the place where the body was found if such a search is likely to produce evidence relative to establishing the cause of death.

A post-mortem examination may be directed if this may prove an inquest to be unnecessary, this takes place generally where there is reasonable cause to suspect that a sudden death of which the cause is unknown is one of natural causes. If this is revealed to be the case by the

---

[3] [1992] 3 W.L.R. 485.
[4] S.I. 1987 No. 2088.

post-mortem examination and there are no circumstances making it desirable to have a public enquiry, no inquest is held and the Registrar of Births and Deaths is informed accordingly. A registration of the death will take place in the normal way. Where a post-mortem examination is directed, it must be made as soon after the death as is reasonably practicable (Coroners Rules 1985, r.5[5]).

If the post-mortem examination results in the necessity of an inquest, there will be considerable delay in the death being registered as it cannot be done until after the inquest verdict is known, which may be as much as a year after the death. Once the verdict has been reached, the Coroner will forward the result automatically to the registrar and the death is automatically registered without the necessity of attendance by an informant. If the inquest is followed by criminal procedeedings, the coroner cannot send his certificate as to the cause of death to the registrar until the outcome of the criminal proceedings.

The coroner will usually issue an interim certificate of the cause of death, which will generally be accepted by institutions such as banks, etc., but insurance companies are more likely to insist on seeing the formal death certificate before they will pay out a claim under a life policy.

If the coroner holds an inquest, the body cannot be disposed of without the coroner issuing a certificate authorising burial or cremation. This certificate cannot be given until after the inquest has been opened, even if it is then adjourned, and any post-mortem examination has been carried out.

If there is to be a cremation, the certificate is also sent to the Registrar of Births and Deaths stating the cause of death and the coroner issues a certificate for the purposes of the cremation (Form E). If there is to be a burial, the coroner issues a burial order generally after the inquest has been opened.

The purpose of the inquest is solely to ascertain the identity of the deceased, as to how, when and where he came by his death, and the particulars necessary for registering the death as required by the Births and Deaths Registration Act 1953.

A coroner's inquest is not bound by strict laws of evidence (*R. v. Divine ex p. Walton*[6]) but such laws are usually observed. Evidence is taken on oath, generally with the coroner asking questions first, then by others who might have an interest, and lastly by representatives of any witness being questioned. There are no closing speeches, but, if sitting with a jury, the coroner sums up the evidence and directs as to the law before the jury can consider their verdict.

After hearing the evidence, a verdict must be returned. If being held by a jury, a majority decision can be accepted if not more than two of the

---

[5] S.I. 1985 No. 552.
[6] [1930] 2 K.B. 29 at 36.

jury members disagree, but if the disagreement is greater the jury must be discharged and another one impanelled.

The verdict must have a finding in respect of the following:

(i)   name of the deceased (if known),
(ii) injury or disease causing death,
(iii) time, place and circumstances at or in which the injury was sustained,
(iv) conclusion of the jury or coroner as to the death, and
(v)   particulars required in order for the death to be registered.

Where criminal charges have been brought before a verdict has been returned, the coroner need not adjourn the inquest until the outcome of the criminal proceedings is known, if the Director of Public Prosecutions informs him that such an adjournment is unnecessary (Coroners Act 1988, s.16(2)). An adjournment may be requested if it appears charges might be brought in connection with the death and a request is made by the Director of Public Prosecutions or police.

In most cases involving coroners and the elderly, the death will have been sudden with the deceased not having seen his doctor for some time so that the coroner has had to be informed, but a post-mortem examination is sufficient to produce evidence of natural causes so an inquest is unnecessary. Where the matter is one which requires an inquest, the coroner will generally order the release of the body to the personal representatives or next-of-kin once the inquest has been opened and adjourned, except in cases where the deceased met their death violently in circumstances likely to involve criminal proceedings such as murder or manslaughter. In such cases the body will be retained for some time in case charges are brought and the defendant wishes an independent post-mortem examination to be carried out.

Some inquests in respect of the elderly are held because their deaths can be related back to an industrial disease such as asbestosis. A lot of verdicts are "accidental death", some because of car accidents, etc., but many because the elderly person has fallen, either in their own home or residential care, and has died of some illness contracted as a result of the fall, often pneumonia.

Some elderly people with dementia go missing and a body is eventually found. A verdict then could be an open one (where it is not clear how they met their death) or possibly one of misadventure.

TAXATION

Pre-death income tax

The personal representatives of the deceased are responsible for clearing the deceased's pre-death income tax position. This will probably entail making returns of income up to the date of death and the personal representative is responsible for the accuracy and completeness of the returns.

If a repayment of overpaid tax is due to the estate, the return must be accompanied by the relevant tax deduction certificates to vouch for the income tax paid. The deceased is entitled to a full year's personal allowance although he may have died part way through the tax year.

If the deceased is liable to pay tax, the personal representative may be expected to complete returns for the six years of assessment preceding the tax year in which the deceased died if it appears that there was fraudulent or negligent conduct on the part of the deceased in failing to make such returns himself. Many elderly people with investments in national savings or building societies have the mistaken belief that they do not have to pay income tax and so receive the income on their investments gross (automatically in the case of national savings and by election in the case of building societies) and never complete income tax returns. Their personal representative is then faced with completing six years' worth of back returns. The Inland Revenue cannot go back more than the six years preceding the tax year of death (Taxes Management Act 1970, s.40), unlike cases of fraudulent or negligent conduct when the tax payer is still alive, when there are powers to go back for longer periods.

Any assessment of tax must be raised not later than the end of the third year of assessment following the year the death occurred (Taxes Management Act 1970, s.40).

When an assessment has been raised prior to death but not paid by the deceased, the personal representative should make an appeal within 30 days of the assessment if possible; if not possible a late appeal will normally be treated sympathetically.

Where tax is payable, this should be discharged as soon as possible to prevent interest running. The personal representative is only liable for income tax to the extent of the value of the deceased's assets which come into his hands.

Any liability to income tax for a period pre-death is a debt which can be taken into account when calculating the net estate for inheritance tax purposes, whilst any repayment due is an asset.

In calculating income of the deceased the Apportionment Act 1870 is ignored. The general rule, as decided in *IRC v. Henderson's Executors*,[7] is that only income received by the deceased during his lifetime is taken into account on his pre-death tax returns. Income which may have accrued during his lifetime but is not actually paid until after his death is taxed as being income of the estate.

Post-death income tax

Whilst the estate is in the course of administration it is the responsibility of the personal representatives to make income tax returns to the Inland

---

[7] (1931) 16 TC 282.

Revenue for each of the income tax periods during which the administration runs until the administration is completed.

The income of the administration period is assessed on the personal representative at basic rate tax. There is no liability to the higher rate or the lower rate, neither is the personal representative entitled to any personal allowances. However, the personal representative may be entitled to mortgage interest relief if a property is the sole or main residence of a surviving spouse and interest paid on any inheritance tax loan may be set off against income tax for the period of 12 months from the date of the loan (Income and Corporation Taxes Act 1988, s.364).

Having calculated and discharged the income tax liability during the administration, the personal representative should issue each beneficiary with a form R185E tax deduction certificate which details the beneficiary's entitlement, the tax paid out and the inspector of taxes to whom the personal representative has made his return. If the beneficiary is a basic rate taxpayer, the certificate is evidence that his liability has been discharged; if a higher rate taxpayer, the Inland Revenue will issue an assessment for the difference between basic rate and higher rate on the beneficiary; if a non-taxpayer or liable only at the lower rate, then it is evidence for the beneficiary to be able to obtain a repayment of the overpaid tax.

If a beneficiary is entitled to a limited interest in the residue then the beneficiary is taxed under the Income and Corporation Taxes Act 1988, s.695. Initially they would be taxed on the amounts paid out as if those amounts were net income taxed at the basic rate applicable to the tax year in which the payment is made to the beneficiary. Once the administration of the estate is complete, the beneficiary's tax position is adjusted. All payments made to the beneficiary during and on completion of the administration which are chargeable to income tax are added together and the aggregate amount treated as accruing on a daily basis during the course of the administration period. From this is calculated the income deemed relevant to each year of assessment and each year's deemed income is grossed up at that year's relevant basic rate.

If the beneficiary is entitled to an absolute interest in residue, payments during the course of the administration are treated as income of the year of assessment when paid and adjustments are made when the administration is complete, to the effect that the amount of residuary income for any one year of assessment is deemed the beneficiary's actual income for that year (Income and Corporation Taxes Act 1988, s.696). If the benefits received by the residuary beneficiary are less than the residuary income when received by the personal representative, then the amount of income upon which the beneficiary is taxable is also reduced.

Widow's bereavement allowance
Any widow is entitled to a full single allowance relevant to a person of her age and income for the year of her husband's death and, in addition, a widow's bereavement allowance which is paid in the year of death and for the next full tax year provided she does not re-marry before the

commencement of that year (Income and Corporation Taxes Act 1988, s.262). Widowers are not entitled to an equivalent bereavement allowance, only to receive their full married allowance for the year of their wife's death. Thereafter they only receive the applicable single person's allowance.

Capital gains tax

As with income tax, the deceased's personal representative is responsible for agreeing and discharging the deceased's liability to capital gains tax to the date of death. Unrelieved losses of the deceased cannot be carried forward beyond the date of death and into the administration or into the hands of any beneficiaries, but can be set off against gains of the deceased for a year later than that in which the loss occurred (the usual rule). Also, losses sustained in the year of death can be carried back and set against taxable gains of the deceased in the three years of assessment prior to the year in which the deceased died, taking later years of assessment first (Taxation of Chargeable Gains Act 1992, s.62(2)).

The value of the deceased's assets are taken as having been acquired by the personal representative for a consideration equal to their market value at death but there is no charge to capital gains tax on this deemed disposal, merely an automatic uplifting in value (Taxation of Chargeable Gains Act 1992, s.62(1)). The personal representative's liability on any subsequent disposal is calculated by reference to any increase in value of the asset in their hands from the date of death.

During the course of the administration of the estate, the personal representative has the capital gains tax allowance applicable to individuals for the year of death and the following two years of assessment (Taxation of Chargeable Gains Act 1992, s.3). Thereafter there is no exempt amount and the personal representative pays at the basic rate of 25 per cent upon chargeable gains made. Personal representatives can therefore benefit the estate during the course of the administration by making use of the annual allowances and disposing of assets which have increased in value during the administration before the end of the second full year of assessment.

Any losses made by the personal representative can be set off against gains arising in the same year of assessment or can be carried forward to be set off against gains arising in subsequent years. If, at the completion of the administration, there is an unrelieved loss, it is simply "lost" and cannot be transferred to one of the beneficiaries. A more effective way of dealing with the loss is for the loss-making asset to be transferred *in specie* to the beneficiary, who might be able to utilise the loss in connection with his own personal tax position.

When assets are transferred *in specie* to a beneficiary, there is no deemed disposal for capital gains tax purposes, but the beneficiary acquires the asset with the base value as at the date of death of the deceased (Taxation of Chargeable Gains Act 1992, s.62).

In calculating the taxable gain, an allowance is given for the appropriate part of the cost of the personal representative obtaining probate. The allowable expenditure is set out in the Inland Revenue Statement of Practice SP 7/81, with variable allowances depending on the gross value of the estate. On estates with a value of over £400,000, the amount allowed is negotiated with the Inland Revenue.

Inheritance tax

As from March 18, 1986, the death duty tax is inheritance tax which replaced and modified capital transfer tax. The basic statutory provisions are to be found in the Inheritance Tax Act 1984 and the Finance Act 1986.

Liability to inheritance tax is calculated by reference to chargeable transfers made by an individual, a chargeable transfer being a transfer of value which is not an exempt transfer (Inheritance Tax Act 1984, s.2). A transfer of value is any disposition made by an individual as a result of which the value of his estate is reduced. A person's estate includes all the property to which he was beneficially entitled, but does not include "excluded property" (Inheritance Tax Act 1984, s.5). Excluded property is property situated outside the United Kingdom if the person beneficially entitled to it is an individual domiciled outside the United Kingdom.

In order to bring a person's estate at his death within the charge of inheritance tax, Inheritance Tax Act 1984, s.4, provides that on death tax shall be charged as if, immediately before his death, the deceased had made a transfer of value equal to the value of his entire estate immediately before his death. The value of the estate includes the value of insurance policies which fall into the estate as a result of the death. Also taken into the calculation are the value of trust funds in which the deceased had an interest in possession (a life interest as opposed to a discretionary interest) (Inheritance Tax Act 1984, s.49), property held jointly with another which passes automatically to the survivor (Inheritance Tax Act 1984, s.171(2)) and the value of any gifts made by the deceased in the preceding seven years (Finance Act 1986, Sched. 19, para. 2). If a lifetime transfer (a potentially exempt transfer (PET) at the time it was made, which had become a chargeable transfer because of the death) becomes taxable, the amount of tax payable depends on the length of time between lifetime transfer and death as follows:

Transfers made between	Percentage of full rate payable
1 to 3 years before death	No change
3 to 4 years before death	80%
4 to 5 years before death	60%
5 to 6 years before death	40%
6 to 7 years before death	20%

From the cumulative total of the deceased's assets will be deducted the debts incurred for full consideration in money or money's worth for the deceased's own benefit. This then produces the net estate liable for tax.

Inheritance Tax is paid on the deceased's estate on the first £154,000 (from April 6, 1995) at 0 per cent (the nil rate band) and on everything over £154,000 at 40 per cent, subject to various exemptions or reliefs. The amount of the nil band is generally increased in line with other tax allowances in the budget.

Exemptions
The usual exemptions are the spouse exemption, where whatever the amount left to a surviving spouse, it is exempt (subject to a limitation of a nil rate band of £55,000 only where the donee spouse is non-domiciled in the United Kingdom), gifts to charity, gifts for national purposes (*e.g.* the National Gallery), gifts for public benefit (*e.g.* land of outstanding scenic, historic or scientific interest, or pictures, prints, books, manuscripts, works of art or scientific collections which are of national, scientific or artistic interest) and reversionary interests.

In addition, there are reliefs relating to the ownership of business property, agricultural property or woodlands.

Quick succession relief
Quick succession relief may be relevant if the deceased had in turn had property transferred to him on an earlier transfer of value within the five years preceding the death. The inheritance tax payable on death in respect of the property transferred by the earlier transfer is reduced by a percentage of the tax charged on the earlier transfer as follows:

Period of Transfer	Percentage of tax charged on first transfer
1 year or less	100%
Between 1 and 2 years	80%
Between 2 and 3 years	60%
Between 3 and 4 years	40%
Between 4 and 5 years	20%

Gifts with a reservation
Where a donor had given away any asset but still retained a benefit which had not been released at or within seven years of death, the reservation of benefit rules come into play (Finance Act 1986, s.102 and Sched. 20). There has been a reservation of benefit where, in respect of any gift after March 18, 1986:

(a) possession and enjoyment of the property is not *bona fide* assumed by the donee at or before the beginning of the relevant period; or
(b) at any time in the relevant period the property is not enjoyed to the entire exclusion, or virtually the entire exclusion, of the donor and of any benefit to him by contract or otherwise.

"The relevant period" is the period ending on the donor's death and beginning seven years previously, or if later, on the date of the gift.

For inheritance tax purposes, the effect of the rules is to treat the property subject to reservation as property to which the donor is still beneficially entitled at death, or until the date when the benefit is given up, if earlier. The most usual examples of this are when a parent gives away his only or main residence to a child or children, but continues to reside there whilst not paying a full commercial rent for the period of the continued residence there, or a settlor of a discretionary settlement who is also a beneficiary of that settlement.

Payment of tax

The time and payment of inheritance tax depends on the nature of the assets in the estate and their disposal (Inheritance Tax Act 1984, s.226). If the death turns a PET into a chargeable transfer, the inheritance tax is due six months after the end of the month of death.

So far as assets in the estate are concerned, unless the assets are such that payment by instalments is available, inheritance tax is payable on delivery of the Inland Revenue account which should be within 12 months of the end of the month of death; interest, however, starts to run from six months after the end of the month of death. The grant of representation cannot be obtained without delivery of the account to the Capital Taxes Office first and the account having been receipted in respect of the tax paid.

There are cases in which the taxpayer can elect to pay inheritance tax by 10-yearly instalments, the first instalment being due six months after the end of the month of death. If the whole or any part of the assets on which tax is outstanding is sold, the outstanding instalments of tax on the part sold, with accrued interest where relevant, become payable immediately.

The instalment option is only available in the following circumstances:

(1) Land—the option applies to all land and buildings, freehold or leasehold wherever situated (Inheritance Tax Act 1984, s.227(2)). Interest must be paid on all outstanding inheritance tax as from the date of the first instalment unless the land is part of a business or agricultural relief is given.

(2) Certain quoted or unquoted controlled shares or securities—if the transferor (deceased) had control over a company immediately before transfer, the instalment option is available on shares and securities in the company. Control means having more than 50 per cent of the votes on all matters affecting the company as a whole, and related property will be treated as though it were the shareholder's own.

(3) Certain unquoted, uncontrolled shares or securities—if satisfied undue hardship would be caused by collecting the inheritance tax in one sum, the Revenue will accept instalments, and, if the sum of tax due on death is substantial, it may be paid by instalments. Substantial means if all the inheritance tax payable by instalments (including the shares or securities in question) comes to at least 20 per cent of the total tax payable by the personal representative.

(4) Unquoted, uncontrolled shares with a market value of at least

£20,000 at the moment of transfer—this applies if either the nominal value of the shares is not less than 10 per cent of the shares in issue at the moment of transfer or the shares are ordinary shares and their nominal value is not less than 10 per cent of the total nominal value of all the ordinary shares in issue at the moment of transfer.

(5) Business assets—including goodwill. The assets must be used in the business; business meaning both trades and professions or vocations carried on with a view to profit.

Interest is paid on unpaid tax as from the due date. So far as land is concerned, it carries interest on all outstanding tax from the date the first instalment is due, for example, no interest will be paid on the first instalment, but, when the second instalment is paid, interest is due on all nine outstanding instalments.

If the death gives rise to payment of tax across several funds (*e.g.* assets in the estate, a trust where the deceased had an interest in possession, joint assets which have passed on survivorship), the funds are added together to calculate the property passing on death and the resultant liability to tax. The total tax is then apportioned to the various funds and should be met out of the estate, settlement or jointly owned asset as appropriate.

The Inland Revenue has a discretion to accept payment of tax in kind (Inheritance Tax Act 1984, ss.230 and 231) but this will generally only be items such as works of art, or land, mainly if capable of being used by the general public, and buildings and objects related to that land.

If inheritance tax is unpaid the Inland Revenue has the ability to place a charge on the property concerned to the extent that inheritance tax and interest remain unpaid (Inheritance Tax Act 1984, s.237). For deceased's estates, this relates to freehold land and buildings in the United Kingdom and all property overseas.

Losses on qualifying investments
Where qualifying investments (quoted investments and holdings in authorised unit trusts) are disposed of within 12 months of death, there is relief under the Inheritance Tax Act 1984, ss.178 and 179 to substitute the total sale prices for the date of death probate values, if lower. This relief can only be claimed by the personal representative if selling during the course of administration and not by any beneficiary to whom an investment has been transferred, or if the personal representative is disposing of holdings which have been appropriated to a beneficiary and which are therefore being held by the personal representative in a bare trustee capacity. The relief can be restricted as all disposals have to be taken into account to claim the relief, including any sales which show an increase in value, and any purchases of additional qualifying investments will reduce the loss by the proportion of the total proceeds of sale which is expended on the purchase.

Land sold within three years of death

Where there is an interest in land comprised in a deceased's estate which is sold within three years for a price less than the probate value at death by the person liable for the inheritance tax on that interest (*e.g.* the personal representative), the sale value can be substituted for the probate value for the purposes of calculating the inheritance tax liability on death so long as a claim is submitted (Inheritance Tax Act 1984, s.190). The sale values of all land sold within three years of death must be substituted for the probate values and if further land is purchased within four months of the last sale, relief is lost proportionately.

No claim is allowed if the difference in price between sale and probate value is less than the lower figure of £1,000 or 5 per cent of the death value. Also, if there is a sale by the personal representative to a person who at any time since the deceased's death has had an interest in the land sold or was a spouse, child or remote descendant of any person with an interest in the land, or trustees of a settlement where any of the previously mentioned persons have an interest in possession, then no claim will be allowed.

Applying for probate

The personal representative is required to deliver an account to the Inland Revenue for inheritance tax purposes giving full details of the estate (Inheritance Tax Act 1984, s.216). There are circumstances where, if the estate is an "excepted estate", these requirements are dispensed with (Inheritance Tax Act 1984, s.256).

To come within the "excepted estate" procedures the estate needs to meet various conditions as set out in the Inheritance Tax (Delivery of Accounts) Regulations 1981[8] as amended. These are:

(*a*) the deceased was United Kingdom domiciled and died after March 31, 1983;

(*b*) the deceased made no lifetime gifts;

(*c*) the gross value of the estate is not more than £125,000 (for deaths after July 1, 1991);

(*d*) the estate contains no more than £15,000 worth of foreign property (for deaths after April 1, 1989); and

(*e*) the estate contains no settled property, only property which passes under the will or intestacy or by nomination or survivorship.

Within 35 days of applying for a grant of representation the Inland Revenue may call for an account and issue forms for completion by the personal representative (CAP 204), but if no account is called for the personal representatives are discharged from any claim to inheritance tax.

---

[8] S.I. 1981 No. 880.

If the conditions are satisfied so that no Inland Revenue account is required, when swearing the oath the personal representative does not therefore swear as to the exact value of the estate, merely that the gross value of the estate does not exceed £125,000 and that the net value of the estate does not exceed the relevant figure as set out in the various bands detailed in the Non-Contentious Probate Fees Order 1981[9] as amended. It is from this net figure, depending in which band the estate falls, that the relevant probate fee is calculated.

If an Inland Revenue account is required because the estate is not an "excepted estate", then generally the form to be completed is either an IHT 200 or IHT 202.

IHT Form 202
This is a simplified version of the IHT 200 and is used only when the deceased's estate comprises property which passes under the will or intestacy, by nomination or survivorship, when all that property is situated in the UK and the total net value of the estate after deducting exemptions and reliefs means that it does not exceed the inheritance tax threshold, above which inheritance tax is payable on death.

The form IHT202 is, therefore, not applicable if there have been lifetime gifts, or where there is an interest in settled property.

IHT Form 200
This is the relevant form used when the deceased died domiciled in the United Kingdom, the estate is not an "exempted estate" and the IHT 202 is not applicable. It is particularly used where the estate is liable to pay inheritance tax, or there are interests in settled property.

If either an IHT 200 or an IHT 202 is necessary and the estate contains either stocks and shares or realty, then the separate form CAP40 or form CAP37 which sets out separate information and details of the stocks or the realty should be completed and exhibited with the IHT 200 or the IHT 202.

Documents to be lodged
When applying for a grant of representation, the application is supported by the following documentation:

(a) relevant oath or affirmation (executor's or administrator's);
(b) original will, if any;
(c) further affidavit evidence, if applicable, for example as to due execution, knowledge and approval or plight and condition in respect of the will;
(d) Inland Revenue account which, if inheritance tax is due for

---

[9] S.I. 1981 No. 861.

payment is shown as receipted on the application, the inheritance tax and the IHT 200 having first been sent to the Capital Taxes Office;

(e) cheque for the relevant amount of probate court fees including any amount payable for additional office copies of the grant.

Post-death variations

If beneficiaries wish to alter the dispositions of an estate, whether there is a will or an intestacy, it is possible to do this not only for genuine family reasons but also to implement effective post-death tax planning.

A variation, provided it complies with the necessary requirements, can be effective for both inheritance tax (Inheritance Tax Act 1984, s.142) and capital gains tax (Taxation of Chargeable Gains Act 1992, s.62), backdating its effects to the date of death and being treated as if the dispositions had been made by the deceased for tax purposes. There are no similar provisions in respect of income tax.

A variation can be effective in respect of any property in the deceased's estate, including jointly held property, but there can be no variation in respect of settled property in which the deceased had a beneficial interest, unless the deceased exercised by will a power of appointment over that property. A variation can be in respect of part only of a beneficiary's entitlement, it does not have to be all or nothing.

Certain conditions apply if the variation is to be effective:

(a) it must be in writing;
(b) it must be within two years of death;
(c) written notice must be given to the Inland Revenue within six months of variation;
(d) there must be no consideration in money or money's worth;
(e) the beneficial interest of a minor must only be increased and not decreased.

Care has to be taken that any variation is not part of a pre-ordained series of steps; if it is found to be such the Revenue will implement the principles set out in *Furniss v. Dawson*[10] so that the variation will be ineffective for tax purposes.

Disclaimer

It is always possible for a beneficiary of an estate to disclaim his interest but this is less flexible than a variation. The major differences are that a disclaimer is possible in respect of any interest, the disclaimer affects all the beneficiary's entitlement in the benefit disclaimed, a person disclaiming is not treated as having received the income between the date of death and the disclaimer, and the person making the disclaimer cannot

---

[10] [1984] A.C. 474.

direct to whom the property in respect of which the disclaimer was made should pass, unlike under a deed of variation where not only can the interest of one person be given up, but the variation can then direct to whom the property should pass instead.

BIBLIOGRAPHY

Chapter 1—Introduction

Age Concern, *The Law and Vulnerable Elderly People* (1986).
Ashton, G., *The Elderly Client Handbook: The Law Society's Guide to Acting for Older People* (1994).
Eekelaar, J. & Pearl, D. (eds.), *An Ageing World: Dilemmas and Challenges for Law and Social Policy* (1989).
Griffiths, A., Grimes, R. & Roberts, G., *The Law and Elderly People* (1990).
Grubb, A., *Decision-Making and Problems of Incompetence* (1993).

Chapter 2—The Delivery of Social Services

Allen, N., *Social Care Legislation* (1994).
Jones, R. (ed.), *Encyclopaedia of Social Services and Child Care Law* (Looseleaf).
Bailey, S.H., *Cross on Local Government* (1993).
Ball, C., *Law for Social Workers* (1991).
RADAR, *Disabled People Have Rights* (1994).
Robinson, C., *Handbook of Local Authority Legal Practice* (1994).

Chapter 3—Community Care

Dimond, B., *Legal Aspects of Community Care* (1994).
Gordon, R., *Community Care Assessments: A Practical Legal Framework* (1993).
Meredith, B., *The Community Care Handbook* (1993).

Chapter 4—The Provision of National Health Services

Age Concern, *The Living Will: Consent to Treatment at the End of Life* (1989).
Brazier, M., *Medicine, Patients and the Law* (1992).
Dyer, C. (ed.), *Doctors, Patients and the Law* (1992).
Finch, J., *Spellers Law Relating to Hospital* (1993).
Holliday, I., *The National Health Service Transformed* (1992).
Kennedy, I. & Grubb, A., *Medical Law* (1994).

Chapter 5—Residential Care

Royal College of Nursing, *A Scandal Waiting to Happen?* (1992).
Wagner, G., *A Positive Choice* (1988).

Chapter 6—Inspecting Residential Care

Carson, D., "Registering Homes: Another Fine Mess" (1985) Journal of Social Welfare Law, 67–84.
Cassam, E. & Gupta, H., *Quality Assurance for Social Care Agencies: A Practical Guide* (1992).
Centre for Policy on Ageing, *Home Life—Code of Practice for Residential Care* (1984).
Jones, R., *Registered Homes Act Manual* (2nd ed., 1993).

Chapter 7—Complaints Procedures

Clements, L., *European Convention on Human Rights: A Practical Guide to the Complaints Procedure* (1994).
Fridd, N., *Basic Practice in Courts, Tribunals & Inquiries* (1993).
Ganz, G., *Understanding Public Law* (1994).
Jackson and Powell on Professional Negligence (3rd ed., 1992).
Jones, M., *Medical Negligence* (1991).
Lewis, C., *Judicial Remedies in Public Law* (1992).
Lewis, N. & Birkinshaw, P., *When Citizens Complain* (1993).
Medhurst, D., *A Brief & Practical Guide to E.C. Law* (2nd ed., 1994).
Morewitz, S. & Livingstone, B., *The Medical Malpractice Handbook* (1994).
Richardson, G. & Genn, H., *Administration Law and Government Action* (1994).
Smith, R., *Medical Discipline* (1994).
S.S.I./Department of Health, *The Inspections of the Complaints Procedures in Local Authority Departments* (1993).
Wilson, Prof. A., *Being Heard* (1994).

Chapter 8—Compulsory Intervention

Bluestone, H. & Trawn, S., *Psychiatric-Legal Decision Making by the Mental Health Practitioner* (1994).
Department of Health, *The Pattern of Delays in Mental Health Review Tribunals* (1994).
Gostin, L., *Mental Health Services—Law and Practice* (1985).
Gostin, L. & Fennell, P., *Mental Health Tribunal Procedure* (1992).
Hoggett, B., *Mental Health Law* (1990).
Jones, R., *Mental Health Act Manual* (4th ed., 1994).
Levy, R., Burns, A. & Howard, R., *Treatment & Care in Old Age Psychiatry* (1993).
Peahy, J., *Tribunals on Trial* (1989).

Chapter 9—Abuse of the Elderly

ADSS, *Adults at Risk: Guidance for Directors of Social Services* (1991).

Decalmer, S. & Glendenning, F. (eds.), *The Mistreatment of Elderly People* (1993).
Eastman, M., *Old Age Abuse* (2nd ed., 1994).
Freeman, M.D.A., *Dealing with Domestic Violence* (1987).
McCreadie, C., *Elder Abuse: An Explanatory Study* (1991).

Chapter 10—Housing Matters

Aldridge, T.M., *Residential Lettings: Enfranchisement, Rent and Security* (1993).
Arden, A., Partington, M. & Hunter, C., *Housing Law* (2nd ed., 1994).
Clarke, D., *Leaseholds: The New Law* (1993).
Megarry: The Rent Acts (11th ed., 1988).
Partington, M., *Landlord and Tenant* (2nd ed., 1980).
Tiplady, D., *Housing Welfare Law* (1975).

Chapter 11—Welfare Benefits and Finance

Arden, A. & Hunter, C., *Local Government Finance: Law and Practice* (1994).
Child Poverty Action Group, *Rights Guide to Non-means Tested Benefits* (1994).
Child Poverty Action Group, *National Welfare Benefits Handbook* (1994).
Disability Rights Handbook (1991–1992).
Ellison, R., "Pensions: Europe & Equality", (1994) Longman Pension Reports.
H.M.S.O., *Annual Report of the Social Fund Commissioner*.
Mesher, J., *C.P.A.G.'s Income Related Benefits: The Legislation* (1994).
Nobles, R., *Pensions, Employment & the Law* (1993).
Rowland, M., *Medical and Disability Appeal Tribunals: The Legislation* (1994).

Chapter 12—Delegation of Financial Responsibility

Aldridge, T., *Powers of Attorney* (1991).
Cretney, S., *Enduring Powers of Attorney* (1991).
Heywood & Massey: Court of Protection Practice (12th ed., 1991).
Law Pack, *Power of Attorney and Living Will* (1994).
Letts, P., *Managing Other People's Money* (1990).
Thurston, J., *Powers of Attorney: A Practical Guide* (1991).

Chapter 13—Wills, Intestacy and Family Provision

Barlow, J., King, L. & King, A., *Wills, Administration and Taxation* (1994).
Butterworths Wills, Probate & Administrative Service (Looseleaf).
Carmichael, K.S., *Spicer & Pegler's Executorship Law & Accounts* (1994).

Miles, G., *Wills, Probate & Administration* (1994).
Parr, R. & Oldroyd, A., *Humphrey's District Registry Practice* (1994).
Pearce, N., *A Guide to Inheritance Claims* (1989).
Ray, R., *Wills and Post-Death Planning According to Family Circumstances* (1994).
Ross, S., *Inheritance Act Claims: Law & Practice* (1993).
Sherrin, C. & Bonehill, R., *The Law & Practice of Intestate Succession* (1994).
Tristram & Coote: Probate Practice (27th ed., 1989).

Chapter 14—Formalities of Death

Tolley's Tax Legislation, *Income Tax, Corporation Tax and Capital Gains Tax* (1994/5).

INDEX

Income
definition of
residential care patients for, 64
support. *See* **Income Support**
tax. *See* **Income tax**
Income Support, 65, 188–192, 210
absence abroad, payments during,
210
applicable amount, 188, 190–191
calculating resources, 191–192
premiums, 188–190
carer, 188, 190
disability, 188, 189
disabled child, 188
family, 188, 189
lone parent, 188
pensioner, 188, 190
enhanced, 188, 190
higher, 188, 190
severe disability, 188, 189
residential care patients, payable
to, 65
Income tax, 211–212, 258–261
allowances, 211–212
pre-death, 258–259
post-death, 259–261
widow's bereavement
allowance, 260–261
Independent Living Fund, 206–207
Industrial Injuries Benefits, 201–202
constant attendance allowance, 201
disablement benefit, 201
exceptionally severe disablement
allowance, 201
prescribed industrial disease
definition of, 201
Informant
person responsible for registering
death, 253
Inheritance Tax, 262–266
exemptions from, 263
land, sold within three years of
death, 266
payment of, 264–265
instalment option, 264–265
interest, 265
personal representatives required
to account for, 266–267
qualifying investments, losses on,
265
quick succession relief, 263–264
Injunction
remedy as, 104
Inquest, 257–258
purpose of, 257
verdict at, 257–258

Inspection
registered homes of, 76–84
Insulation grants
availability of, 162–163
Intent
assault, to, 148
Interim relief, 104
Intestacy, 240–243
no surviving spouse where,
242–243
surviving spouse where
issue and, 241
no issue, 241
rights of, 241
Invalid Care Allowance, 207–209
carers, paid to, 207
limitations on, 207
not means tested, 207
overlapping benefit, 207–208
pensionable age over, 208–209
taxable, 207
Invalidity Benefit, 198–200, 209
hospital stay, payments during,
209
inequality of men and women, 199
invalidity allowance, 198–199
invalidity benefit, 198–199
incapacity benefit, to replace,
199–200
retirement pension and, 199
severe disablement allowance
payment if ineligible for, 200

Judicial review, 21, 24–26, 44, 91–97,
100–104, 142, 179
community care plans, of, 21
grounds for intervention, 101–104
local authority
community care assessments
improperly carried out by,
24– 26
complaints procedure, of, 97
homelessness, challenging
decision by, 179
Mental Health Tribunal decision,
of, 142
relief available on, 104
scope of, 100–101

Laches
equitable defence of, 158
Land
residential care patients for, 62–63